Write Right!

Write Right!

Creative Writing Using Storytelling Techniques

Kendall Haven

1999
Teacher Ideas Press
A Division of
Libraries Unlimited, Inc.
Englewood, Colorado

TEACHER IDEAS PRESS
A Division of
Libraries Unlimited, Inc.
P.O. Box 6633
Englewood, CO 80155-6633
1-800-237-6124
www.lu.com/tip

Library of Congress Cataloging-in-Publication Data

Haven, Kendall F.
    Write right! : creative writing using storytelling techniques /
Kendall Haven.
    xv, 211 p. 22x28 cm.
    Includes bibliographical references (p. 205) and index.
    ISBN 1-56308-677-8
    1. English language--Rhetoric--Study and teaching. 2. Creative
writing--Study and teaching. 3. Storytelling. I. Title.
PE1404.H393 1999
808.3'07--dc21   98-33110
                                                            CIP

To every child
who has felt a burning need to write;
to every adult who has encouraged them;
and to every person at any age
who has poured heart and soul
into the writing of their story,
regardless of the final result.

Contents

List of Exercises

Introduction

A few disturbing tidbits have crossed my desk this year. Did you know that 1988 was the last year in this country when there were more checkouts from public libraries than from video stores? Since then, video checkouts have soared. I understand that as of 1996, the ratio of library checkouts to video-store checkouts is more than 20 to 1. Worse still, "library checkouts" includes videos which were checked out from libraries. So the ratio of videos to books is even more lopsided!

Do you know what single volume was stolen most often from U.S. public libraries in each of the four years 1991 through 1994 (the only years for which I have seen this statistic)? The annual *Sports Illustrated* swimsuit edition. Seemingly, this is what Americans want to "read" enough to make it worth stealing.

Did you know that, in each of the years 1992 through 1995 (again, the only years for which I have seen this statistic), more money was spent on chewing gum in the United States than on books? One hardbound picture book would buy five years' worth of gum in my house. Either many people are chomping on great and continual wads of gum, or not many people are buying books. The Department of Statistics researcher who complied this bit of data said, "At least with gum you know what you're going to get." Don't people realize what wonders and delights they can expect from a book?

A 1992 Harvard University study found that the one personal parameter that best correlated to general work success was a large vocabulary. Yet a 1986 national survey of high school seniors claimed that the average vocabulary of those graduates dropped during the 40 years from 1946 to 1986 from 40,000 words to 10,000 words.

What do all these depressing tidbits have in common? Each is a small indicator of a generally declining trend in language skills in this country—not just in schools, not just in classrooms, but in this country as a whole. They indicate a decline in the precision of our language, in our emphasis on mastering it, and in our ability and desire to manipulate and control it.

I have found, though, that everyone still loves a story, which is pure language. I support my family by traveling to schools and telling stories. Everyone delights in my arrival: It's story day! We all intuitively, innately respond to stories and recognize what makes a story fun to read, fun to listen to, as if a "story gene" were woven into the spirals of human DNA. After I've told my stories, I can convince almost any student to create a story, to *want* to create a story.

However, they aren't as enthusiastic about reading stories. Nor are they particularly enthusiastic about actually writing stories. Still, they love to create stories and to share stories—even if they don't think they are very good at it.

Research shows that development of any of the major language-arts skills improves them all. Arm kids to more consistently, efficiently, and effectively create successful stories and they will have more enthusiasm for developing the full range of language skills. I have seen it work too many thousands of times not to know it's true.

I have written this book to share a new, and I think better, approach to creating stories. Hundreds of in-class trials of my system show that it accomplishes this goal. I believe that each of us holds a wealth of stories deep inside our heart and imagination. I believe that each of us wants to write and share these stories. I believe that each of us would, except that many of us feel woefully incapable of creating a story—any story. Many of us feel overwhelmed by the prospect, embarrassed to try and not to succeed.

Writing stories is like singing, like playing a sport, like dancing, like making music. Some people are naturally more talented than others. The activity comes more easily, more gracefully, to some. Still, everyone is capable of competently performing each of these activities—*if* they are exposed to it early in their development, and *if* they are shown the skills and techniques that form the foundation for the activity.

Story writing is no different. Every adult can adequately communicate their unique stories. Each of us is capable of weaving together the tapestry of an engrossing tale. So is every child. They just need someone to teach them the fundamental skills of creative writing.

In this book, I split creative writing into three separate acts: creating, writing, and rewriting. Research shows that the mechanical act of writing is the single greatest impediment to creativity. The continual presence of this great mechanical beast shifts the focus away from creating a powerful story. Story development is avoided in favor of struggling through the act of writing.

I have conducted thousands of workshops with students, and hundreds more with teachers. Each of these workshops addresses the same general questions: What is a story? What elements are at its core? Without fail, I see students' eyes light up with excitement as they begin to understand that there are specific, dependable building blocks to story writing, which they can master. Once they understand what really makes a story work and what a reader or listener needs from their story, they realize that they are capable of writing—that they can do this!

I have written this book as a guide for classroom teachers, school librarians, reading specialists, and others who share the task of teaching the effective use and application of language to students. The exercises and approaches in this book have all been tested in school classrooms and have all proven themselves effective in helping students learn to write. I often use the word *you*, which refers to the teacher, and *your students*, which refers to the story writers. However, the exercises, techniques, and concepts presented here are equally valid for all writers.

In assembling this book, I feel a little like Samuel Morse. We all know that Morse invented the telegraph. Did you know that he did not invent or develop even *one* component or subsystem of his telegraph and long-line transmission system? Half a dozen scientists scattered around the western world invented the individual components of the telegraph—the battery system, the keypad circuits, the booster batteries on the transmission lines, the insulators on the telegraph line, and so on. Joseph Henry, the first director of the Smithsonian Museum, is credited with inventing four separate subsystems of Morse's telegraph. Samuel Morse's contribution was having the vision to see how other people's inventions could be assembled to create an entire workable system.

In this same way, the individual writing and storytelling concepts and techniques in this book are centuries old. The principles behind the exercises are, too. What I have developed is a system for blending and applying oral-based storytelling principles to facilitate student creative writing, and a specific set of effective exercises to demonstrate and teach these principles. I have assembled the available concepts and components to create a more workable system.

My formal training is in science. Fourteen years ago, I jumped ship to become a full-time storyteller and story writer, but I kept my scientific passion for tearing things apart and determining what makes them work. I focused this analytical drive on stories and storytelling: Why does one story move and enthrall an audience while another leaves them restless and bored? Why does one telling of a story enchant an audience while another telling of the same story seems lifeless and uninteresting? What aspects and elements of a story is an audience most hungry to receive?

These questions cannot be answered by writers sitting alone in their offices. They are answered by performers who deliver their material to a live audience and receive, line by line, unmistakable feedback. They are answered by someone who watches live storytellings.

I have presented more than 5,000 storytelling performances and have closely watched another thousand by other storytellers. Because I write all the stories I perform, I am able to control, adjust, and manipulate them as a direct function of the audience reactions I observe. My understanding of the structure and form of a story is based on these observations and on review and analysis of what the story and the performer do to create these reactions.

My understanding of student writers, and of the process of guiding them toward more successful story writing, is similarly based on review and analysis of the thousands of student writing workshops I have conducted, and on review and analysis of the post-workshop feedback I received from both students and teachers. I have seen the techniques in this book work for students all across the country. I am confident they will work for yours.

A grammatical note: In this text, I routinely refer to individual student writers in the third person. The correct pronouns are either *he* or *she*, *him* or *her*, *his* or *hers*, *himself* or *herself*. When the gender of the student is unspecified, though, it becomes "he or she," "him or her," or "he/she," and "him/her," and so on. I found this to be awkward and disruptive. "Each student writes his or her own story" reads worse to me than "Each student writes their own story." Too, "After the student writer completes this process, he or she . . ." is more disruptive to my ear than "After the student writer completes this process, they. . . ."

In many places, I use the plural pronouns *they*, *them*, and *their* instead to refer to the unspecified singular student as well as to the plural. Yes, this is technically incorrect, but the language is changing to accept such nongender pronoun usage. Many other books successfully integrate such usage, and I think the text reads more smoothly and clearly this way. I also shifted some "he/she" and "him/her" references into passive voice to avoid using a pronoun altogether. I admit that this scheme pulls energy from the text, but it does sneak around many of these awkward unspecified pronoun problems.

I owe a great debt of thanks to the 100-plus teachers who let me use their classes as guinea pigs to test these exercises, and to the 300-plus teachers who tried these concepts and provided feedback on how well they worked. This material is workable in large part because of their efforts. I also owe a great debt to two talented women—Roni Berg, the light of my life, and Donna Clark, a good friend and talented writer—who reviewed and critiqued this manuscript, vastly improving it in the process.

How to Use This Book

Write Right is packed with a vast array of information, concepts, exercises, and student writing activities. It would probably overburden an academic year to introduce and develop all these ideas. There is probably more here than your students can absorb in one year anyway. I don't want *Write Right* to appear overwhelming. Rather, I want it to be comprehensive. To give this one book the widest possible applicable range of grades and student writing-skill levels, I have included more detail, and more advanced writing concepts, than many teachers will need in their classrooms. Begin with those elements and concepts that best meet the needs of your students and then slowly work toward including the other concepts.

I recommend that you read the entire book to get a sense of the *Write Right* approach and then identify those aspects that will be most beneficial to your students. Often, I have indicated which concepts, approaches, and exercises are appropriate for younger student writers and which for older. In places, I have also noted which specific aspects of a more comprehensive approach or activity should be introduced first, and which may be added later, after students have developed an understanding of the basics.

Still, every group of students and every classroom is unique. Use what is appropriate for your students, for their grade level, and for their present writing ability. Then try to lead them as far along the *Write Right* path as possible during the year.

Part I

Not as Hard as You Think

Where Student Writers Go Wrong

 **Story Stew**

There is an ageless adage that floats through the world of writing conferences. It begins, "There are only three rules to great writing." Anyone who hasn't heard it leans forward, eagerly clutching pen and adjusting paper: Ah, finally—the real inside scoop! Finally, the secrets of the masters will be revealed! Those who have heard it lean back smugly, arms folded, and chuckle. The second half of the saying is, "Unfortunately, nobody knows what any of them are." Everyone groans and laughs.

This saying survives because there is a sizable grain of truth in it. Name any of the common rules dictating how to structure and write a story, and someone who knows literature can find a dozen stories that successfully violate the rule. The apparent conclusion is that there must not be any rules to story writing. It must be that creative writing is something writers simply *do*, not something taught as an essential life skill to all students, such as arithmetic. This view holds that writing ability is a gift, a God-given talent. Either you have it, or you don't. Either you "get it" on your own, or you never will.

We can offer a better vision than this. Our students deserve better. There *are* "rules" that hold true for all successful stories. But *rule* is probably the wrong word. These are not government or societally imposed mandates. They are universal truths that can be easily mastered and easily taught. They are "laws" of stories in the same sense that gravity is a law of the physical universe. In the same way that Newton's laws of motion allow us to mathematically uncover a host of truths about the physical universe, so, too, do these laws of stories allow us to dissect and understand stories in a new and much more useful way. They describe how stories work.

It is unfortunate that we have tended to overlook these powerful truths in our rush to proclaim creative writing an unteachable art form. Once students understand the universal truths that govern the power and effectiveness of stories, traditional rules take their rightful place as useful guides based on the experience of generations of successful writers.

I view a story as being like a flavorful meat-and-potatoes stew. Smelling and sipping the rich broth is delightful, but you probably will not be able to detect how it was made to taste that way. The secrets of the stew, its "rules," lie in the general principles of cooking and in its specific recipe. We can teach the general principles of story cooking and the ingredients that make a basic story stew successful. If you help students master these principles, you can expect consistently more successful creative-writing efforts, just as you would expect them to become more successful in basic math or American history once they understand the principles of these subjects.

The Myths of Story Writing

I constantly see students being snagged by one or more of a small collection of insidious myths about creative writing. Like all popular myths, these seem reasonable, even reassuring, on the surface. They hold a hopeful ring of truth. Students want to believe them. Like so many myths, they lead student writers in exactly the wrong direction.

Before we can delve into the inner workings of stories, we must investigate where and how students so regularly fail in their writing efforts. Most student stories are boring. Every writer is certainly entitled to write boring stories. Every working writer has. The percentage of student stories that are boring, though, is far too large. Too many adults have come to accept, even expect, mediocre stories from their children.

I keep hearing a set of story-writing myths from students and teachers that, I believe, are the source of much of the misdirection in student writing. These myths sound like innocent truths and rational guidelines. Like Southern kudzu, they have deep roots and spread rapidly to cover the countryside. I hear them everywhere. I see how they warp students' views of story writing.

There are nine story-writing myths I must debunk. I'll list them first, using the language I most commonly hear:

1. "To write: *write!*" (Creative writing is all about writing.)
2. "It came to me in a flash." (Good story writing flows through the author in a burst of spontaneous creativity.)
3. "It comes out perfect the first time for good writers." (Good writers achieve perfection—or near perfection—in the first draft.)
4. "Fiction writing should be fun."
5. "Too much planning spoils my creativity."
6. "Too much editing makes the writing lose its freshness, makes it stale."
7. "The story will reveal itself to me as I write." (There's no need to know the exact direction of the story or its ending before beginning it. The story will unfold during the writing.)
8. "If I put lots of *action* in my story, the reader will like it better."
9. "The place to start my story is with the question, '*What* will happen in my story?'"

Do any of these myths sound familiar? Do you believe any of them? Do you object to calling any of them "myths"? Have you taught any of them to your students?

What makes these myths insidious and allows them to persist is that most contain a solid grain of plausible truth. These truths, however, are misinterpreted and exaggerated into dangerous writing myths:

1. **"To write: *write!*"** Creative writing is not about writing. It is about creating. Writing is the end product, the form of the final version. Writing is how writers document and revise their work once it has been created. This myth implies that writing is both process and product. Believing this myth will prevent students from fully exploring and developing the creative process for their stories and will shove them prematurely into writing the first draft.

   Writing is an important skill. Student writers should write every day. The more students write, the better they become at writing, and the more control they develop with writing tools and techniques.

   The act of writing must be viewed as an important tool used in the process of story creation. The central act, however, is that of creation. The mechanical act of writing can actually hinder the process, and certainly does not facilitate it as well as other, verbal activities do. A number of these proven activities are discussed in this book.

   Writing should be emphasized because it is the most important tool for the expression of creativity. However, writing and creation should never be viewed as synonymous. This myth is interpreted by many students as implying that they are.

2. **"It came to me in a flash."** Far too many students believe that great stories are the result of creative flashes of inspiration rather than methodical planning. The grain of truth here is misinterpreted. The muses *do* offer flashes of inspiration and insight to a writer. For the vast majority of writers though, these flashes only come after they have carefully planned the foundation for a successful story.

   Too many students use this myth to excuse themselves from any story planning at all. Many have heard stories about well-established writers who write first drafts of stories without any conceptual planning, and use this as evidence to support their case. Again, the grain of truth is misinterpreted. There are writers who write free-form exposition as a first step in the story-planning process. They write first and then sift through their draft, searching for a worthy story on which to focus. Most of this rough first draft, sometimes even all of it, is discarded. Writing is a plausible but not very efficient way to begin the creative process. For elementary and middle school students, who are still struggling to master narrative structure and the mechanics of writing, it is a poor choice compared to the available alternatives.

3. **"It comes out perfect the first time for good writers."** Good writers don't get it right the first time, they just get it right. This process is more likely to require twenty rewrites than it is to require one.

   The dangerous inference of this myth is that, if students write an ineffective first draft, they are justified in assuming they are lousy writers. Hundreds of sad-faced and somber students have told me that they love to write but that they know they aren't any good at it. Their proof is always the same: They wrote a story and it was boring. Of course it was. It was a first draft that hadn't been properly and thoroughly preplanned. This kind of first draft is virtually always ineffective.

This myth survives because every student envisions the great writers scribbling perfect, flowing prose every time they set pen to paper. Hemingway revised, rewrote, and edited. So did Steinbeck, London, and Twain. I'm willing to bet that Shakespeare rewrote and edited—extensively.

Good writers commit themselves to making a story as effective and powerful as possible. The more preplanning done *before* the first draft, the fewer rewrites required after the first draft. This is why I advocate extensive story preplanning. It greatly reduces the amount of editing a story will require. Still, editing will be required. Stories do not live up to their fullest potential on the first draft. If you lead students to expect the necessity of editing, their first drafts will no longer be a source of disappointment.

4. **"Fiction writing should be fun."** Preplanning activities for a story should feel like energizing, exciting discovery and play. Writing the first draft should be a time of sweeping passion and energy. Both should be, and commonly are, fun—but then comes the necessity of editing. Editing is just as essential to the writing process as the first draft. Editing is only fun in that it makes the story stronger and more effective. Editing is mostly tedious work.

If students believe the myth that writing should be *all* fun, they'll shun editing. If writing the first draft is like smearing polish on a scuffed shoe, editing is like buffing that shoe with first brush and then rag. Editing is that necessary part of the process that brings out the luster and radiance of a story. Editing, not drafting, makes the story shine like a mirror. If you teach students that editing is a normal part of the writing process and give them appropriate tools for successfully completing this task, they won't feel like they have failed when their first draft doesn't work.

5. **"Too much planning spoils my creativity."** Planning *is* the creativity. Planning both sparks and harnesses creativity. If creativity isn't channeled into the story during the planning stages, it probably won't ever enter the story. The planning activities and exercises presented in this book are specifically designed to channel a student's creativity into their story characters and situations.

This myth survives because of the idea that planning involves the imposition of rigid structural mandates upon the story. The opposite is true. Planning allows the writer to shove aside mental limitations and barriers while stretching open the world of possibilities for their story characters.

Planning is the most effective and appropriate time for allowing new ideas to flow into and reshape the story. Story-planning activities should encourage and foster creative, original thinking about story seeds, which will then sprout into full bloom during drafting and editing. Creative ideas will come to mind during drafting as well. However, if allowances haven't been made during planning, most of these ideas won't come forward, and the story will never take shape.

6. **"Too much editing makes the writing lose its freshness, makes it stale."** Freshness, passion, and energy are infused into a story during drafting. Precision and efficiency are polished during editing. Editing doesn't spoil freshness, originality, and creativity—it enhances these qualities. I believe that this myth survives because students don't understand the editing process or the use of effective, appropriate editing tools. Once they see how the editing process can methodically improve and refine their story, this myth will evaporate.

7. **"The story will reveal itself to me as I write."** This myth tells students that they don't need to know the direction or ending of a story before or while they write it. If you don't know where you're going, how will you ever get there?

   Students often claim to know of writers who say they write to see how the story will unfold. The words are true, but the inference is not. Most writers believe that, during drafting, they will have ideas that alter the direction and outcome of a story. I certainly do. The key word is *alter*. At any given moment, good writers know the exact direction of their story. They also know that their ending is likely to change before the story is finished.

   It is also true that many writers begin to draft a story when various plot details are not yet fixed. (How will Prince Fred get inside the castle in time to overhear the wizard's assistant mutter the magic spell? How will Sir Bob know which path to take in the forest?) Within a planned and fixed story line, there can be many such questions still hanging in the air when writing begins. Writers know that specific details will present themselves as the story progresses. However, they always know the direction and ending of their story and what role these details will play.

   The distinction is subtle but important. Without a clear vision of the structure and direction of a story, the writing will be vague, aimless, and stagnant. It will be all the things students are secretly terrified that their writing is. It will be boring. They have to know where they are going if they are to carry the reader along a well-defined path, if they are to create purposeful movement in the characters.

   The targeted ending can change, but no writing should be attempted without a clearly defined ending in mind. Each change of ending, of course, requires more extensive editing and revision to adjust the early portions of the story to match the new ending.

8. **"If I put lots of *action* in my story, the reader will like it better."** This myth parallels the Hollywood notion that gratuitous special effects, action, and violence will save a floundering script and keep viewers in their seats to the end. The problem is, stories are not about action. As we shall see, they are about characters. Action only has meaning to a reader within the context of the story characters and their goals and struggles. Action is a useful tool. Action can be exciting and fun. It is a well-crafted story character that creates this excitement and enjoyment, not the action itself. The more students focus on action as a solution to problems with the structure of a story, the more likely they are to fail.

9. **"The place to start my story is with the question, '*What* will happen in my story?'"** "What" is a plot question. Unfortunately, we teach our students to think in terms of plot. We assign them plot questions. ("Write about *what* you did over summer vacation.") Every story will have a plot. Yet no story is *about* its plot. Plot-based stories are typically pointless and boring. Stories are about characters, and about the struggles and conflicts of these characters.

   Beginning a story with a plot question bypasses the foundation of the story. The story, like a house, cannot stand without a solid foundation. The foundation is found in specific core character information. Plot must be subservient to, and built upon, these character concepts. Begin stories with the question, "*Whom* will my story be about?"

The Hard Parts

Over the past decade, I have begun more than a thousand student writing workshops by asking the same question: "What is the hardest part of writing a story for you?" Initially, I used their answers as springboards for the topics I would cover. I soon realized that class after class, in grade after grade, they answered this question the same way. The parts that were hard for second-graders were still hard for eighth-graders. No new concerns had arisen. By eighth or ninth grade, only one concern had dropped off the list of complaints.

I believe that these student complaints are universal, or at least national. They cross all ethnic, gender, regional, and age boundaries from second grade through middle school. These complaints are the aspects of story writing they struggle with and worry about most. In order of frequency of mention, the seven hardest aspects of story writing are:

1.   Getting an idea for what to write about.
2.   Mastering the mechanics of writing.
3.   Figuring out how not to be boring.
4.   Figuring out who the characters are.
5.   Creating a title.
6.   Writing dialog.
7.   Figuring out how to start the story.

These student complaints probably seem familiar. You have probably heard them regularly. Of these seven, only two are age specific. I have not heard students below third grade complain about dialog. They place little, if any, emphasis upon it. Neither have I heard students above seventh grade claim that it is hard to create titles for their stories.

There is one common elementary school complaint I have omitted: "Drawing the pictures." It usually ranks second or third on their list. However, this is a book about writing, not drawing. All I can say to these students is, "I agree. Drawing is hard for me, too. That's why no one gets to see the pictures I draw to help me write a story."

Try Exercise #1, "The Hard Part" (p. 106), with your students. How do their complaints compare with those of the mass of students I have quizzed? The goal of this exercise, partially, is to have them give title to their story-writing difficulties. It also sets the stage for future discussions and exercises that lead them to understand the real problems, which concern their approach to story writing, that lie beneath and create the surface problems they identify.

Interestingly, with one exception, teachers do not complain about these same aspects of their students' creative writing. In private, away from their students, many teachers have complained that their students' stories are boring. I have asked more than a thousand teachers to list the most common and serious problems of their students' stories. Their complaints (*criticisms* and *requests* might be more accurate words) fall into four categories:

1.   Lack of adequate description and detail.
2.   Lack of a cohesive, single story line (plot).
3.   Use of weak word choices (especially for verbs).
4.   Lack of imagination and originality.

There is some overlap between student and teacher lists, but surprisingly little. More significantly, I began to realize that neither list is directly useful for the students. It would be easy to fix all the students' complaints (except for not being boring) without significantly improving the quality or effectiveness of their stories. They would still struggle and still produce mediocre stories.

The teacher list isn't useful because, though the criticisms are accurate, none of the listed complaints translates easily to direct student action. Students already know that their verbs are weak and that they lack originality. What they don't know is how to fix these problems. What they need is a translation of these two lists into the real misunderstandings and misinterpretations that lie at the core of their story-writing problems.

Where Students Really Go Wrong

The general problem with these two lists of complaints is that they don't facilitate corrective action. If you tell a student writer to add more description and detail to their story, two questions will flash through their mind: *What* detail? and Where am I supposed to get it? These questions suggest a more fundamental problem with the way students approach story writing. It is not a matter of adding an extra dash of seasoning. It is a matter of changing to a completely different recipe for their story stew.

I once thought that students intentionally withheld descriptive detail to torment their teachers. They would write wonderful stories, show them to their friends, and then, with a sadistic giggle, chop out all the action verbs and powerful detail as they wrote the final version. I've since decided that this isn't true. Students don't include detail because they haven't created the detail to include, because they began writing the story before they could vividly imagine, in multisensory detail, the story and each character.

Similarly, students don't "shotgun" their stories (include a number of story lines, hoping that one will hit the mark) because they think each of their plot lines is a worthy idea. They do it because they have neither a clear image of what their specific story is about, nor a clear idea of what a story, in general, is about. Again, a fundamental shift, rather than a slight adjustment, is needed. This shift must occur in the way students are taught to think about and approach stories.

When students are shown how to better visualize their story, and how to better understand the anatomy of a story, they automatically choose more powerful, accurate, dynamic, descriptive words. All students are replete with imagination and creativity. What they need to better understand is the form of a story, so that they can successfully apply their imagination and creativity to this unique structure.

It occurred to me that this situation is very similar to what happens when experienced storytellers critique beginning tellers. Beginning storytellers grab a new story and want to begin developing the nuances of performance technique immediately, skipping the real work associated with story development. They complain that developing effective gestures, physical characterization, and vocalization are the hard parts. These are the oral equivalents of the student writing complaints.

Coaches complain that beginning storytellers lack expression and conviction in their delivery, and that they haven't developed a clear image of their story characters. Beginning storytellers don't lack these qualities deliberately. They lack them because they overlooked them in their rush to develop final story delivery.

Because these two situations are surprisingly similar, I wanted to know whether the exercises and techniques used to help student storytellers might also work for student story writers. I used established storytelling concepts as guides to translate the student and teacher writing complaints (symptoms) into the underlying, fundamental problems concerning the way students approach and write stories.

This process led me to identify seven problems that I believe are the real culprits in derailing students' creative-writing efforts. These seven problems create the symptomatic problems students and teachers complain about, and they obscure the potential of student stories. The deadly seven are:

1.   They think plot before and above character.
2.   They write about undefined and underdeveloped characters.
3.   They write without knowing the ending.
4.   They write "blind."
5.   They focus on outcomes rather than struggles.
6.   They create and write at the same time.
7.   They lack a knowledge of systematic editing and revision.

Once I had identified these seven deadly sins of student creative writing, I began to research them. I found that these seven underlying problems are as old as writing itself. What is new in this book is the adaptation of storytelling exercises and techniques to solve these writing problems.

Solving these seven problems, I believe, is the key to liberating students to create stories that are as consistently powerful on paper as they are in the writer's mind. Note that the first five of these fundamental problems must be solved before students begin to write. Only one problem (#6) is corrected *during* the story-drafting process. This is accomplished by distinguishing story creation from story drafting. Only one problem (#7) is corrected *after* the story-drafting process.

The *Write Right* approach to writing, then, is heavily weighted toward prewriting activities. This allows the student to define and clarify their story, and solve story problems, before they begin to write.

Part II

A Better Path to First Draft

From Idea to Completed Draft

 **What Is a Story?**

We have identified seven problems that seriously hinder most students' creative writing. How do we overcome them? The answer is surprisingly easy, once we change our view of stories themselves. In this book, I want to change the way you and your students think about the word *story*. I want to change your expectations and beliefs about stories. Experience in hundreds of classrooms has shown that, if I accomplish this one goal, the effect on students' writing will be immediate and profound.

We have allowed the word *story* to encompass such a wide range of narrative forms and structures that it no longer has a useful meaning. Almost all writing, it seems, now qualifies as a story. Such a broad definition, however, doesn't help student writers create the kind of successful, enchanting stories they want. If we rethink and narrow our definition of *story*, the term becomes a powerful guide for student writers.

During workshops, I often ask students to define a story. Their answers are usually vague and general, and always uncertain. When I ask them to define a *good* story, they confidently identify a series of specific, important characteristics. I propose that the students' definition of a good story is closer to what we should use as the definition of a story itself. Tightening our definition of "story" will exclude many narrative pieces that would normally be classed as stories. We can give these pieces a different name.

The shift I propose means that we must stop thinking that every narrative piece is a story. Most aren't. This does not mean that stories are automatically exciting and delightful. It is still unfortunately easy to create a boring story. If the piece fails to meet the specific set of criteria that establish our new understanding of a story, though, let's no longer call it a story. Such a narrative piece can never achieve the captivating, mesmerizing, magnetic draw we seek in a story.

The first task of *Write Right*, then, is to create a new definition for *story*. Call it a "working definition" if you want. Call it a "writer's definition." From this moment forward, though, in this book, the word *story* will not refer to the all-inclusive popular definition; rather, it will refer to our new, sharply focused, and more useful definition—but what is this definition? What is a story?

A story is a unique and specific narrative structure, with a specific style and set of necessary characteristics, that includes a sense of completeness. The structural demands of a story create its incredible power and allure. Stories pass on wisdom and experience. Stories shape beliefs and values. Stories are the building blocks of knowledge, the foundation of memory and learning. Stories model effective use of words, of language. Stories create empathy and connect us to our humanness. Stories link past, present, and future by teaching us to anticipate the possible consequences of our actions, by teaching us cause and effect.

These are descriptive characteristics of a story, but not a definition of one. The question remains: What is a story? As a culture, we accept the existence of story and our vague sense of story without truly understanding what a story is. Understanding begins with a clear definition. Not every narrative piece is a story. A story carries structural demands and expectations that set it apart from other narrative forms and give it incredible draw and power.

I have asked thousands of students and teachers for their definition of a story. Most of the answers I hear revolve around plot:

"A story is when you tell about something that happened."

"A story is something you make up about something and write down."

"A story is when you tell about a series of events."

The most frequently offered answer, though, is this: "A story is something with a beginning, a middle, and an end." True; but what *doesn't* have a beginning, middle, and end? A magazine article does. The phone book does. So do a sewer pipe and a peanut butter sandwich.

My favorite definition came from a fifth-grade boy in western Pennsylvania. My asking the question "What is a story?" seemed to trigger one of those rare life epiphanies. For one brief moment, my question brought the universe and everything in it into clear, sharp focus for this kid. His face glowed with the glory of true insight. He raised his hand so hard that it lifted him out of his seat. His legs snapped straight, shooting his chair backward to clang against the radiator. He cried out, "I know what a story is! It's when you have a subject and a verb!"

I didn't have the heart to tell him he was wrong. I had to say that yes, that was the definition of a short story—a very short story—but that I was asking for the definition of a *longer* story. He was satisfied, and the class wasn't too misled.

All these definitions are plot-based definitions. Even the dictionary defines *story* using plot-based language: A story is a "narrative account of a real or imagined event or events." This is the old, general definition and is plot-based.

The problem with dictionary and other plot-based definitions is that they simply do not identify what gives a story its appeal and power. They do not identify what separates story from other narrative forms. Plot is not what allows readers to understand and internalize a story. Plot is not what readers crave and require from a story. Plot is not what uniquely separates story from other narrative forms.

Worse, plot-based definitions lead students to believe that all they must do to create a story is describe the action of one or more events. Not true. Plot-based definitions imply that a reader is satisfied if a sequence of events is adequately described. Again, not true. Describe any book or story you have enjoyed. I'm willing to bet that you would begin your description by identifying a *character* and not some disconnected bit of action.

So, what is a story? When does a narrative piece become a story? What differentiates a story from an article or an essay? What gives a story its amazing power?

Try Exercise #2, "What Is a Story?" (p. 107) with your class. Let them struggle with defining the elements that create a story. It is appropriate for you to question and requestion their answers. Likely, they will *describe* a story rather than identify and *define* those aspects of a story that set it apart from the rest of the narrative world.

The question may still remain. Have students really defined a story? What elements of a story create a unique listening or reading experience? It is time to have students identify the elements they think are critically important to creating a story. The best way to do this is to have them identify the moment when a last, critical bit of information is stirred into the mix, transforming a series of paragraphs into a story. Have students also identify what is still missing from the story-to-be as it slowly builds toward becoming a story.

Exercise #3, "Is It a Story Yet?" (p. 109) is designed to accomplish this task. Try it with your class. It is best to use this exercise while their definition of a story from Exercise #2 is still fresh in their minds. Compare the results of these two exercises upon completing Exercise #3.

"Is It a Story Yet?" is a very telling and important exercise. It helps students clearly identify character and conflict as the core of every story. It helps students identify character (and their reactions), problems, and struggle as three of the key elements that draw a reader into a story. These are the elements from which to form a definition, but this definition still hasn't been formed. What *is* a story, finally?

My definition is four letters derived from the elements identified in "Is It a Story Yet?":

> *story*
>
> a narrative account constructed
> around four central elements:
>
> C, C, S & G.

These four letters, I am certain, were on the tip of your tongue. The mathematically inclined may call it "C-squared SG" (C^2SG). Those inclined toward chemistry might call it "C-two SG" (C_2SG). The British might say "Double-C S&G." The letters stand for

Character
Conflict
Struggle
Goal

As we proceed, we'll examine each of these four elements, explore their components, and construct strategies that students can use to easily and effectively create them. These elements are common to all stories, and they uniquely define the form of story. They are the elements that draw us into a story. They are the elements we demand from a story.

1.   Characters

Characters are the central organizing element of all stories. Stories happen to characters. Characters are the driving force of a story. Characters take the actions, experience the conflicts, and undertake the struggles of a story. Characters are at the core of every story element and event. No other element has meaning and relevance without a character.

2.   Conflicts

Stories happen to characters, but they are *about* the problems and flaws that story characters must face. Problems and flaws are the elements that create conflict. The more dangerous the conflict, the better. Conflict implies adversaries. These opponents may be external or internal. They may be living beings or forces of nature.

Yet it is not the adversities, the problems and flaws, that rivet readers to a story. It is the *risk and danger* associated with the problems and flaws that readers really care about. Characters must have a vested interest in the outcome of their struggles. They must have something at risk for which they struggle. There must be some danger to characters. This danger need not be physical. Danger to their emotions, to their reputation, or to their self-image is every bit as valid and interesting. If characters risk nothing, face no danger, and have nothing to lose, the reader will never feel compelled to stick around to see how the story comes out.

Conflict, then, consists of the internal flaws and external problems a character must face, and the risk and danger associated with each.

3.   Struggles

Struggles are the actions a character takes to overcome conflict. No action (internal or external) means no story. The character must *do* something. It is during these struggles that risk and danger are realized, that meaningful action happens, that excitement and tension build. Struggles require character and conflict to have meaning for a reader, but it is the struggles themselves that readers come to watch.

4.   Goals

The character's struggle to overcome the story's conflict and associated risk and danger must be undertaken to achieve something the character cares about, to achieve the story's *goal*. If a character has no goal, no need, there is no reason for them to struggle or to face the conflicts before them, no reason to confront risk and danger. Conflict, struggle, and risk and danger must be undertaken for a reason. This reason is a character's story goal.

The approach to stories implied by my definition is far more important than the actual wording. Stories are about characters. All elements of a successful story evolve from the characters and their goals, conflicts, and struggles. All elements are dependent upon the characters. Plot derives from character and struggle. Setting is defined by the needs of the characters. The beginning, the middle, and the end are written to serve the needs of the characters.

Yet, in our culture, we tend to think first of plot when we think of story, even though, as readers and listeners, we demand and crave information about the characters. We have been indoctrinated to think first of plot, even though the human mind interprets stories through the perspectives and viewpoints of characters. Even though successful stories are character-based creations, still we think the focus of stories as being plot-based.

Try an experiment with your class: Have students make up a story—quickly, sponta-
neously, with no time for planning and little time for thought. They will think first of a plot
event or action and will then struggle to identify what the story is about, its plot, and how it
will end. If they were to begin by creating characters and their goals, conflicts, and struggles,
they would simultaneously define all parts of the story, including the plot, the ending, the climax, and the theme. This will be further demonstrated in Exercise #9, "The BIG Three."

My definition of story excludes many narrative pieces that others routinely call a story.
What are they if not stories? What are these written accounts in which characters, goals,
conflicts, and struggles are not clearly defined? We will call them incidents.

An incident is simply an event, something that happens. We tell each other about incidents every day. Few real stories happen to us, but incidents happen regularly. Rational humans work very hard, in fact, to keep incidents from becoming stories by avoiding the
conflict and struggle, the risk and danger, that are required of a story. Most of what we share
in informal, daily conversation and storytellings are really incidents. Incidents can, and often
do, contain tragedy, trauma, and loss. They describe and engender strong emotions. Still,
without identifiable conflict and struggle, an incident is simply something that happens.

Incidents become stories when the writer redirects the presentation, away from plot and toward the characters. Only after the writer makes this conversion will characters, and their goals
and motives, conflicts and flaws, risks and struggles, be brought to the fore to engage the reader.

In my graduate-level *Write Right* classes, I have participants pick a story from their
family history to write. Most struggle through the first days, realizing that their story
lacks tension, power, interest, a climax, and a theme. What they really lack is a story.
They are trying to write an incident because this is the form in which events are routinely
recorded and passed down through most families.

Incidents are plot- or event-based. Stories are character-based. Incidents can usually
be converted into stories, but this won't happen until the student understands the difference
between the two. The best way to keep your students from beating their heads against a boring incident that won't lend itself to successful development is to regularly review with
them the elements that make a story a story.

Some writers and storytellers define a story as *change*. I disagree. Change does not always create a story, and change is not necessary to create a story. Change could be desirable. A girl grows taller. That's change, but there will be no story until there is conflict: A
girl grows taller, taller than her older brother. She can outrun and outwrestle him. He's
twisted into a fit of jealousy. She's embarrassed by being the tallest in her class. Now we
have the makings of a story.

Really, it is *unwanted* change that creates stories. Why? Because characters *struggle*
against unwanted change and become immersed in internal and external *conflict* with the
agents of that change. Their *goal* is to avoid or reverse the unwanted change. Of course, change
isn't really necessary for a story to occur. The threat of change is enough conflict to incite characters to struggle. Clearly, it is character, conflict, struggle, and goal that create stories.

What Readers Want

By defining a story, we have identified several of the most important elements for student writers to focus on when they write. Before using this information to help students
overcome the first five of the seven writing problems they face, we must further explore
what a reader wants and needs from a story. Characters, conflicts, struggles, and goals are
some of a reader's needs. Are there more?

Few students have ever considered whether their stories meet a reader's wants and needs in order to feel satisfied. Fewer have tried to identify what these wants and needs are, even though, as story readers, each student has personally experienced each of them.

Exercise #4, "What Makes a Story Real?" (p. 113) is designed to help students identify those aspects of a story that a reader wants and needs. This exercise asks the question, What makes a story seem real? Actually, this is the same as asking, What makes a story appealing? The qualities that make a story seem real are the same qualities that draw us into a story.

Said another way, what draws readers most deeply into a story is a sense that the story seems real. Above all else, we want a story to seem real. Even fantasy stories of tap-dancing frogs, of grouchy trees who won't share sunlight with bushes and grasses at their feet, or of talking worms who wear fancy suits can be made to seem real. It happens all the time.

Every group with whom I try the exercise "What Makes a Story Real?" bases their votes on the same few reasons. First-graders, middle school students, teachers, senior-citizen groups: They all evaluate whether or not a story seems real using the same few criteria. Amazingly, they almost always mention the criteria in the same order.

What makes a story seem real? The first reason mentioned for believing one story over another is usually *details*. It tops the list of listener and reader demands. The second element of the story readers are drawn to, is some aspect of character information. We all gravitate toward stories that include character feelings, histories, reactions, motives, and relationships. These stories seem more real. We also gravitate toward humor. Stories that make us laugh are more appealing. Somehow, humor generates authenticity. Finally, we tend to believe that all of a story is real if it includes some factual information.

Because "What Makes a Story Real" is an oral exercise, some of the reasons mentioned will relate to *how* the story was told. Typically, these are couched in language such as "sounded more comfortable," "sounded more confident," "seemed to be more sure of herself," and so on. The focus of the exercise, however, is the story itself. Though listeners occasionally base their vote on other reasons, the central four are details, character information, humor, and factual information. This short list summarizes what readers want and need from a story. The story rises from the character information identified in the C, C, S & G definition of story.

Two additional considerations are significant to this exercise. First, no one has ever voted that a story seems real because they liked or believed its plot. There will always be a plot, and it must be logically plausible, but plot is not what readers or listeners are drawn to first. Second, the central four elements will be automatically built into each story when students overcome their seven writing problems.

Students quickly learn how to win "What Makes a Story Real?"—that is, how to collect the most votes. Within a couple of rounds, the real story (told by the student to whom the story really happened) is always the dullest. Every student who has the freedom to embellish their story will lavish physical detail and character information upon the basic story line. Their stories become wonderful—so wonderful, in fact, that listeners are certain no one could have made up all that detail, certain that the story must have really happened that way.

The keys to making a story seem real are the same keys uncovered when we tried to define a story: detailed character information, conflicts and problems, character actions (struggles) and reactions, and detailed descriptions of the scenes and actions. Each of these key elements needs further examination before we can create a successful progression of writing activities that leads student to writing better first drafts.

Fiction Is Folks

Try making up a story—quickly. You'll find that you tend to think first and describe first what will happen in the story. We begin with the plot. Yet plot alone never has, and never will, engage a reader. A searing summer sun blazing down its wilting heat during a long summer drought that has cracked the parched earth is, at best, mildly interesting. Add a main character—a young worm named Wilby who must cross this cracked and withered landscape, with a vial of medicine tied around his neck with a red ribbon, to save his dying grandfather. Add a flock of fierce, starving crows circling low overhead, casting black, fearsome shadows across the dirt. . . . Now we want to know what happens. It is always the characters, their conflicts, their struggles, and their goals that hook us and make us care about the plot.

Plot is the servant of character: Fiction is folks; stories are about characters. If any reader doubts the truth of this statement, consider that Americans consume more than 8 *billion* hours watching television soap operas every year. Yet nothing ever happens on the soaps. You can miss one for months and return only to find the same telephone conversations still in progress. Soap operas are character studies. This is why we sit transfixed in front of our televisions every day. We know every secret, flaw, goal, and twisted motive of every character; the more we learn, the more irresistible they become. Stories are about characters.

The question with which to begin our quest for a better approach to writing stories, then, must be: How does a student create an interesting, compelling character? The answer isn't luck, and it isn't raw talent. The answer is a specific set of information that every student can create.

I was well into my third year of analyzing stories and struggling to find the keys to their success before I found the first and foremost key: Forget plot and focus on characters. I was at a national storytelling conference in Jonesborough, Tennessee. The audience for an evening storytelling concert were all practitioners of the art—adult professional storytellers. Five tellers performed. One was a man who had a wonderful reputation as a master storyteller. He told a simplistic children's story. The entire plot can be easily summarized: Two children fall into a book, land on a cookie, meet some raisins and their king, fall out of the book, and go home. There is precious little I have omitted.

As he began to tell his story, I thought, Oh this poor, misguided man. We're a sophisticated audience and he's telling us a mindless children's tale. Everyone will hate it.

Well, everyone loved it, myself included. I sat awake long into the night analyzing that story and its plot. Again and again I reached the same conclusion: Nothing of significance happened in that story. How could we be so satisfied by a story in which nothing happens?

Then it hit me. We didn't love the story; we loved the characters. We loved the raisins and the kids. If an audience or a reader likes the characters, they will like the story. If they don't like the characters, they won't like the story. There is no way plot and action alone can pull them into the ranks of the satisfied.

Perhaps that storyteller missed a golden opportunity to tell a magnificent story because he didn't create something more elaborate for those delightful characters to do. Yet, with characters alone, his story was the hit of the night. This storyteller's success reveals the truth that stories are about characters. The plot will become apparent once the characters are understood.

Have your students begin understanding the central role of characters by pondering the same question I began with: What makes a story fun? Use Exercise #5, "What Makes a Story Fun?" (p. 115) to begin this process.

Did you have much success with your students? Were they stuck thinking that plot, action, and excitement are what they really like in a story? Many students think this and are quite insistent that they are right. In a sense, they are right. However, it is not action itself that they like. It is action done by or to a character they care about, action relevant to the character's goals and associated obstacles, that they like. Unfortunately, students tend to focus on the action aspect.

Helping students change the very core of their thinking about a story, from plot-based elements, such as action, to character-based elements, such as goals, motives, obstacles, and reactions, is difficult. Don't expect the shift to occur during one preliminary exercise. Part of the reason students don't give story characters their due is that they tend to think of character development as being mundane and boring rather than empowering and exciting. They approach characters the wrong way, just as they approach stories the wrong way.

To help demonstrate this for your class, use Exercise #6, "Character Myths" (p. 117). Through this exercise, students have the opportunity to compare three sets of character information: what they think someone else would want to know about them, what they want to know about someone else, and what they think creates an interesting character. These three sets of information will be substantially different. What students write down about themselves and what they ask to know about another student tends to be superficial information, insufficient for creating an interesting character. Still, it is valid, accurate information. It is one layer of a character.

The information they invent when trying to create an interesting introduction tends to fall into two categories: 1) an exaggerated, sensationalized version of the superficial information they discovered about another student, and 2) a fictionalized version of some of the more substantial information that helps create an interesting character. Students typically fictionalize their introduction information because it never occurred to them to request it of another student. Only the need to create an *interesting* character introduction brings new categories of character information into their mind.

What information creates an interesting story character? Humans aren't transparent, simple organisms. They are complex and often contradictory. They are surprising and multifaceted. They act differently in different situations. Characters, like humans, are created by concentric layers of history, belief, experience, and interpretation. Layer stacked upon layer—like the layers of an onion—creates a character. It is the sum of these layers, rather than any individual layer, that creates a compact, sturdy, interesting, believable character. The question can now be better stated: What layers of information create a character, and which automatically create an *interesting* character?

The place to begin this investigation is with Exercise #7, "Campmate" (p. 119). This exercise asks participants to list the information they would want to know about someone with whom they were being bunked at camp for a week. Older students list the information they would want to know about someone with whom they were being set up on a blind date. The lists are fun to create in groups and often become quite extensive. Still, all the requested information can be divided into four categories, or character layers:

- **Sensory image**, or information available directly to the senses.
- **Personality**, or how the character relates to and interacts with the world.
- **Activity**, or what the character does.
- **History**, or what the character has done in the past.

These are four of the five layers of a character a writer must address. They, and the basic character information they create, are shown in figure 1, "The Layers of a Character."

Fig. 1. The Layers of a Character.

The Core of the Character

The four layers of a character identified in the exercise "Campmate" define a character's physical being and make them real. They allow us to understand their reactions and feelings. However, there is a fifth, deeper layer that is both more basic to every character and more important to every story. This innermost layer involves the **core elements** of a character.

We tend to overlook the core elements of a character, just as we do for our friends and family. These elements are buried too deeply to observe, even in ourselves. They form the very core of who we are, and who we think we are. The place to begin creating characters is at their core.

One theory about what gives stories their incredible power is that, because a story only concerns itself with a few select aspects of a character's life and history, we can penetrate to the core elements of the character. By understanding these innermost aspects of a character, we see story characters with a clarity and insight that is perhaps never available to us with human beings. Through this core information, we are perhaps able to understand and relate to story characters more completely, more intimately, and with greater fulfillment than we do with human beings, whose core elements are less vulnerable to penetration.

The elements of the core layer shape all the layers above them and give them meaning within the context of the story. Though the core elements of a human being form an intricate web of competing and interrelated goals, motives, flaws, and foibles that would require perhaps a lifetime on a psychiatrist's couch to understand, a story character is reduced to having only those few core elements that relate to the story itself.

How are the core elements of a story character presented?

> *Sixteen-year-old Caroline wanted, more than anything, to learn to read. But in Colonial America in 1768, women did not read. Caroline's parents forbade her to even talk about it. "Society would ridicule any female," they said, "who wasted her time in idle reading." They were a poor family and needed every able-bodied member to work in the family candle shop. Through the small window where Caroline dipped tapers into liquid tallow, she watched the sons of rich merchants carrying books back and forth, discussing various passages. And she burned with envy and resentment. When one young man left a book on a nearby bench, Caroline rushed out of the shop, snatched that book, and clutched it to her chest. Silently she swore that, no matter what the consequences, with this very book, she would learn to read!*

This passage contains Caroline's core elements. What are they? Try to identify each as they are introduced and discussed below. Figure 2, "The Core of a Character," illustrates these core elements.

Fig. 2. The Core of a Character.

1. **The character.** A story character is created by interweaving layers of information—core information, personality, history, sensory image, quirks, habits, schemes, hopes, dreams, routines, fears, and so on. Where does a writer begin creating this mountain of imagery? What does the writer create first? The answer is to begin with a first impression, a quick, thumbnail sketch solely to identify the character.

    The first impression does not create a character. It identifies just enough information to begin the creative process of fleshing out a complete character profile. Six bits of information can be used to create a first impression of a character:

    1. **Species.** *What* is the character? A tree, a snail, a human being, or a shoelace? Begin by identifying the species.

    2. **Age and gender.** Age need not be in exact years. Words such as *old, baby, young, fully grown,* or *teenager* create a sufficiently accurate mental picture of the character.

    3. **Name.** Names are important. We all have many names: formal names, nicknames, what friends call us, what family call us, names used when others tease us, names we call ourselves. Some of these names we like; some we despise. Which names are used to identify a character, and how the character feels about those names, provides the reader with information about how the character views him- or herself and how others view him or her.

    It is empowering to search for a formal name that describes a character's personality. Upon hearing or reading such a name, one instantly "knows" the character's nature. Devote some time to ponder names for major characters. Sift through phone books, name books, and other lists of names. More importantly, though, I think the writer should consider the *variety* of names, nicknames, and titles used by and for a character.

    4. **Appearance.** Create one or two prominent aspects of the character's physical being.

    5. **Vocation.** Identify one aspect of the character's activity. It can be their job, their role in society, or a favorite hobby.

    6. **Personality.** Find one word that creates an overall impression of the character's dominant personality trait. Is the character *pushy, meek, friendly, quiet, hardworking,* or *lazy*? Some writers wait to create this one aspect of a first impression until after they create (or while they are creating) the other core elements, because many of these elements (goal, conflict, reactions, etc.) will reflect the character's personality. Some writers prefer to create a one-word personality impression first and then base other core information upon this personality trait. Either method works.

    How is a character's first impression presented?

    Piney, a sad, aging fir tree whose branches had grown bent, withered, and scraggly.

    A young, cocky frog named Shirley with an extra-long tongue that could clip a fly out of the air at four feet. Her friends called her "Sure Shot." Other frogs called her "Surely Stuck-Up."

*Born Samantha Vanderslice III, she was now a 28-year-old, frazzled house-
wife with four kids. Everyone called her "Mom," or "Mrs. Frank Frudgel."
She hadn't heard anyone use her own, real name, the name she had cher-
ished all her life, for five years.*

These are first impressions. First impressions can be very brief and simple, or they can become more elaborate as the writer explores different names for a character and their reaction to each. The top of figure 4, "Character Profile Sheet" (p. 34), includes space for a first impression.

Caution students to remember that the first impression is just a place to begin character development. Even this limited bit of information can empower creativity, and many students are tempted to immediately begin creating story events involving the character. A first impression does not define a story. It merely introduces the writer to a character so that they can proceed with creating that character's core information.

2. **Goal.** We all have more wants and goals than we could ever fulfill in one lifetime. Some of our desires and goals are noble, almost saintly, and deserve to be announced from the pulpit. Some we conceal in the deepest, darkest recesses of our souls and don't dare share them with anyone. Some are so private we hide them even from ourselves. That's why Americans spend hundreds of millions of dollars every year with analysts trying to discover why we do what we do, and what it is we really want in the first place. We struggle to discover our own hidden core elements.

Every moment of every day is governed by a complex set of competing goals. Should I take a day off and play hooky, or go to work? Should I be helpful and supportive, or be deliciously selfish for a change? Do I want to answer the phone, or let it ring and pretend I'm not home? We weave our way through a continuous minefield of competing wants every day. This is the way we human beings manage our lives. If we are to appreciate story characters, we must know what they want in the story.

What characters want to do and want to obtain in the story is their *story goal*. If readers don't know the story goal of the main character, they can never appreciate the events of the story. Story events only assume meaning for readers when they see the events either helping or hindering the main character from reaching their goal.

This seems simple and obvious. Some modern fiction overtly states this information: "Once there was a young frog named Fernly who wanted a raspberry fudge ice cream cone." The writer has introduced character and goal. In many stories, though, goals are anything but obvious. Goals are often buried and inferred. In many folk and fairy tales, character goals have been altered or lost through the ages, so that only plot elements remain.

"Goldilocks and the Three Bears" is a good example. In the opening paragraph, Goldi commits felony breaking and entering. Why does she do it? Why does she risk five to ten in the slammer, or death by bear claw? Stop and ponder this delinquent girl for a moment. Do the obvious answers make any sense? Ask your class to analyze Goldi's goal and then probe their responses for merit.

The three most common goals ascribed to poor Goldi are curiosity, hunger, and fatigue. Yet none makes any sense. Do you know any kids who would break *into* a house, at great personal risk, for a bowl of oatmeal? Most of the kids I know would break out of a house to get away from oatmeal. She can't be *that* hungry. Besides, there is no indication that she smells porridge before she busts in. Finally, if she's so hungry, wouldn't she search the cupboards for something better? If she's so hungry, why does she eat only the porridge in the *smallest* of the three available bowls?

Curiosity makes no real sense either. Goldi doesn't act curious either inside or out. The story never tells us that she curiously rummages through closets, drawers, and medicine cabinet after she's inside. Besides, curiosity is an exceedingly mild emotion to incite a major spree of vandalism and destruction. Unless poor Goldi is uncontrollably, obsessively driven by a curiosity compulsion, curiosity is too mild a motive to support the risks and dangers she willingly faces. The adrenaline rush of committing an ultra-dangerous crime, though, is not a mild emotion. The emotional charge of breaking and entering would overpower curiosity long before Goldi crossed the threshold.

I know. I once broke into a house, a good friend's house. I was 11, and his family had left for the weekend. I needed to borrow his four baseball mitts for a game. The heart-pounding, hand-trembling adrenaline rush of illegally tiptoeing across that familiar house lasted for hours. Imagine what it might be like breaking into a strange and dangerous house! The emotional surge of committing a crime would overpower mild curiosity every time . . . unless Goldi is already a hardened criminal who needs the jolt of a morning felony to get her day started because coffee alone just won't do it anymore.

Finally, put yourself in Goldi's place. You've broken into the bears' house. You've eaten their food. You've stayed long enough for any of the neighbors to call 911. You've smashed most of the furniture in the living room. One swipe from any paw of any resident and you're dead. Can you honestly say that, at such a moment, you would consider wandering upstairs to take a nap? She would have to be one cool customer to be able to sleep at a time like that!

I have no idea why Goldilocks broke into that house. That's why I will never tell the story. If you were to write, or tell, the story, though, and you had concluded why you think she broke in there, you would instantly create a more powerful and engrossing story. You would allow readers to glimpse the character's goal. They would no longer be simply watching events unfold. They would understand the significance of each event and become much more involved in the outcome.

As an example, I offer Goldilocks's goal as told to me by a ninth-grade girl. During a character-development workshop in an overcrowded alcove of the school library on a stifling-hot May day, I used Goldi's story as an example and asked why Goldi broke into the bears' house. One girl raised her hand and said, "I *know* why Goldilocks went in there. She was trying to commit suicide. That's why she picked the bears' house."

Of course, I am *not* advocating the suicidal version of "Goldilocks and the Three Bears." Still, it makes sense. I can see her standing at the foot of the stairs impatiently glancing at her watch. "Where are those bears? They were supposed to be home 20 minutes ago. Guess I'll go upstairs and lie down till they come home and do the deed."

Tell "Goldilocks and the Three Bears" to a room full of middle school students, clarifying at the beginning that Goldi doesn't plan to come out of that house alive. The audience will hang on your every word. Why? Because now they understand Goldi's goal, and that goal is real and important to the character, and relevant to the audience.

This is as close to magic as story writing comes. If a student writer makes the main character and their goal seem real and relevant to readers, the story will hook them. Incidentally, this criteria of relevancy is why kindergartners accept curiosity as being Goldi's goal. Five- and six-year-olds are curious, and they don't yet have the ability to anticipate the consequences of their curiosity. So curiosity is relevant and plausible to them.

No, you cannot say that Goldilocks has no goal. Nothing is ever done without a reason. If Goldi goes into the bears' house, she must have some reason for taking this action. It is the writer's job to uncover reasons and motives. We often don't search for underlying reasons and motives. We often refuse to admit to the real reasons and motives. Still, there always is one. Always. When a writer doesn't bother to find the goal for a main character, they instantly discard much of the potential power and allure of their story.

The main character's goal tells us when the story will end. It will end either when the character reaches their goal, or when the character realizes that they will never reach their goal. These are the only two story endings possible. Goal creates the ending.

The main character's goal tells us what the story is about: "Once there was a young frog named Fernly who wanted a raspberry fudge ice cream cone." This goal defines whether or not each event is relevant to this story, and thereby establishes the structure of this story. It tells us how to interpret every story event. The goal gives meaning to every event. The reader will interpret everything that happens as either helping or hindering Fernly from getting his ice cream cone.

Guide your students into the habit of creating character and goal at the very beginning of their story planning. The story can't move forward without these two key elements.

3. **Conflict.** Story conflict is the composite effect of two story elements:

    1. **Obstacles—problems and flaws.** The main character can't have reached their goal yet, or there wouldn't be a story. A man wanted a thousand dollars; he had a thousand dollars. There's no story there. It only becomes a story if the character hasn't yet reached their goal. This means that something must be keeping them from attaining their goal.

These somethings are called obstacles. There are only two possible kinds of obstacles: those that originate from outside a character (problems), and those that originate from inside a character (flaws). If the bears come home, Goldilocks has a problem. If the cops arrive and arrest her, she has a different problem. Whatever drove her to break into the bears' house, though, is a flaw.

A flaw is any internal drive, feeling, or motive that prevents a character from obtaining a goal. Flaws can be, but do not need to be, negative. Certainly, there are enough negative flaws to fill a thousand years' worth of literature: the seven deadly sins; the flaws warned against in the Ten Commandments; countless possible vices: fear, hate, revenge, superstition, anger, laziness, cowardice, prejudice, lack of self-esteem or poor self-image, and so on. The list seems endless.

Flaws can also be neutral (ignorance, misunderstanding, misinformation, etc.) or even positive (self-sacrifice, conflicting goals, nobility, etc.). Putting one's family or nation ahead of oneself can be as much an obstacle to obtaining a personal goal as fear or self-doubt. Neutral and positive flaws are still flaws in the context of a story.

Usually, flaws and problems are coupled. That is, the onset of a problem forces a character to confront a dreaded flaw. To solve the problem, the character must also overcome the flaw. Flaws and problems exacerbate each other and are far more formidable in tandem than either would be alone.

A knight of old must rescue the fair princess from the evil wizard and his henchmen dragons. The wizard, though, lives in the top of a twisting turret high upon a jagged mountain cliff. Not only does our hero have a dreadful fear of heights, but he is allergic to dragon breath. Still, he really wants to save the princess. . . .

Obstacles are the root cause of story conflicts. Conflict drives stories. Problems and flaws (as was true for goals) must seem real to the character and be relevant to the reader. Further, not all problems and flaws are created equal. The bigger the problem, the deeper the flaw, the more readers like it, and the more engrossing the story. The second element of conflict determines what makes a problem or flaw bigger or deeper.

2. **Risk and danger.** It really isn't the obstacles themselves we care about. The bears Goldilocks waits for might be koala bears—declawed koala bears—tame, circus-performing, declawed koala bears. Takes the punch out of the story, doesn't it? The evil wizard mentioned above might be a bumbling weakling who hasn't cast a spell correctly in 20 years and is afraid of his own shadow. His dragons might be friends of Puff the Magic Dragon. The knight's fear of heights might only be activated after he eats spicy food.

No, it isn't the actual flaws and problems we care about. It is the risk and danger they represent for the main character that holds us rapt. Danger is a measure of the severity of the consequences of failure. Risk equals the probability of failure. Increase the danger (what *might* happen to the main character), or increase the risk (the *likelihood* that that danger will be realized), and the story more strongly captivates the reader.

The flaws and problems that create conflict are an essential element of a story. Dominant risk and danger are characteristics of a *good* story. It is possible to have a story with little or no risk and danger. It would almost certainly be a *boring* story, but it would still be a story. I prefer to include risk and danger as core elements of a story because no writer intends to create a boring story. Without risk and danger, a writer will almost surely reach this disappointing outcome.

Relevant, unavoidable risk and danger hooks readers and won't let them go. Books described as "page-turners," books that the reader "can't put down," are stories in which risk and danger are used to their fullest effect.

In every story, have your students search for ways to burden the character with flaws and problems. Have them search for ways to increase the physical and emotional risk and danger associated with each obstacle. This means that students must be mean and cruel to the characters they create. However, students are loath to do this. Once they have created and given story birth to a character, they want to arm that character with extraordinary powers to ensure them an easy, successful story life.

You must help students shift their thinking. They must focus on flaws, problems, risk and danger, struggle and conflict, rather than character successes. In fact, the more cruel your students are to their main characters, the more thankful readers will be. An excellent way to help students understand this is to have them play a game in which they try to be as cruel as possible in creating story situations for a character. One such game is the focus of Exercise #19, "Getting Into Trouble," which will be introduced later.

The risk and danger a writer creates need not afflict only the main character. It may, and often does, afflict the character's family, community, or country. Someone on a quest to save a community is a much more gripping situation than someone on a quest to save only their own skin. Why? Placing an entire town in peril creates more total risk and danger than placing just one person in peril. More risk and danger creates more interest.

Typically, writers think of and work with flaws, problems, and their associated risk and danger as an interconnected whole. The term *jeopardy* is often used to describe this powerful combination. Jeopardy creates conflict. Every story, at its heart, centers upon a character and the jeopardy they must face. The greater the jeopardy, the more we care about the character, and the better we like the story.

4. **Crucible**. A crucible is a technical and less important core element of a character. Still, it is an essential consideration. If your students succeed in creating incredible obstacles for a character, with deadly risk and danger, some reader will inevitably ask, "Why doesn't the character just walk away and say, 'Heck, I didn't want that goal, anyway'?" We'd probably walk. We constantly do exactly this, watching goal after goal drift past while we sit unwilling to risk what's required to achieve them. The reader's temptation is to conclude either that the jeopardy must not really be that great (because if it were, any sane character would simply leave), or that the story is unbelievable, that its basic premise doesn't seem real.

Something must force the main character to confront the jeopardy your students have carefully laid in waiting for them. We all need a helping outside push to rise to heroic levels. That outside boost is a crucible.

The most common crucible is time. The kidnapper says, "Get the money here by eight o'clock, or I'll kill the hostage." The doctor says, "We have to find a matching kidney donor within 24 hours, or your brother will die." In either case, the race against time has begun. There is no longer any time to hesitate or back away from the danger. Fears and problems must be confronted now. There is no other option.

Pride, loyalty, fortune, and love are also commonly used as crucibles. Almost any flaw or problem can be used as a crucible if it is constructed as a conditional threat: "If you don't _____, then _____ is gonna happen!" A crucible conveniently forces the main character to take a deep breath, face the jeopardy, and engage the conflict, thereby creating a winning story.

5. **Struggle—actions and reactions**. Sir Isaac Newton first discovered it as one of his universal laws of motion. For every action there is a reaction. It is a basic law of nature, and of characters. To seem real, story characters must both act and react. Why? Because as human beings, *we* both act and react, and we use the actions and reactions of others as our primary means of understanding them. We are what we do.

To have a story, the main character must act, must do something. Their goal, what they want, is blocked by some jeopardy. No story can progress until the character is willing to take some action to obtain their goal. Readers want and need to know what this character is willing to do and risk to reach a goal. This is one of the most important aspects of the story to a reader. It is the glue that binds us to characters and their story. We judge characters by their actions. We relate to characters largely through their actions. The story plot is about the actions of the main character. Plot equals the actions the character takes to overcome obstacles and reach their goal.

It's possible to have a story in which the main character does nothing but sit frozen into inaction while they watch their goals and dreams collapse. It's possible, but it's very difficult to make such a story seem believable, interesting, or appealing. "Hamlet" is as close to such a frozen-into-inaction story as Shakespeare ever came. In scene after scene, Hamlet stews in seemingly endless consternation and turmoil and does *nothing* as other characters act around him. Eventually, though, even Hamlet had to act. The Elizabethan audiences would have pelted the actors with rotten fruit in protest if he hadn't.

Reactions are a subset of actions. Reactions are those unconscious, automatic movements (gestures, facial expressions, and utterances) made at the moment something happens, or within the first few seconds after it happens. Reactions are a form of reflex action.

Whenever something stressful happens, we automatically react, whether the stress is positive or negative. A favorite basketball team scores a basket. You react. You leap from your seat, shake your fists triumphantly in the air, and screech incoherently at the players, "Atta' baby wayta slam it yo' hot!" You never plan to do it. You never consciously think about it. You simply react. The other team scores. You react again, differently.

Someone trips and sprawls on the floor in front of you. You react. You laugh, stoop to help, flush with embarrassment, or snub the victim with your nose and turn away. A car crashes through the wall of your living room. You react. You scream and jump; you freeze in silent terror; you bellow in anger. In whatever way fits your personality, you react. You laugh, scream, flush beet-red, sneer, duck and hide, whine and complain. Even under the least bit of duress, we all react.

Stressful story events create opportunities for character reactions. There is nothing a reader craves more than character reactions. Yet we don't care about *all* reactions. Reactions to emotionally charged and stressful moments are what we want in a story. This is why a writer must search for ways to create and intensify the jeopardy. Obstacles, with their risk and danger, create stressful moments. The more such moments, the more opportunities we have to watch the main character react, and the better we like the story.

Character reactions are our primary guides to emotional interpretation of both the characters and the story events. Character reactions guide readers in deciding how they would react in a similar situation, and in interpreting a character's personality and attitudes.

Reactions are not statements of a character's emotional state. They are statements of action. The reader learns little with a statement such as "She was sad." We need to *see* what she does (Does her lip quiver? Does she clench her fists and tighten her shoulders? Does she laugh to cover the deep hurt? Do her eyes cloud or blaze with passion?), and we need to *hear* what she says when she is sad. These are reactions.

Character reactions also present the most surefire opportunities for slipping humor into a story. Exaggerate a character's physical and verbal reactions and the moment will be funny. It works almost every time. It is especially effective to repeat such a reaction throughout a story. Many stand-up comedians make their living exaggerating reactions to every imaginable situation. Studying successful stand-up comedians is an excellent way to study effective character reaction and overreaction.

Character reactions, however, even more than overtly stated goals, almost never appear in student stories. Students aren't accustomed to thinking in terms of character. They're busy thinking about *what* happens, and they forget about considering the ways their characters react to these events. Reactions to events are far more important to the reader, and to the story, than the events themselves.

Guide your students into the habit of thinking about how their characters react to each story event. Exercise #8, "React to This!" (p. 121) is designed to help students become aware of their reactions, as well as what makes these reactions interesting and humorous. After completing this exercise, encourage students to continue identifying reactions and the kinds of situations that generate them. The more aware your students are of the reactions they see around them every day, the easier it will be for them to create interesting and believable reactions for their characters. They will also learn how to weave reactions into the fabric of their stories.

The BIG Three

Of the core character elements discussed previously, three form the key to defining a story. The BIG Three are character, goal, and the problems and flaws that define conflict. Character is first. It identifies who the story will be about. Goal, what this character wants to achieve, is second. It identifies what the story will be about (its scope), the purpose of the story and each story event, and the ending. Conflict (defined by problems and flaws) is third. Risk and danger follow from conflict to create the immediacy and power of the story. Struggle, actions and reactions, follow from conflict, goal, and risk and danger to identify the plot of the story.

Actions are what a character does to overcome obstacles and will therefore follow from the story obstacles. Reactions must be plausibly consistent with the defined personality traits of a character and are used, reflexively, to *reveal* these traits.

The BIG Three thus identify the scope, purpose, ending, and plot of a story. Exercise #9, "The BIG Three" (p. 124) demonstrates this concept for students. It is an important and powerful exercise for reorienting the way students view stories into an approach that produces more successful writing. I recommend that you repeat this exercise often enough to establish the thought process it represents as a mental habit for your students. It is the single most important key to greater success at story writing.

The use of this exercise can help students substantially overcome four of the seven student writing problems. (#1: They think plot before and above character. #2: They write about undefined and underdeveloped characters. #3: They write without knowing the ending. #4: They focus on outcomes rather than struggles.) This system for approaching stories forces students to consider and develop characters before they consider plot. It lays the story's ending in a student's lap by forcing them to identify the main character's goal. By identifying conflict and jeopardy before considering plot, story focus is shifted toward struggles, and away from outcomes and meaningless story events.

Layers of the Character

A character's core layer is critically important to the character and to the story. However, this one layer neither defines nor creates a complete, interesting character. Core information gives writer and reader a thumbnail sketch of the character and defines the story. The other four layers of character information (sensory image, personality, activity, and history) flesh out the character and make them compelling and complete.

The writer needs to consider each of the five layers of each main character to visualize and describe a vivid character. The reader needs to see enough of each of these layers to understand and relate to this character, and to visualize a compelling image in their mind. Collectively, these layers make a character seem real and believable.

These multiple layers don't apply only to writers creating long novels. In a short story, a writer must visualize characters just as completely, and perhaps more completely, because the writer has fewer opportunities and fewer words with which to create a compelling character. They cannot include the majority of the details they have created for their characters. Because they must create an entire characterization with a few, select details, the writer must choose these details much more carefully to accurately portray the essence of the character. This requires the writer to envision their characters just as thoroughly as if they were writing a novel.

Beginning with the outside layer of this character onion and working inward to the core, the other four character layers consist of the following information:

1. **Sensory image.** Sensory image includes any information you could learn through your sensory organs, without mental interpretation—what something looks like, sounds like, smells like, feels like, and what it tastes like. You don't need to be Sherlock Holmes to observe whether a character is left-handed or right-handed, whether they walk casually or with quick, nervous steps as if they feared they were being followed, whether they smell like axle grease or reek of cheap perfume.

   Sensory information creates the physical reality of a character. It includes how they dress, their grooming habits, prominent features, expressions, how they laugh, how they keep and structure their environment, how they walk, sit, and talk. It includes the sound of their voice, the words they use, and the way they structure their dialog. It includes what they eat, how much they eat, and how they eat. It includes scars, bumps, twitches, habits (nervous or otherwise), and whether the character would be noticed if they walked into a crowded room. It includes their physical strength, as well as the strength of their jaw (facial shape) and the strength of their tongue (verbal audacity). It includes whether they maintain eye contact, as well as the color and shape of their eyes.

   The writer will never report all the sensory detail they create for main characters. They will communicate much of it through stereotypes. Stereotypes have the power and potential to cause much damage. However, they also have the power and potential to efficiently communicate sensory information. If I introduce a character as being a bunny rabbit, you would instantly invoke an image having not only size and shape, but also temperament, personality, and particular eating habits. These images are stereotypes. *This* rabbit, though, might have an insatiable sweet tooth and break into candy stores at night. It might be a vicious killer bunny who carefully files his long front teeth into razor-sharp points—not to chomp through carrots but through victims he plans to rob.

   Stereotypes are any specific qualities, attributes, or characteristics ascribed to an individual solely because of their membership in a particular group. If I introduce Lea as being a 12-year-old Eskimo girl, I don't need to tell you that she has straight, black hair; dark eyes; and a round face. You have already pictured these characteristics based on your stereotypical image of an Eskimo. If these characteristics are accurate for Lea, I can stop with the stereotype, having painted an accurate physical picture of this character. Many stereotypes, though, aren't as benign: a dumb blond, an Irish Boston cop, a California surfer, a teenage gang member, a cold-hearted bank executive, a kindly grandmother. These common stereotypes all carry some negative connotations that are often inaccurate.

   If I introduce a character as being a great white shark, you assume that the shark is a vicious, aggressive killer. This is a stereotype, but it's inaccurate. Stereotypes are very useful for efficiently communicating large sets of sensory and personality information. However, they must be used with caution and care to ensure that they do not denigrate, belittle, or malign either an individual or a group. Each writer is responsible for ensuring that they do not perpetuate negative, inaccurate stereotypical imagery. Each writer is also responsible for effectively and efficiently communicating their story to the reader. Used properly, stereotypes can help accomplish this.

2. **Personality.** A character's personality profile is a description of how they choose to interact with the world. It is a description of how they interpret themselves, express themselves, and interact with other characters. Are they honest, trustworthy, sullen, cruel, kind, glib, shy, quiet, boisterous, introverted, extroverted, foolhardy, or timid? Are they secretive, sensitive, hard-nosed, apologetic, or quick to blame? These are a few of hundreds of personality traits. Combined, they create a personality profile.

   Remember that characters may act one way in one situation and differently in another situation. An office executive might be loud, gruff, and demanding at work, but meek and submissive at home (which, by the way, is a stereotype). Personality elements often appear to be inconsistent and complex. Characters won't necessarily "be themselves" in every situation.

   The personality layer includes more than just one-word labels for how a character treats others. It includes what excites them, what bores them, their passions, their self-image, and their sense of humor (or lack thereof). It includes what they are afraid of, what they long for, their loves, their hates, their doubts, and their beliefs. These personality elements create motives for a character's actions and reactions.

3. **Activity.** The activity layer is really a subset of the history layer. It is, in effect, "present history." It is an accounting of the present pattern of activity in a character's life. It includes the character's job, hobbies, chores, and games. It may also include such information as their possessions, and how often they wash their hands and brush their teeth. Activity and personality are interrelated and should be plausibly consistent.

4. **History.** Writers often call a character's history their "back story." History is what happened to the character before the time frame of the story, the events that helped shape them into the character they are at present. Why should your students care about a character's history? The events that happened to a character in the past, and how the character interprets these events, is a (if not *the*) major determinant of their present beliefs, attitudes, goals, fears, hopes, and personality affectations. A character's history tells us why they are who they are, and why they do what they do. Who we are today is largely determined by what happened in the past.

   Likely, your students will not want to invent an encyclopedic character history. The key questions to ask when creating a character's back story are: Why do they think and act the way they do? What events helped shape their thoughts and actions? Usual targets in creating a back story include traumatic moments, major life events and significant moments, the character's origins and family structure, how they were treated by others, their relationships and friendships, and how they interpret their past performance at work, chores, and studies. It is the *unique* and *critical* events from a character's checkered history that a writer must invent. These are the events that define who a character is at present.

Interrogating a Character

   We have now identified a massive amount of information to consider when creating a character. Questions will surely arise: "Do I *have* to make it all up for every character?" "How long does it take to make all this stuff up?" "Where does it all come from?" If asked to answer their own questions, most students will grudgingly answer that character information must come from their own imagination, as if they had just been stuck with some onerous and impossible task. The truth isn't quite that simple, nor is it that difficult.

Three concepts will help ease this burden for your students:

1. **Characterizations should be grade appropriate.** First, the complexity and completeness of character profiles must be scaled to the grade level and capacity of the student writers. Middle school students will want to devote substantial time and effort to developing characters. Their stories will be at a level and sophistication that require substantial characterizations.

   First- and second-grade writers will still want to create basic core information for characters. They will still want to create enough sensory, activity, and personality information to communicate their story and their main characters to the reader. They will still want to search for those details that make their characters unique and interesting. However, they will do all this at a level of detail consistent with their language and story abilities. Though they often skip the history layer of character information completely, I have observed that their stories improve when they are guided to consider history through simple "why" questions: "Why do you think the character wants that?" "Why do you think they feel that way?"

2. **Main characters only.** Detailed, multi-layered character information is usually created only for one or two main characters. The information created for one layer often suggests information for other layers. Once a student has decided how a character will react, this information reveals much about the character's personality type, and vice versa. The character's physical description will limit the actions they will be capable of performing. The five layers must interrelate coherently and be plausibly consistent for the reader to understand and appreciate the character. Understanding this will make it easier for students to create all five layers.

3. **Let the characters of the world do the work.** Characters need be only partly created by the writer from imagination. A large portion of the necessary character information can come from observation. As soon as students have a brief sketch of a character, they should begin to watch and listen to the people around them. Can the ways these people look, act, speak, laugh, or blow their nose be used as models for the main character? Do students see any interesting actions or reactions in the people they meet? If their character is a dog, have them watch dogs for a while to see what they do. Have them watch themselves. How do they respond, react, and think? What do they fear, hate, and crave? Why not have their character adopt similar values and attitudes?

   Many elements of the best characters come from observations. I often spend months collecting observations for my characters before I begin to write a novel-length story. Students don't typically have the luxury of this much time, but they always have *some* time.

   More importantly, students don't need to wait for a story assignment to begin their observations. They can begin keeping a notebook of character observations now. Encourage them to log every interesting person, action and reaction, and dialog they observe. When given an assignment, they need only review their notebook of observations to find appropriate elements for their story characters. As an additional bonus, they'll find that the more they observe people, the easier and faster they'll be able to invent elements for a new character.

   A large portion of character information for any fictional character is certainly invented by the writer from their imagination. There are tricks to make this process easier for students. Have them hold an imaginary conversation with the character and ask them questions. The student should picture the character answering in the character's own voice and unique phraseology. Have students visualize their character and let the character provide the needed information.

Have your students pretend that they are a police officer interrogating a suspect. As a skeptical cop, the student should demand answers of the character and be very suspicious of the first, easy answers that come to mind for the character's response. Don't trust characters to readily reveal their true inner feelings, just as we humans do not. Challenge the character with tough questions. Reject the first answers and demand others. Continue until an interesting, story-worthy answer is obtained.

This search for character information is really a search for qualities and elements that make a character unique and interesting. The reader won't care to know how one character is like every other. The reader doesn't want to know everything, just what is special, interesting, and relevant about the character.

Figure 3, "Interrogating a Character" (p. 32), offers suggestions for the types of information your students should seek in analyzing their main characters. Remind student that these are suggestions intended to serve as guides in the process of creating interesting characters. Students should open themselves to other ideas and suggestions they encounter. If characters make the story, then interesting, unusual character traits, quirks, personalities, histories, actions, and reactions make the character.

I recommend that students begin creating their characters by creating the core elements, and then hang the other four layers of information onto that framework. Many ideas will flood into their mind as soon as the first impression, goal, jeopardy, and struggle have been created. Some of these ideas will be useful. Some will not.

It is often most useful to begin with a quick exploration of the character's history, the events that have led them to the point at which the story begins. Exercise #10, "Character Creation" (p. 127), provides a proven format for this first exploration into a character's history and, through that history, into the other layers of character information. This exercise helps students create a story solely by creating a character profile based primarily on the character's history.

The character profile is launched by collectively creating an identity for a main character and then a goal for that character. From this modest beginning, a long series of "why" questions guide the participants in uncovering character elements and traits that have brought the character to wanting the chosen goal. These simple "why" questions act as a guide to locating character information relevant to the story. Each new bit of information raises new questions about different layers of the character profile. A well-defined character and a well-defined story soon emerge.

Though the process of creating character information may seem daunting to your students, and though it may be initially frustrating for them to set aside their eagerness to immediately create the plot, they will soon find that the time they invest in creating characters pays handsome rewards. Well-defined character information helps them define the story, and actually reduces their overall writing time. It adds power and interest to the telling of the story.

Two additional character exercises are included in this book—Exercise #24, "Be Your Character," and Exercise #25, "The Character Game," both introduced later. Both are presented as small-group exercises in a comprehensive progression of writing activities that guides students from idea to first draft. Both help students expand their options for creating multi-layered character information.

Interrogating a Character

Questions to Ask	Your Answers Will Make the Character Memorable If It:
1. What does the character want to do or get?	• creates risk and danger for the character • is relevant to the audience
2. Why does the character want it?	• is based on deeply held feelings • expresses strong passions
3. Why doesn't the character already have it?	• exposes character flaws • represents conflicts of basic character goals • represents problems with great risk and danger
4. What is the character willing to risk and do to get it?	• requires the character to risk great loss • involves extreme (desperate) actions
5. What has happened in the past to make the character feel this way?	• reveals past traumas • reveals past hurts and injuries • reveals unfinished old business (skeletons in her closet)
6. What is the character's personality?	• describes unique and interesting characteristics • show how the character reacts • show what the character cares about and fears

Fig. 3. Interrogating a Character.

Additionally, figure 4 shows a typical "Character Profile Sheet" (p. 34). I have seen a great variety of these forms offered by various writers. They have ranged from half a page to eight pages in length. The form I include here is modeled after those I have developed for my own use. It is, I think, sufficiently comprehensive to help your students create a complete, well-defined character. Have students use it as a guide, rather than as a framework, which might limit the kinds of information they consider creating for their characters.

Spilling the Beans

Many students complain that, if they were to include in their story all the information they invented for their character, it would ruin the story, making it too slow and boring. They are right. The first truth about characters is that a writer must create much more information about each than they will ever use. However, if the writer creates only that information absolutely needed in their story, the characters will never seem real, nor will they be interesting.

Your students' first job in creating a story is to create complete main characters. This act requires them to create multiple layers of compelling character information. The more character details they create, the more effective their story details will be. Which details should they include in the story? The details that reveal the unique, relevant, and interesting aspects of the character. Additional information is sprinkled into the story, as needed, to create vivid images of the character and their actions.

How should they reveal character information to the reader? First, they should reveal information as needed by the reader to understand and visualize the characters and their actions. There is no need to paint a complete picture in the opening scene. Intermix action with narrative description. Tell the reader something about the characters, then show the reader some action involving the characters, and then repeat the process.

Second, to the extent possible, students should let the characters do the work for them. A writer doesn't need to provide all the essential character information in long narrative passages. Let the characters reveal themselves through what they say, what they do, how they do it, their expressions while they do it, what they think, how they react, and the names they use to describe themselves. Let characters reveal one another through their thoughts about them, their actions and reactions towards them, and their dialog with and about them.

This approach to revealing character information is part of the general maxim writers call, "show don't tell." Rather than telling the reader that a character is clumsy, the writer shows the character dropping and fumbling various objects. Readers will conclude on their own that the character is clumsy.

If students follow these guidelines and suggestions for creating characters, they will populate their stories with vivid, interesting characters. The five-layer system for creating character guarantees the remedy of student writing problem #2: They write about undefined and underdeveloped characters. Along the way, the creation of core character information focuses the story on character rather than plot, thereby identifying the ending and focusing the story on struggles rather than outcomes. Thus, this system also remedies student writing problems #1, #3, and #5: They think plot before and above character. They write without knowing the ending. They focus on outcomes rather than struggles.

After a final note about character, we'll remedy student writing problem #4: They write "blind." Then your students will be ready to write.

SENSORY

NAME:_____

Nicknames. By self:_____By others:_____

Age:_____Sex:_____Height:_____Weight:_____

Hair:_____Eyes:_____

"Look" or impression:_____

Physical "sense":_____

Key / unique physical characteristics_____

Key / unique physical habits:_____

CORE

Wants / Goals:_____

Fears:_____

Passions:_____

Flaws:_____

Problems:_____

PERSONALITY

Personality type:_____

. Attitude toward work:_____ Friends:_____

School:_____Play:_____

Clothes preference:_____

Food preference:_____

Guiding beliefs:_____

Quirks / habits:_____

Reactions—When something goes wrong:_____

         —When something goes right:_____

HISTORY

Family structure:_____

Family history:_____

Major life traumas:_____

Major life successes:_____

Past work / function:_____

Unique past activity:_____

ACTIVITY

What character does:_____

Hobbies:_____

Sports:_____

Volunteer efforts:_____

Unique activities / hobbies:_____

Fig. 4. Character Profile Sheet.

Key Characters

One last character-related question: Must students complete multi-layer character profiles for every character? No. For a novel-length (chapter-book) story, a writer will probably want to create a complete profile for each major character. For a short story, students might only profile two characters—the main character, or protagonist, and the character against whom the main character struggles, or antagonist. The main character is that character whom the story is about. The story ends when the main character's goal is resolved. That is, the story ends when the main character either gets what they want, or realizes that they will never get what they want.

The antagonist is that character against whom the main character must struggle. The antagonist is the embodiment and personification of the conflict and jeopardy the main character faces. The antagonist is the one we love to hate. The antagonist must have their own wants and goals in the story. They must have purpose and motive. They must intentionally or unintentionally block the main character from reaching their goal.

Must the antagonist be a person? Of course not. In many stories, the antagonist is an animal. A cat might be the ideal antagonist in a story about a mouse. Lions, bears, tigers, and cobras have all played the role of antagonist. The antagonist might not even be a living thing. A mountain that must be climbed or crossed might be the antagonist. A river or a raging winter storm might be the antagonist.

The antagonist might even be the main character. It is said that the best fight is always the fight against oneself, and that we are often our own worst enemy. This is said because it is often true. If the greatest obstacle facing the main character is an internal flaw instead of some external problem, then they are their own antagonist. One part of the character's personality will fight against another part. This battle becomes the central focus of the story.

> *Little Goldilocks promised to be a good girl, and she meant it. "I'll be good Mommy!" But she was so curious she just couldn't resist exploring anything she hadn't seen before. "No, I won't go in the bears' house. I promised to be good. . . . But just one peek won't hurt. . . . No! I won't. . . . But I might find something wonderful. . . . No! Yes! No! Yes!"*

In this version, Goldi is her own antagonist. The real fight is between two internal drives or wants. Everything else in this version results from this internal flaw.

To identify the antagonist, examine the story's obstacles. Find the greatest obstacle, the one with the most risk and danger, the one that will be the most difficult to overcome, the last obstacle encountered during the story's climax. This obstacle is the antagonist. The climax of the story should be the scene in which the character confronts the final obstacle standing between them and their goal. This obstacle should be the antagonist, because stories build toward the greatest conflict and confrontation at the climax.

Is there always an antagonist? Must there be an antagonist? Yes. Stories are about struggles. Stories without struggles become incidents. Stories without an antagonist become rambling incidents. If the main character struggles at all (as they must), they must struggle *against* something. This something is the antagonist.

A question I am regularly asked during writing classes is, "But what if there isn't an antagonist in *my* story?" My answer is, "Then you have written an incident, not a story, and focused on events (plot) rather than characters. The antagonist is there. You are just politely avoiding the confrontation with them. Go back to your main character. Define their goal. List the obstacles that block them from that goal. The biggest is the antagonist. If you have no obstacles and no struggles, then you have no story."

Can there be more than one antagonist? Yes and no. Antagonists are the embodiment of obstacles, and stories can have many obstacles. However, it should always be clear to both writer and reader which obstacle is the greatest and most dangerous. That greatest obstacle is the real antagonist of the story. There should always be one enormous obstacle looming in the background. As the main character bravely (or not so bravely) overcomes each of the lesser obstacles, the reader should be thinking, Sure, you got by *that* problem, but [antagonist's name] is still out there, and you still have to face [it/him/her]!"

It is much easier for the reader to focus on one major obstacle and other immediate but lesser obstacles, than to focus on several equally threatening obstacles. If a writer does include more than one antagonist, all must be confronted and overcome at the story's climax. If all the antagonists are worthy opponents, seemingly impossible to overcome, the reader may well begin wondering how the main character could possibly defeat all of them at once. We readers will begin doubting the ferocity of these multiple antagonists.

The single routine exception to the one-antagonist guideline occurs when an internal flaw becomes the main character's greatest obstacle. The main character acts as their own antagonist. In such stories, there is still room for an external antagonist to torment the main character. A problem can be personified into an antagonist. Then the main character must confront both their internal flaw and some other antagonist during the climax.

So why should a student writer care about the antagonist? Now we come to the real point, the value of "bad guys." I call this portion of the discussion "Thank You Darth Vader." I'll use Luke Skywalker and Darth Vader from the *Star Wars* trilogy to show the value of antagonists.

Luke Skywalker is a whiny, insignificant figure, a farm boy who doesn't want to get involved. He doesn't want to stay home. He has no fighting skills. He bumbles and stumbles badly and needs constant saving throughout the first episode of the trilogy. He is rightly called "kid." Certainly, Luke is a central character in the first episode. He's certainly on the screen a lot. Han Solo, Princess Lea, and Obewon are the real heroes, though. They have the skills to lead the fight, to save the day, and to plan the escapes.

By the second episode, it becomes clear that Luke will have to be the one to confront Darth Vader. Instantly, Luke becomes our hero. Instantly, he is admired and respected—not because of anything he has done, but because of the antagonist he must face. By this time, Darth Vader is an all-powerful, unconquerable monster. How can little Luke ever beat him? We are hooked—not because of the main character, Luke, but because of the enormity of the antagonist he must face.

By the third episode, Luke has risen to superhuman stature. He *must* become superhuman to have a chance against Darth and the even-more-evil emperor. Imagine how different and boring the story would be if Darth continually lost power as Luke gained it. In the third episode, Darth would be a confused, powerless, toothless old man as all-powerful Luke Skywalker crushed him with a triumphant sneer.

It would be a very different story indeed. Luke Skywalker would become a villain, for only villains take unfair advantage of the weak and helpless. The thing that makes Luke Skywalker a hero is not Luke. Heroes can never proclaim their own stature, or they would be reduced from hero to braggart. A hero is made by the enormity of the antagonist they must face. A hero can never be more powerful than their antagonist, or the tension would evaporate from the story. There would then be no doubt in the viewer's mind about the outcome.

If your students are to make their main characters into heroes, if they are to build suspense and tension into their stories, the way to do it is not to develop a heroic main character. It can't be done. The way to do it is to develop a seemingly unbeatable antagonist. Then the main character automatically becomes a hero.

Stories are about struggles. A writer who develops and enhances the struggles automatically develops and enhances the main character. In many respects, the antagonist is more important to a student's story than the main characters. Heroes can only rise as high as their foe, the antagonist, will allow them to rise.

Want another example?

If the Lone Ranger arrests a wimpy, bungling, apologetic, deaf-and-blind bank robber, he gets no credit. We want him—we need him—to face a dozen grizzly, mean, well-armed brutes. We want the Lone Ranger to be out of bullets when he does it and have only a plastic pocket comb with which to defend himself. We want him to have to capture all 12 of the desperadoes within the 10 minutes before the dynamite they hid blows up the whole town. We even want him to be tied up in barbed wire lying on the train track with an express train barreling down on him as his 10 minutes begins.

Now the Lone Ranger gets to be a hero. Same main character, different antagonist and jeopardy— but he's only a hero in one of these two stories.

Jeopardy, and especially the antagonist, are the keys to creating a memorable main character and to creating gripping tension and suspense in a story. The value of a gloriously diabolical antagonist cannot be overemphasized. The more power your students give to their antagonist, the more power they allow for the main character.

Seeing Is Believing

There is a common misconception among student writers that, if they begin to write as soon as they have an idea, the story will emerge and take shape in their minds as they proceed. I mentioned this misconception previously as writing myth #7: "The story will reveal itself to me as I write."

There is a grain of truth here. Many writers *do* use preliminary story writing as a vehicle to explore the story and develop both story and character. However, developing a story this way requires more, and more extensive, rewrites. Further, research shows that developing a story in this way is not nearly as effective for writers who still struggle with, and must concentrate upon, the mechanics of writing. Yes, free-form drafting of a story *can* work as a tool for story development—but it does not work well for grade-school students.

Most importantly, though, the act of writing does not tend to develop an expanded and more vivid image of scenes and characters in a student writer's mind. This creative expansion is blocked by the mental effort devoted to the mechanics of writing (physically writing and controlling pen or pencil, word choice, spelling, grammar, etc.). Telling a story, talking about a story, drawing pictures of a story, acting out a story—these have all been shown to increase a writer's visual detail. Writing a story, though, does not.

If students have not formed a story in their mind as a vivid, detailed "movie" before they begin to write, it probably never will develop, either in their mind or on the page, without a considerable rewriting effort—an effort most students have neither the time nor inclination to perform. The writing progression I recommend (and present later) for stories emphasizes prewriting activity. Oral-based, prewriting activity has been shown to develop the vivid imagery students need to write convincingly.

A central theme to these activities is that student writers must be able to see their story in their mind as if they were really there watching it happen. This concept is embodied in a nine-word sentence. In workshops, I write the first letter of each of the words on the chalkboard and let the students try to guess the sentence. The nine letters are: **I. Y. C. S. I., Y. C. W. I.**

Try this with your class. Can they guess the sentence? I am routinely surprised at how many writing classes can nearly guess the correct sentence without any prompting. If a class is stumped, I lead them to guessing the first word. Then the students always guess the rest. They will usually guess that the sentence is: If You Can See It, You Can Write It.

I usually have the student who first guessed this repeat it several times, so that everyone hears it. Then I say, "You're wrong. But you were *close*. You are missing only two letters, one on the end of each of two words in the sentence."

Soon, someone guesses the correct sentence: If You *Can't* See It, You *Can't* Write It. This negative statement is more correct than the positive corollary because a writer still may not be able to write a story even though they can see it. However, if they *can't* see it—vividly, completely, in multisensory detail (including sound, smell, etc.)—they will never effectively communicate their story to a reader.

What does this sentence mean? A student who writes without the benefit of a detailed, multisensory mental movie of their story is no more able to make this story seem tangibly real and alive for a reader than they would be able to describe a forest they walked through with their eyes, ears, and nose closed. They just can't do it. Reality comes from the details. Details come from vivid sensory impressions and images.

Unfortunately, many students "write blind." That is, they write without being able to see the story in detailed, vivid technicolor in their mind. It is as if they were trying to describe the world around them while wearing heavy blinders that hide the world from their eyes. They have an idea and immediately begin writing. They write without seeing the scenes and characters they are trying to describe. Writing blind is student writing problem #4. It is corrected by remembering the sentence: I. Y. C. S. I., Y. C. W. I.

There is a simple test your students can use to ensure that they do not write blind: If they can see each scene as well as they can see their own bedroom, they are ready to write. Sounds simple—but have them pause a moment and consider how much they know about their own bedroom. They know the physical layout and all the colors of each object in the room. They know where there are spots, chips, nicks, and stains. They know the history of each object. They know whether sunlight pours through their windows in the morning or afternoon, and how shadows slide across the walls during the day. They know whether the room is stuffy or drafty, hot or cold, bright or dark. They know what smells they would smell and sounds they would hear in the morning while getting dressed, and in the evening while doing homework. They know how and where dust collects. They know the identity and history of every bit of clutter. They know an amazing amount of details about this room.

Using what they know of their own bedroom as a guide, students need to create similar degree of detail for the scenes of their story. Let's use the kitchen scene in "Goldilocks and the Three Bears" as an example. A student might say, "She walks into the kitchen, eats porridge, and walks out. I don't need to know much about that room." Wrong.

This is a scene in the story, and the writer can't make it seem real without first seeing it in detail. What kind of bowls do bears use? Metal mixing bowls? Rubber dog bowls? Ceramic or china bowls? Are there plates beneath the bowls? Are there placemats? Napkins? Silverware? Do bears use spoons and napkins, or do they simply stuff their faces into the bowls? Are the bowls on a table, a breakfast bar, or just lined up on the floor? Where is the sink, the counter? Are these clean, or covered by last night's dirty dishes? Is the kitchen lighted? Are there electric lights or candles, or does the sunlight come through windows? How many windows? Are there curtains? What kind? Are the windows clean, or covered with a moldy film of musty bear hair? Does the kitchen smell like porridge, honey, dirty dishes, or bears? What's on the floor? Black-and-white checked linoleum? Where's the refrigerator? Is it covered with pictures that Baby Bear has drawn, stuck there with small bear magnets?

After answering these questions, a writer can see the kitchen and add the detail to make it come alive for the reader. The writer needs to see, hear, smell, and understand each story character as well as they understand members of their own family. If they know specific details about a family member, they should create similar details for their characters.

The writer's job is to create a story and then create in their mind a detailed, vivid, multisensory, exacting movie of that story. Most of a writer's prewriting activity should focus on the development of this vivid imagery. The most beneficial outcome of this process will be a bounty of rich details that the writer can sprinkle liberally into the story, invoking a similarly detailed image in the reader's mind.

Description and Detail

Teachers clamor for them. Readers crave them. Students struggle with them. Description and detail, the Big D's. What is description? What is detail? Are they the same? Should student writers use both?

First, let's define our terms. Have your students each write *their* definition of the terms *description* and *detail*. Have them discuss their definitions to arrive at a consensual definition for each word. Compare their definitions with the following definitions from *Webster's Collegiate Dictionary*:

> **Description:** An account of something in words; discourse intended to give a mental image of something experienced.
>
> **Detail:** The small elements that, collectively, constitute the whole; a small or minor part considered separately from the whole.

These terms are often used interchangeably. Really, *description* is a more general term. What we, as writers, mean by the term *detail* is a bit more specific than what Webster's defines. Details are a carefully chosen subset of description. Details both describe specific element(s) of some things *and* imply or invoke some larger context, usually either the scene (the entire physical place) or the characters. Dew drops clinging to a lacy spider web can conjure an image of an entire morning meadow. The image of a crumpled sheet of paper, blackened on one side by frantically pencil-scribbled notes that have been crossed out, only to have been written in a new form, only to have been viciously scribbled out again, can invoke an image of a desperate writer's desk. These are details.

Every reader wants to vicariously experience the events, stresses, and triumphs of a story. They need three things to be able to do this:

1. A character and their core information (discussed previously).
2. A perspective and viewpoint that will pull the reader into the action of the story (discussed shortly).
3. The details that bring the story to vivid life and make it seem real.

Writers search for ways to describe scenes, events, and characters that provide specific sensory imagery and also provide clues about the entire scene and its characters. When they find a way, they have found details. Details are what writers seek. Details create reality in the reader's mind.

Exercise #11, "Description and Detail" (p. 129), will help clarify the difference between description and detail. Try it with your class. Do they struggle more with creating description, or with selecting detail from that description? Be sure that your students understand the purpose and nature of details, and that they can recognize effective detail, before proceeding to other activities.

Even with our definition, the concept of detail is still difficult for students to grasp. Answering four common questions will help:

1. **What does a writer describe?** The details a writer chooses for their story describe where the story happens, what happens there, and the characters. Details describe what each of the five human senses would record if readers were within the story to experience it for themselves. Details describe that which sets something apart, that which is unique about something, that which is interesting and relevant about something.

2. **How does a writer describe something?** A writer describes by finding *sensory* details that the reader will understand. These details should be specific, not general. They should describe the unique attributes of something. Description may include direct sensory details: "Her eyes clouded over and she wept." Or, if it will create a more vivid image for the reader, the description may include similes or metaphors to reference to a common thing, experience, or phenomenon: "Her eyes darkened like a stormy sea, and glistening tears trickled down her cheeks and dripped off her chin as if from a leaky faucet." The goal of every detail is to help create a vivid, precise, and interesting image of the story in the reader's mind.

3. **What forms can description take?** Detail can take many forms. Specific nouns are a form of detail. The noun *pants* is neither specific nor descriptive, but *Levi's Dockers* is. Adjectives, prepositional phrases, and dependent clauses provide more specific information to separate a specific noun from others of its type. There are many pairs of Levi's Dockers in the world. The specific pair we want to identify is the *tattered* pair of Dockers with *two neon orange hearts stapled over ragged holes to keep her underwear from showing through.* Now we have specific detail, identifying a specific pair of pants while creating visual imagery to help the reader see it. I didn't include detail about the zipper, stitching, or pockets because there is nothing unique and interesting about them for this specific pair of pants.

    Specific action verbs are also a form of detail. "She entered the room" provides no specific image of the action taken. "She blasted into the room," "She crept into the room," or "She slithered into the room" each provide a clear image of the action taken and shows how her entrance was unique and different from other people's entrances. Adverbs describe verbs and can be used to provide more specific detail when a verb alone will not suffice.

    Detail can also take the form of references to common things, experiences, or phenomena. "She cried a lot" doesn't create nearly as unique and vivid an image as "She cried a waterfall." Similes and metaphors (discussed in Part III) are the grammatical forms a writer uses to create these references. "She cried a waterfall" is a metaphor.

4. **What creates good detail?** Details may include almost any word and take almost any grammatical form as long as it creates a strong, vivid, and specific image of what is unique, interesting, and relevant about the thing, character, or action being described. Here are four questions your students can ask themselves about the detail they plan to include in a story to help them evaluate its effectiveness:

    1. Is the description general or specific? (Compare "He was tall" to "He was just tall enough to bonk his head on the doorframe when he forgot to duck.")

    2. Does the description refer to a common trait or to something unique about the thing being described? (Compare "He had long, black hair that reached to his shoulders, as did every male in this Athabaskan town" to "He was the only Athabaskan in Ketchqua who curled his long, black hair with a curling iron.")

3.   Does the description include either direct sensory details, or a simile or metaphor referring to some common thing, experience, or phenomenon?

4.   Does the description include direct sensory details that the reader's own senses could gather if they were within the story, or does it *tell* the reader about internal character information (feeling, mood, attitude, or personality)?

Good detail is specific, unique, and sensory, conveying an impression obtained through one of the senses—sight, smell, taste, touch, or hearing. Good detail may be either direct sensory information, or simile or metaphor. Typically, direct sensory information is used far more often than simile and metaphor.

I sometimes have students in storytelling classes play a game called "What Time Is It?" One team member tries to convey a specific hour of the day to their team as quickly as possible by miming what they would do at this exact time of day. No words may be spoken. The winners are rarely the best mimes or actors. The winners are usually the students who select the most descriptive, most identifying detail to mime. Given the right detail, the team correctly guesses the hour in a few seconds. General, non-specific details, even well mimed, rarely lead to correct guesses. It is the unique, interesting details that create vivid images in the mind of the viewer (and reader).

Effective detail, however, is more than just unique, interesting sensory information. Truly effective story detail of action, place, or object also gives readers insight into the characters associated with the action, place, or object being described. Effective detail leads readers to conclude particular internal information about the characters.

Effective detail describing a character's room will also give the reader information about the character. Choosing the most interesting detail of a man's car will effectively describe the car and also reveal some of the man's personality. Creating a vivid description of how a girl jumps rope will not only allow readers to mentally watch her, but will also allow them insight into what kind of a person she is.

Exercise #12, "Detail Alert!" (p. 130), helps students distinguish description from detail, and demonstrates the power of effective, descriptive detail. Use it repeatedly with your class. Also, the following list of seven guidelines can be used as a quick recap to keep your students' detail on track:

1.   Name names. Be as specific as possible.

2.   Avoid common, ordinary details.

3.   Use multiple senses (sight, smell, taste, touch, and hearing).

4.   Use details that distinguish the thing being described from other things of the same type.

5.   Choose details that reveal combinations of setting, action, and character.

6.   Vary your details. Use both direct sensory information and simile or metaphor.

7.   Ask yourself, "What is the most unique, descriptive, relevant, and interesting detail I can find for the thing I need to describe?"

Try Exercise #13, "The Detail Game" (p. 133), with your students as an opportunity to review the principles of good detail. After each round of the game, have the class try to identify more effective details than those the Contestant used. This will encourage each student not only to try to guess the object being described, but also to review and critically evaluate the detail used by the Contestant. Effective detail will soon be second nature, solving the most common teacher complaint about student writing.

Limits of Detail

Detail is a powerful, alluring element of a story. Detail creates reality. So, detail is essential, right? The answer is yes, and no. Detail is essential, but it has a price. Writers don't get to pepper detail into their stories for free. The price of detail is the quantity of extra words required. It can slow the pace of the story. Compare the three versions of the story passage in Exercise #12. Count the words in each. The third version is certainly more exciting. It's more visual, more appealing—but it's also much longer than the other two.

Using detail becomes a compromise, a balancing act. Too little detail makes a story vague, unreal, and boring. Too much detail makes a story sluggish, tedious, and boring. Too much detail kills the energy and excitement of action sequences and hides the power of sharp dialog. All stories need detailed descriptions. What they really need, though, is the minimum possible amount of detail to effectively and vividly communicate the scenes, actions, and characters.

How will students know how much detail to include? It is better to err on the side of excess when first drafting a story. One of the tasks of editing is to check for excessive and unnecessary detail. It is much easier to remove the excess than to try to create new detail and wedge it into an undefined and vague scene.

There are two keys your students can use to better balance their detail in the initial drafts of a story:

1. Concentrate descriptive detail where you can afford to slow the pace of the story. Keep action sequences and powerful dialog interchanges relatively free of description. Find ways to include necessary detail in the scenes and passages that precede these exciting and fast-paced story segments.

2. Use the best descriptive detail you can find to create the biggest bang for your buck. Detail always slows the story's pace, but creating vivid visual imagery for the reader is well worth the price of a minor lag. The strongest detail reveals both physical imagery and action, or both physical imagery and character, or even all three in one precise word or phrase.

These two keys are the reason students will never use all the detail they create for a character. A writer must create complex character profiles and images, and then sift through this stockpile of information for the few details that best represent the entire multi-layered character package. The more information a student creates and has available, the more likely they are to find the perfect details to use in their story.

Detail is part craft and part art. Students will not master it in a few easy stories. The good news is that detail constantly surrounds us. Students can practice choosing vivid details every moment of every day. They should practice this wherever they go. How would they describe the "scene" they are in if it were part of a story? What details would they choose? What words would they use to form these details? What details would they exclude? What actions and movements do they see, and how efficiently and precisely can they describe it? What details would they use to describe the "characters" near them?

Student writers should make a habit of searching for interesting, revealing details. The more they do it, the easier it becomes.

Dialog

Dialog is actually part of character. I discuss it in a separate section because student writers routinely list dialog as being a major writing problem. What is dialog? It is an exact listing of what characters either say or think. Including dialog in a story is one of the most powerful and effective ways to reveal a character to the reader. Dialog is, in a sense, a form of character detail. The way characters speak defines who they think they are, and who we think they are.

As with detail, there is a price for including dialog. Dialog also slows the pace of the story. Generally, more words are required to present information in dialog form than in direct exposition or narrative. The benefits of using dialog are fourfold:

- Dialog pulls a reader into a story and makes it more immediate and gripping.
- Dialog makes the reader feel closer to (empathetic), and more sympathetic toward, the characters.
- Dialog creates energy and is an excellent source of humor.
- Dialog reveals characters and makes them seem more real.

Still, there is a balancing act to perform. We are not writing scripts, but stories. There is an old adage about dialog: Use dialog for the sake of the character; use narrative for the sake of the story. This means that, when a writer needs to present a substantial portion of the story quickly and efficiently, they should use narrative. When a writer needs to reveal character, or to include a character in the events of a scene, they should use dialog.

Students struggle with dialog. It is extremely difficult for them to write dialog that sounds real. It is difficult for them to write dialog that includes information necessary to move the story forward. It is difficult for them to weave narrative and dialog together as unified and mutually supportive parts of a scene.

The reason behind these struggles is that dialog is its own language. Conversational English tends to use sentence fragments, to be highly repetitive, to be informal and casual, and to jump from topic to topic. Narrative English is more structured, linearly sequential, and formal.

Dialog is somewhere between these two. Dialog must sound like unrehearsed conversational English. Yet it must efficiently move the story forward like narrative English. Dialog is a new language, a new way of structuring and organizing words. Students are not familiar with this language, even though it uses vocabulary they already know. Writing effective dialog, like mastering any new language, is an acquired skill. It comes with practice.

What a character chooses to say, and not to say, gives the reader direct insight into the character's intelligence, their education, their age and interests, and their attitudes and concerns. Not every character will notice the same things, think of the same things, or talk about the same things, even in exactly the same situation.

If a student has created a rich, vivid character, they should be able to see and hear that character speak in their mind. Just as we all can anticipate what a family member would say in a given situation, writers should be able to anticipate and hear what their character would say, and how they would react. As your students create a conversation, have them ask themselves the following questions:

- What would each character want to talk about, to say?
- What would they notice?
- What do they want the other character to know?

What a character says will depend mostly upon the history, activity, and core elements the writer has created for that character.

The writer must also consider *how* a character says something. More than the sound of the character's voice, the writer should consider dialect, sentence length, sentence connectivity, sentence complexity, and grammar. In other words, the writer must consider how a character combines words into thoughts and sentences. How a character speaks is primarily determined by the personality and sensory profile created by the writer.

An example will be helpful. Six characters (four animals and two humans) arrive at a rolling field sloping down to a wide pond. Have your class infer as much information as they can about each of these characters, based solely upon what the characters choose to say and how they choose to say it:

Character #1: *It was easy pickin'. Fat City. No lookouts, no nothin' to slow me down. Tall grass for hiding. Good rocks for sunning. And lots of fat bodies for the snatchin'! I did see one horse. But a couple of rattle shakes and he'll spook. Good water, and easy hunting by the water. This place is mine!*

Character #2: *The grass was sweet, and, well, it was like I remembered once over in the north county when I had a whole pasture. You should have seen me then, young muscles rippling as I ran. Everyone stopped and watched back then, I tell you. But I was saying somethin'. Let me see. By golly, it was about the meadow, the grass, waving in gentle ripples, brilliant green. Reminded me of the first time I traveled up to Kentucky for a race. Eight states I traveled through just to show off in races. I was somethin' to see back then. But what was I saying about the pond? There was somethin' about that meadow and pond I wanted to tell you. . . .*

Character #3: *The fort goes there. We can have a flag and swords and charge down the hill to destroy the pirates on the lake. We'll even have a cannon and a catapult by that tree. I can reach the bottom branch of that tree. I'll climb to the top and probably find an eagle's nest or a dragon or something. Maybe we could camp out here and roast marshmallows.*

Character #4: *Well I declare. It looked like such a sweet spot. Lots of tall grass for cover from birds, and a good supply of water. What was that? Did you hear something? No? I guess I've just got the jitters. But listen to me ramble on. There was plenty of grains to eat and nooks for hiding in. A lovely spot, really. And I didn't see any signs of snakes or owls, either.*

Character #5: *There were bugs everywhere. And I like didn't want to touch anything. I couldn't even see a road or a house. All there was were weeds and like a scummy old pond. And I said to myself, So, duh. Like what are you doing here? Mud and grass stains were all over my legs. There wasn't even music or electricity or anything.*

Character #6: *Oh sure, sure, there was work to be done. There always is. But I could see the possibilities. Dominant breeze out of the northwest. That would minimize wave erosion on the dam. It definitely needed repair, but had a solid core. I can organize three work details to begin hauling logs. We can take advantage of the downward slope to accelerate log movement. I wish the trees were closer to the pond, but the peculiarities of nature can't be helped. There's still three hours of daylight. No time like the present to begin the tasks at hand.*

Were your students able to guess the identity, age, personality, interests, intelligence, concerns, attitudes, and relative position of each character? What aspects of the dialog reveal this character information? Did students use common stereotypes to connect dialog to character identity? Most likely, they did. What if the stereotypes don't apply to these characters? Can students create character histories to justify their interpretation of these characters based on this dialog?

Finally, writers must develop a sense of what *natural conversation* sounds and looks like, that is, what it sounds like when two or more people talk together naturally. The keys to conversation are the motives and personalities of the characters involved. If students first develop a sense of the sound of each character's voice, then of their personality, and finally of exactly what each character wants from the conversation (what they want to say, learn, hide, reveal, etc.), dialog will be much easier to write.

An example will be useful here, and for the exercises that follow. I include no narrative with this dialog so that the reader must rely wholly upon the dialog for information about the situation and the characters.

Jennifer: Mom, Carol is having a party to—

Mom: No. Don't even ask. I'm still mad about the last time you went out with that bunch.

Jennifer: It's not exactly a "party" party. Just a get-together. We'll probably talk about school projects. I really want to go. Can I?

Mom: You have a lot of homework to do tonight. Homework before social get-togethers. Why didn't you say something earlier?

Jennifer: Carol's mom said it would be okay for a bunch of us to come over. We won't go out, or anything. Maybe I could finish my homework over there.

Mom: This is the third time you've pulled this stunt this month. You know you won't do any work once you start gabbing with your friends.

Jennifer: Just this once, mom. I really need to be there tonight. I won't stay out late. I promise. Pleeeeease!

Mom: Tomorrow *is* Friday. You *can* sleep in on Saturday. Sixth-grade homework isn't that critical. . . . Just don't stay out 'til eleven o'clock again, or this is the last time ever!

What story information can you learn from this dialog? What character information can you learn about Jennifer and her mother? What can you infer about their personalities, their history, and their family dynamics from this conversation?

Conversations, like stories, are built on goals, obstacles, conflict, and tension. What do you think Jennifer and her mother each want? What obstacles must each overcome? Is there conflict in this conversation? Tension? What creates them? Interruption, opposition, sudden jumps to a new topic, unanswered questions, and emotionally charged words and statements all create a sense of conflict and tension. They make the dialog more powerful.

Note that Jennifer and her mother don't often directly answer each other. Rather, they put forth their own position and their own arguments. Note also that there is much unsaid history between these two (as there should be in such a conversation), which the reader must infer from the spoken words.

I have included two exercises to help students with writing dialog. Once they understand the aspects of dialog, mastery is only a matter of practice. The three most difficult aspects of dialog for students seem to be the following:

1. Making it sound real.

2. Using dialog to move the story forward and present essential story information.

3. Making dialog concise and rapid to keep the pace from dragging.

Exercise #14, "Narrative to Dialog" (p. 135), is designed to help students overcome the first and second problems. Exercise #15, "Compression" (p. 138), is designed to help students overcome the third problem.

In Exercise #14, students are forced to weave all essential story information into dialog as they turn a narrative passage into script form. The first goal of this exercise is to include all necessary information in the dialog in such a way that the dialog sounds natural and real and reveals essential character information. The second goal is to do it in as few words as possible.

The previous dialog passage between Jennifer and her mother contains no narrative. All necessary information about the events of the scene is contained in the dialog. Dialog doesn't contain as much scene and event detail as does narrative description. However, there should be enough information in the dialog for the reader to understand what is happening.

Exercise #15 helps students learn to say what they need to say in dialog quickly and efficiently. It is impossible that a character could needlessly ramble when there is a tight word limit for each line they speak. After students try these exercises several times, their dialog becomes sharper, more revealing, and more powerful.

As an example of dialog compression, the conversation between Jennifer and her mother has been compressed below using a seven-word limit per line:

Jennifer: Mom, Carol's having a party to—

Mom: Don't even ask.

Jennifer: It's just a get-together.

Mom: I'm still mad about last time.

Jennifer: Her mom said we could.

Mom: You have homework.

Jennifer: We won't leave her house, or anything.

Mom: Homework first.

Jennifer: I'll finish it over there.

Mom: You've said that before.

Jennifer: I won't stay out late. I promise.

Mom: Just don't stay out 'til eleven o'clock again. . . .

Jennifer: I said I promise!

Mom: Or this is the last time!

In compressing this dialog, I cut the number of words to less than half the original number. Some of the story information is of course lost in this compressed version. However, the emotion and power of the interaction is heightened and emphasized. In a story, dialog never stands alone. Narrative passages around the dialog set the scene and tell us about the events. Dialog reveals information about the characters, their passion and energy. Compressing dialog helps remind the writer to focus dialog on its primary mission—revealing character.

Working with Dialog

It takes practice and work to write tight dialog that carries the energy of a story, propels it forward, and reveals character. Here are some hints to help your students make their dialog more successful:

1. **Consider the goal of each speaker.** What does each speaker want to accomplish in the conversation? What does each speaker want to hide? How much are they are willing to reveal? How do they want others to view them and the topic of discussion? Don't force characters to answer each question asked of them. There are many times when *we* don't directly answer a question but rather talk about something that explains our position in an attempt to steer the conversation in our own favor. Let characters answer with silence sometimes if they can't think of a way to answer that will benefit themselves. Have each character say what is in their own best interest. Don't make them say anything they don't need or want to say.

2. **Beats.** Beats are the bits of narrative detail a writer weaves between lines of dialog. In a play, beats are called "stage business." Beats give the actors something to do, and they build movement into the dialog. Beats show readers where the characters are and what the characters are doing while they talk.

   In the following example, the beats are italicized:

   John flopped onto the couch. "Do you think mom will be home soon?"
   Caroline opened a can of Coke and glanced at the mantle clock. "Not for another hour."
   John turned to stare toward the kitchen. "But I'm hungry now."
   Caroline slid onto the couch beside her brother. "Don't even think about it. Mom said no snacking before dinner."
   John rubbed his chin and then smiled. "Dessert isn't a snack. It's dessert. I could eat my dessert now. Then I won't have to worry about saving room for it during dinner."

Beats provide visual detail. Beats anchor a reader into the scene and setting during passages of dialog. So beats are essential, right? Yes and no. Beats are an excellent way to include needed detail for the reader. As you can see in the passage above, though, too many beats become tiresome and detract from the dialog. Beats can dilute the power of dialog.

What's a writer to do? First, use beats judiciously. Include only those beats that are necessary to create a vivid, accurate picture of the characters and their actions. Second, don't spread out beats one per line of dialog. Group them so that three or four lines of dialog can flow unimpeded and undiluted. This will free the natural energy and power of dialog and will help keep the pace of the story from dragging. The above passage would read better if the beats were rearranged as follows:

Caroline opened a can of Coke. Her brother John flopped onto the couch and asked,
"Do you think mom will be home soon?"
"Not for another hour."
"But I'm hungry now."
"Don't even think about it. Mom said no snacking before dinner."
John rubbed his chin and smiled. "Dessert isn't a snack. It's dessert. I could eat my dessert now. Then I won't have to worry about saving room for it during dinner."

Beats provide vivid information. Beats are valuable. Beats are almost necessary—but don't beat the dialog to death!

3. **Character tags.** Every writer searches for another way to write "He said" and "she said." He said, she said. We all agree that *said* is a flat, boring verb. We all fear that we use it too much, but what are the alternatives? We still must let the reader know who's talking. The verb used to identify the speaker of a line of dialog is known as a "tag."

There are four alternatives to repeating *said* for every tag. First, use different, more descriptive verbs. Instead of *said*, try *claimed, alleged, stated, commented, asserted, implied, offered, added, commented, declared, noted, remarked, promised, affirmed, shouted, announced, asserted, described, proclaimed, intoned, vocalized, called, whispered, mumbled, groaned, whined, cried, sang, cheered, panted,* and so on. There are hundreds of verbs to choose from. Depending on what a character is doing and how they are speaking, there are always one or two verbs that more accurately convey the character's action than *said.*

Besides providing variety, action-verb tags themselves are a form of detail. However, as with most other aspects of writing, descriptive tags must be used judiciously. Use none and the story becomes boring. Use too many and the writing seems forced and ridiculous. Use descriptive tags sparingly. Save them for times when that other verb becomes the perfect detail to describe both character and action. In the first John-and-Caroline passage, I would definitely include one descriptive tag, and possibly a second. I would have John *whine* his first line, and possibly have Caroline *threaten* or *warn,* "Don't even think about it . . . ."

Second, a writer can use beats as substitutes for character dialog tags. Notice that no character tags are used in the first version of the John-and-Caroline passage, and only one (*asked*) in the second. If dialog follows a beat, the reader will assume that the character described in the beat is doing the talking.

Third, when only two people are involved in a conversation, the reader will assume that separate lines of dialog alternate between speakers, unless the writer tells them differently. The writer can group three or four lines of dialog together without any tags without losing the reader. This technique brings out the natural power and speed of dialog. I use this technique in the second version of the John-and-Caroline passage.

Finally, a writer can let unique dialects or speech patterns identify the speaker. If one character (and only one character) stutters, the reader will know when that character is speaking if the writer writes the stutter into that character's dialog. Again, a caution: Don't use this technique often to avoid using *said*, and don't use it with more than one character in a story. The reader can follow a character's conversation this way, but it is work. If the writer makes the reader work too much and too often, they will resent it and stop reading.

Though powerful, effective alternatives to *said* exist in the writer's bag of tricks, students shouldn't be afraid to use good ol', plain ol' *said*. It's clear; it's concise; and it doesn't compete with the dialog for attention as do some descriptive tags and beats. If a writer includes dialog, this dialog should be the star. Tags should support and enhance the dialog, not try to overshadow and upstage it.

4.   **Read all dialog aloud.** Dialog is what characters *say*. It must sound real and natural when it is said. There is no better or more effective way to make dialog sound real than to read it aloud. The writer should say the dialog repeatedly, adjusting the wording to sound real and natural when read. Then the writer should have someone who hasn't heard it read the dialog aloud. If the dialog is good, someone who doesn't know how it should sound will still read the right emphasis, tone, and pace into the dialog.

If this reader doesn't read it the way the writer intended them to, the writer has two ways to correct the situation. (No, one of them is not to find a better reader. A good story will be read correctly by any reader.) First, the writer can change the wording of the individual lines of dialog to clarify the feeling and intent of each speaker. Second, the writer can insert descriptive tags and beats to clarify the feeling and intent of the speaker, as well as how the reader should interpret the line.

The more often a writer reads their dialog aloud, the stronger and better it becomes. The same is true for the number of people who read it—the more the better.

5.   **Indirect dialog.** There are times when a writer doesn't want to invest the time and the words required to have a character directly say something, but still must tell the reader and other characters what that character said. Furthermore, the writer may still want to use the attractive power of dialog. What is the writer to do?

Try indirect dialog. This is used when either the writer or another character summarizes or paraphrases what another character said. Indirect dialog reads fast and efficient like narrative, but still sounds like dialog, still carries much of the energy of dialog.

Indirect dialog is a useful compromise—but beware. Like pungent spices, indirect dialog should be used very sparingly. A little adds a subtle, rich flavor. Too much is overpowering and spoils the stew. Indirect dialog should only be used in those rare moments when a writer can't afford to slow the story's pace, but still must report what a character said.

Dialog is an incredibly powerful tool for every writer, from the first-grade student to the professional. Replacing narrative with dialog increases the energy and interest of the story, adds character detail, and draws the reader into the story. It is worthwhile for students to become comfortable writing dialog. It solves a great variety of story problems and provides much of what students want from their own stories, as well as what teachers and readers want from them. It just takes practice . . . practice . . . and a little more practice.

Dodging the Potholes

We have addressed each of the first five of the seven student writing problems. Before presenting an overall progression of story-writing activities that incorporates the concepts we have discussed into a comprehensive program for story development, I want to address several common student complaints. These complaints don't qualify as major writing problems; rather, like potholes in an urban street, they are annoyances that rattle the teeth, slow the trip, and make the ride less comfortable.

Title

Many students, especially younger students, think that they should write a story's title first, because the title comes first when they read a book or story. The opposite is true: Save writing the title for the absolute last task in story writing. I believe that students should leave a blank space at the top of the first page of their final draft (and I mean *final* draft). After this final version is finished, they should search through the story for wording, concepts, or themes to use as a title.

For most of my published stories, I created the title long after I had written, edited, and reviewed the story. Really, the title is not part of the story. It is a separate, but related, piece that advertises the story.

We all want our titles to be catchy and memorable. We want titles to pique reader interest, to make the reader curious about the story's content. There are several patterns that have proven themselves consistently successful. The most common of these are the following:

1. *The* [Noun]. This title form is simple, direct, and easy to remember. *The Crucible*, *The Jackal*, "The Triumph."

2. *The* [Adjective Noun], or *The* [Adjective, Adjective Noun]. Adding one or more adjectives gives the reader a better sense of what the story is about and the general tone and mood of the book. *The Killer Brussels Sprouts*, *The Awful, Terrible, Really Bad Day*.

3. [Noun] *and* [Noun]. This title form lets the writer establish a comparison between, or a linking of, two dissimilar concepts, themes, or characters. It is catchy and gives a potential reader pause to ponder the content of the story. *Pride and Prejudice*, "The Lion and the Mouse," "Samson and Delilah," *The Old Man and the Sea*.

4. [Noun] *of* (or other preposition) [Noun]. This title form is easy to use. Often, either the central theme or main character can be categorized in some greater context. Writers can use this relationship as the basis for a title. *The Heart of Darkness*, "The Commissioner of Balloons," *Marvels of Science*, *All About Eve*.

5. [Prepositional Phrase]. We use prepositional phrases often in our everyday speech. They are familiar and comfortable, and can provide a curiously engaging idea of the story's content. "Above the City," *Along the Waterfront*, "Into the Lion's Den," *Of Mice and Men*.

6.   [Question]. Questions create suspense, interest, and tension. Why not hook the reader with a title that asks a question? *What Ever Happened to Baby Jane?* "How High Can an Elephant Fly?" *Why Do Clocks Run Clockwise?*

First Paragraph

If the title is the last thing to be written for a story, the first paragraph (or first few paragraphs) should be the next to last thing written. The first paragraphs of a short story (or the first chapter or two of a novel) have more tasks to perform than any other part of the story. Some of these tasks can't be clearly understood until the story has been completely written.

These tasks of the first paragraph(s) of a short story (a story of 1,000 words or less) include the following:

1.   **Make a good first impression on the reader.** The first paragraph is like a first date. You want to make a good impression so that the reader will want to stay for a second date. Finding the wording to create the right impression is easier once you clearly know the entire story.

2.   **Set the tone and mood for the story.** Readers want an immediate "sense" of the story. Will it be funny, scary, a farce, a fantasy, a true story? The writer must ensure that the tone set at the opening of the story accurately reflects the mood of the rest of the story.

3.   **Introduce the main character and their goal.** We have already seen that character and goal are at the heart of every story, that they define the story's purpose and structure. Readers become bored and irritated when kept in the dark. Let them know immediately what the story is about, so they can jump in and become involved with the story and its characters.

4.   **Pull the reader into the middle of the action.** The modern trend is to begin telling a story in the middle of the action rather than with background and introductory information. This was not always the popular style, but it certainly is today.

5.   **Set up the last paragraph.** Many writers overlook this important task of the first paragraph. Have your students examine stories they like. Frequently, the wording, sentence structure, and theme of the first paragraph match, or at least parallel, that of the last paragraph. This structure gives the reader a sense of satisfaction and provides a sense of proper closure for the story. Garrison Keilor regularly uses this technique to signal the end of his *Lake Woebegon* stories.

That's a lot of pressure to put on a few simple lines of text, especially when most student writers struggle with the act of beginning, itself. This is the best reason not to worry about getting the first paragraph right when beginning to write the story. Writers must begin writing *somewhere*, though, and this is usually with the first paragraph. However, students should consider the first paragraph as being merely a place holder, a set of words that helps them begin writing and holds a spot for the *real* first paragraph, which will come later, after the rest of the story has been written.

There are two quick exercises your students can do to help them develop a better sense of writing first paragraphs. Have students trade stories after they have completed their first drafts and read only the first paragraph (or about the first 10 percent) of the story. Each student then states what and who they think the story will be about. Have them decide how they think it will end and if the story will be serious or humorous, an adventure story, a scary story, a mystery, a romance, and so on. Have them guess as much as they can about the story based on their impressions of the first paragraphs. The story's writer then decides how accurate this first impression is—or is not—and adjusts the first paragraph accordingly.

For the second exercise, have students reread the first page of three stories they like and know well. Have the student write an explanation of how each opening shapes their expectations and guides their understanding of the story. The more students analyze successful openings, the better they will become at creating their own.

Perspective and Viewpoint

Most students have never thought about the perspective and viewpoint from which they write. Yet there are few tools at the writer's disposal that revitalize and reenergize a boring story faster and more easily than shifting perspective and viewpoint. First, have your students try to define perspective and viewpoint and then differentiate them from each other.

Perspective is really a measure of where the writer forces readers to place themselves within the story while reading and imagining it. If the story were a movie, perspective would define where the camera is placed to film the movie. The writer, of course, creates the story's perspective. The reason for, and the effect of, creating a perspective is to place the reader in a specific vantage point as they watch the action of the story. Perspective is created by *where* the writer is allowed to go, and *whose mind* the writer is allowed to enter. The effect on the reader of such a seemingly simple decision is staggering.

Viewpoint refers to the story character through whose eyes the reader views the story. Every story is written from some perspective. Some perspectives, though, do not have viewpoint characters.

A number of systems have been devised for defining and describing the possible perspectives a writer can use. The goal of considering perspective isn't to create a new list of terms for students to memorize, but rather to assist the student writer in creating a stronger, more effective story. Students should focus on three questions when they consider perspective:

1. Should I follow one character throughout the story, or must I jump from place to place and character to character?

2. If this story were a movie, where would I place the camera to film it?

3. Which character can most effectively tell this story, or should it not be told from the viewpoint of one of my story characters but instead by some unnamed narrator who describes the story?

The following list of six possible perspectives can assist students in answering these three key questions:

Omniscient perspective. Writing from an omniscient perspective, the writer can go anywhere, know anything, and enter every character's mind and thoughts. The writer can instantly cross continents and oceans, leap tall buildings, and enter inside every character's mind without asking permission. It is as if the writer were an observer floating high in the sky, far above the action, able to see everything, go everywhere, and know every character's thoughts. This is the perspective students automatically use, not because they need to, not because they want to, but because it never occurred to them to do anything else.

> **Plusses:** Omniscient perspective is the most flexible, convenient perspective for the writer. Nothing is hidden from, or inaccessible to, the writer.

Minuses: Omniscient perspective distances the reader from the action of the story. It pushes them up to that same high vantage point the writer uses. No one's heart ever pounded reading a story written in omniscient perspective. It carries the least energy. It makes it more difficult for the reader to become deeply involved in the story and its characters.

Objective perspective. This is a relatively new perspective, and has become popular only during the past decade. Objective perspective is the ultimate statement of the "show don't tell" philosophy. In this perspective, the writer may only report what the reader's senses would record if they were there to watch it happen. In objective perspective, the writer can go anywhere, see anything, overhear anything, but may not enter *any* character's mind to learn their thoughts and feelings. As Sgt. Friday said, the objective writer only reports "the facts—just the facts."

Plusses: Objective perspective is a sensory-laden way to write. Rich details abound. The reader is allowed to—must—do all interpretation to decide how characters feel and what their secret motives are. This makes the reader feel more involved with the story.

Minuses: Stories written in objective perspective tend to be slower and wordier than those written from other perspectives because the writer can't summarize or interpret anything. Pace and energy often lag in objective perspective. The reader is also denied a viewpoint character to identify with in objective perspective. Stories written in objective perspective are told by a faceless, invisible, objective reporter.

Third-person perspective. Instead of floating high above the action as with omniscient perspective, the camera for third-person perspective follows one specific character. Readers are linked to that one character throughout the entire story. The writer may only go where that one character goes, and may only enter that one character's mind and know that one character's thoughts. However, it isn't this character who reports the story. The story is told by an observer, or viewpoint character, hovering at the perspective point, who tells about the actions of this main character and can objectively comment on all story events.

Two subgroups of third-person perspective are often distinguished from each other: *distant* and *close*. In distant third-person perspective, the camera is tied to a kite floating high above the character. Like omniscient perspective, distant third-person is an overview perspective. This perspective follows one specific character, but the reader has the freedom to see fairly far afield.

For close third-person perspective, the camera hangs over the character's shoulder like an umpire hangs over the catcher's shoulder during a baseball game. The writer reports not what a meadow or forest looks like (as they might from an omniscient or distant third-person perspective), but rather what individual flowers or the dust on the trail looks like. The reader sees and experiences exactly what the character sees and experiences, and is thus pulled very immediately into the action of the story.

Plusses: Relative to omniscient and objective perspectives, third-person perspective, and especially close third-person perspective, creates immediacy, power, suspense, and tension. The reader is always near the central action, and feels every emotional tug and twinge of the main character. The indifference of omniscient perspective is gone. Every up-close-and-personal detail of the story is made vivid, immediate, and real for the reader. This is a flexible perspective and still allows the writer to report objectively about the main character and their actions.

Minuses: Third-person perspective is a limiting perspective. The writer can report only what the main character experiences. The writer can go only where the main character goes, and can enter the mind of only that character. Other character's thoughts and feelings can only be implied through what those characters say and do.

Second-person perspective. Very few stories use second-person perspective. It is awkward and difficult to maintain. In second-person perspective, the reader becomes the main character, and the writer talks directly to the reader: "You walk down a dark alleyway and hear the rattle of trash cans rolling through the inky blackness behind you. A cat howls ahead of you." What is awkward about this perspective is that many readers will think, *I* don't hear a cat howling. *I* wouldn't walk down that dark alley. The reader may lose interest and reject the story. I recommend that student writers avoid using second-person perspective.

Plusses: Because second-person perspective directly places the reader into the story, it creates immediacy and power.

Minuses: This is the most limiting perspective. The writer continually tells the reader what they do, feel, and experience. It is extremely difficult to pull the reader through an entire story without having them revolt and say, "Not me!"

First-person perspective. Here the writer writes as if the story were happening, or had happened, to them. Instead of writing, "He walked down a dusty trail through a meadow of wild flowers," the writer writes, "*I* shuffled down a dusty trail through a meadow of wild flowers." Everything reported in the story is filtered through the observations, beliefs, and understanding of the main character—as played by the writer.

Plusses: First-person perspective creates all the power and immediacy of close third-person perspective, and has a bonus advantage: First-person perspective creates impeccable legitimacy and authenticity. If the story is happening to the writer, the writer is the official expert and thus knows exactly what is really happening. As with all close-in perspectives, the reader is thrust into the core of the action.

Minuses: There are three limitations of first-person perspective. First, the writer may experience only what the main character experiences, as with close third-person perspective. The writer may enter the mind of only the main character. Second, the main character must survive the story to be able to tell it to the reader. They can't die. The reader knows this, and so the threat (risk and danger) of death is eliminated.

Third, and most significant, there is no longer an objective observer reporting the events of the story. Neither the writer nor the reader may ever leave the mind of the main character. Events, places, and characters (including the main character) are not reported objectively, but rather in accordance with the observations, beliefs, and understanding of the main character. The reader must interpret truth based on what this self-serving main character reports. There is no absolute truth in first-person perspective. There is only what the main character chooses to tell the reader.

Multiple perspectives. Many writers want to use the power of third- and first-person perspectives but can't make their story work within the limitations of these perspectives. One solution is to use multiple perspectives, which is as close to having your cake and eating it too as a writer can come. In multiple-perspective stories, the writer writes part of the story from one perspective and other parts from some other perspective. Most commonly, these shifts all remain within third-person perspective, but shift between viewpoint characters. Multiple perspectives are most common in chapter books. Several chapters are written from one perspective. Then the writer shifts to a different location and a different character for a chapter or two before returning to the original perspective.

> **Plusses:** Using multiple perspectives eliminates the awkward limitations of third- and first-person perspectives by allowing the writer to go where the main character is not, cannot go, or will not go.

> **Minuses:** There are two cautions when using multiple perspectives. First, each perspective shift is a disruption for the reader. It pulls the reader out of the story while they adjust to the new perspective. Second, the reader can become confused if the shift isn't made clearly and cleanly. Perspective shifts are a useful tool, but bring with them a price that both writer and reader must pay. They should be used only when there is no other way to tell the story.

What do these various perspectives look like in print? Here is an example of a scene as it might be reported in three of these perspectives. Have your students create plausible versions for second-person, third-person, and multiple perspectives.

> **First person:** *I was kickin' up dust as I skipped across the meadow. Not even having to waste the afternoon traipsing out here to Granny's flea-bitten cabin could bother me today. Wild flowers lined both sides of the trail like guards. They smell okay, but I'm not wild about wild flowers. They just grow in splotches anywhere they feel like it, and most of the year they're dead. They should put plastic flowers out here like Mom and I have in our condo. I hate that Granny has to live way out here in yucky nature instead of in a neat condo in town. I sneezed from the dust and pollen, but had lost my handkerchief. Yuck! I had to wipe my nose on one sleeve.*

> **Objective:** *Little Red shuffled through the dust of the meadow trail, bordered by brilliant wild flowers shimmering in the soft breath of early morning air. The sun shone down through a clear blue sky. Her shadow stretched out to the trees lining the meadow's edge. Her red hood and cape fluttered gently as she walked. Little Red sneezed from the blowing dust and pollen.*
> *Her grandmother also sneezed and sighed as she tucked the covers tight around her chin in her cottage bed. Hot summer wind whistled through the cracks of her rough, wooden walls.*
> *Little Red threw back the red hood on her cape and wiped her nose with her sleeve. A wolf in the line of trees licked his tongue across his lips and smiled.*

> **Omniscient:** *The rolling forest stretched on for miles, dotted by occasional, small meadows, looking like missing teeth in the forest's solid mouthful of dark-green trees. Through one of these meadows, a girl in a bright-red hood*

and cape walked a narrow trail on her way to visit her grandmother, who huddled in bed in her small cottage one mile ahead. Bright splotches of wild flowers dotted the meadow. The girl sneezed and wiped her sleeve across her nose and face. Both girl and grandmother sighed. The grandmother because she felt lonely, the girl because she hated wasting a summer afternoon visiting her sickly grandmother. But the wolf smiled with greedy pleasure. Either the basket of goodies or the girl would be his dinner tonight!

Review the rules for each perspective after reading these passages. How does the choice of perspective affect your feeling of involvement as a reader, and your impressions of the characters? How does it control the information a writer can present?

Exercise #16, "Where's the Camera?" (p. 140), is a demonstration designed to help students better understand these perspectives and their major advantages and disadvantages. After doing this exercise several times, students will be more likely to consciously consider perspective when planning a story. A fresh, powerful perspective is one of the best and easiest ways to enliven a static, boring story. Not being boring is one of the most fervent prayers of student writers.

As mentioned previously, viewpoint refers specifically to the character through whose eyes readers view the story. A second-person story can't really have a viewpoint character. The writer speaks directly to the reader. No character intercedes to interpret and report the story. Omniscient and objective perspectives don't use a viewpoint character. The writer presents the story to the reader through any and all of the characters. The story is not reported by one of the characters, but by an impartial, objective, unidentified observer.

Viewpoint characters come into play in first- and third-person stories. The question to ask is, Which character is in a position to best see and tell the story? Whether the story is written using first- or third-person perspective, the writer must still decide through whose eyes, or over whose shoulder, readers will watch the story, and through whose thoughts readers will best interpret the story's events and characters. Selecting a single viewpoint character is a powerful way to draw the reader into a story, to make their experience more personal and direct.

Separate Creating from Writing

One of the simplest and most helpful tips you can give your students is to separate story creation from the mechanical effort of story writing. Lack of adequate vocabulary and grammatical struggles often prevent story ideas from exploding into their full creative potential. Having to spell words, construct sentences and paragraphs, and match subject with verb often act like a closed damper on a wood-burning stove, keeping the creative coals merely smoldering instead of burning brightly. So often, students have a great idea and then forget it while looking up the spelling of the first word. Nothing dissipates creative energy faster and more completely than the frustration of creative genius forgotten and forever lost.

The mechanics of writing is difficult work. So is the process of creating a story, although this work is considerably more fun. Having to do both at the same time often means that students do neither well. Worse, research shows that the part of the brain that controls the mechanics of writing can shut down the creative part of the brain. When push comes to shove, students routinely shove aside creative expression (story creation) in favor of mechanical correctness. Creativity, passion, energy, and originality are all lost for the sake of grammar and spelling.

Separate these two processes. Create first; write second. Students should be encouraged *not to write* their first draft. They should *say* it. So as not to forget the wondrous story they are creating, they should say the first draft into a tape recorder. They shouldn't worry about constructing complete sentences, or about jumping backward and forward through the story as ideas flood into their mind. They should simply blurt out their story.

This "first draft," of course, is not the first time students have thought through or even talked about their story, nor is it the first time they have said it. As we shall see in "A Better Recipe" on page 60 the first draft comes only after considerable story planning, character development, and scene and character envisioning. At this point in the development of the story, they have already created a story. They are now trying to find organization, structure, and wording to effectively communicate the story and its energy, detail, emotion, and humor.

Small, cheap tape recorders are available for $15 or less in dime and variety stores everywhere. The smaller and cheaper the recorder, the better. Then, when a student is horrified by the sound of their voice on tape, they can blame the awful sound on the equipment instead.

There are three significant plusses to taping first drafts. First, students can give their creativity free reign. Nothing encumbers or impedes the creative process. Second, taping a story is an oral activity. Research has shown that *saying* something improves the richness and detail of the speaker's images. Each time a student *says* a story, they create more detailed multisensory images to use when they later write the story.

Third, taping is time-efficient. It only takes five minutes for an elementary school student to say their story. If they realize that the story is a dud, they have invested very little time into this version. Undaunted, they simply rethink the story and record a better version. Students can easily afford to record three or four versions of a story, improving their imagery and detail with each version, before proceeding from oral activity to committing their story to paper.

When later writing the story, a student can listen to their final taped version one sentence at a time. Their focus then becomes word choice, spelling, and other mechanical considerations for best presenting this one thought. They won't fear forgetting the story—it's preserved on tape. When they have this one thought on paper exactly the way they want it, they listen to the next sentence and continue their writing.

Story Seeds

"An idea! My country for an idea!" Shakespeare's Richard III was lucky. All he needed was a horse. All he had to do was fight a battle. He didn't have to find an idea for a new story.

Actually, story *seed* is a more accurate term than story *idea*. Idea implies to many that this one thought will reveal the story's theme, plot, and purpose. We have seen that core information about the main character reveals these key story elements. What students really need is a place to begin, a seed to focus their thinking. They then need a comprehensive progression of activities to lead them from this seed to a fully developed story (the next section of *Write Right*).

A story seed doesn't dictate what the story will be about. It is simply a place begin, a focal point. A seed can be any idea around which to construct a story, the idea from which a story sprouts. Good story seeds have several common characteristics. They must be ideas that are

- accessible to all students,
- within the experiences of all students,
- of interest to all students, and
- relevant to all students.

Story seeds are like a jump start for a story. They start a student's creative engine and accelerate them into story-creation mode. The cruelest thing teachers can do is to tell their class to write a story about anything they want. Students will then spend 98 percent of the available time spinning their wheels, searching for an idea.

Lacking an idea for what to write about is students' major story-writing complaint. We have seen that stories are about characters. The way to create a story is to create character, conflict, struggle, and goal. Which character, though? Which conflict? Which struggle? Which goal? A story seed gives students the focal point around which to begin creating character, conflict, struggle, and goal.

Usually, seeds are situation- or incident-based: "What would happen if a girl fell down a rabbit hole to another world?" (from Lewis Carroll's *Alice in Wonderland*) is a seed. So is "A boy's friends start turning into frogs," (from my book *The Wrong Side of a Neighborhood Witch*) or "Two children skipped rocks at the edge of a lake. One rock came skipping back" (from Chris Van Allsburg's *The Mysteries of Harris Burdick*). A seed can be a sentence, a phrase, or even a single word that outlines or suggests a situation. A seed does not need to include character information because creating the character information is the first step in writing any story. A seed precedes the creation of character information.

Story-starter kits, books, boxes, and displays now abound at almost every commercial booth at every reading conference. Teachers can make their own lists from the experiences, concerns, hopes, dreams, and interests of their students, or by making up "what if" questions. My favorite story seeds, though, are ideas that students create themselves. Why should this burden fall upon teachers when students are fully capable of creating their own seeds?

I have used the following seven story-starter exercises with students of all ages:

Exercise #17, "Word by Word" (p. 142)

Exercise #18, "Love/Hate" (p. 144)

Exercise #19, "Getting Into Trouble" (p. 147)

Exercise #20, "Who Could Struggle Most?" (p. 149)

Exercise #21, "Picture Personality" (p. 151)

Exercise #22, "Write Abouts" (p. 153)

Exercise #23, "Guided Visioning" (p. 155)

My personal favorites are Exercises #17 and #23. They always work, always help students create appropriate seeds, and are always great fun for students to do. I have also found consistent success with the other five. Try them all and use those that best resonate with your students. Good story seeds excite students and make them eager to create and write a story. These seven exercises consistently accomplish these goals.

A Better Recipe

All previous discussion in this book has led us here, to a "new-and-improved" recipe for creating and drafting a story. We have discussed the individual concepts, pieces, problems, and concerns that encumber and misdirect student creative writing. All that remains to do is mesh together the individual solutions into an orderly and comprehensive progression of activities to lead students from seed through first draft.

If character-based story writing is the heart and lifeblood of *Write Right*, then this progression is the body that surrounds it. This 11-step progression of activities leads students through the writing process, to a complete first draft of their story. It does not include story revision or editing. The student editing progression is presented in Part III.

This progression is a guide designed to assist your students, not a dictate or mandatory rule designed to regiment them. The goal is to lead students to creating successful stories that they are proud of, to have students enjoy and become excited by the prospect of story writing. This progression has proven itself to greatly increase the chances that student writers will succeed.

Still, there is no need to initiate all the steps of this valuable progression at once. If you have a class of new writers, or are working with a primary grade, begin simply. For their first few stories, have them define core and sensory character information, identify the story's ending, define a general sequence of events to overcome chosen obstacles, do several quick exercises to make the story more visual and tangible, and tape and then write the story. You might have students entirely skip theme, viewpoint and perspective, scenes and sequels, and complete character profiles, as well as subsequent revision and editing.

As students master these basic steps, add viewpoint and perspective and more complete character profiles. Emphasize the importance of the antagonist and the role of other, supporting characters. Add theme, suspense, and the story question. Later, add scene cards and sequels and complete the 11-activity progression. Finally, after students have completed the first draft, have them systematically evaluate and revise their work (Part III).

Add new steps as students are ready for them. Each step helps students define and refine their story, and communicate it more effectively. Still, encountering a maze of steps and concepts all at once can be overwhelming and counterproductive.

Note that step 11 of this progression is the first time the story is actually written on paper. Notes are made during earlier steps, but the formative process of a student story should be oral-based. Oral and physical exercises help students expand and refine their vision of the story material. The formal act of writing does not. Writing is the end product, the chosen final form of the story. The process of story *creation* is better accomplished with oral and physical activity.

The *Write Right* story writing 11-step story-drafting progression is summarized in figure 5, and described below.

The *Write Right* Story Writing Progression

1. **PLANT A SEED.** Create an idea that launches the story.

2. **CREATE THE MAIN CHARACTER(S).** Define the core, personality, activity and sensory layers of the main character. Create the history layer as needed to explain the other layers.

3. **DEFINE THE STORY THEME AND STORY QUESTION.** Identify a story theme and, from goal, create a story question.

4. **LAY OUT STORY STRUCTURE.** From goal define the ending point. From obstacles create a sequence of events (Plot). Identify associated risk and danger.

5. **DEFINE AND CREATE NECESSARY SUPPORTING CHARACTERS.**

6. **WHO TELLS THE STORY? (VIEWPOINT & PERSPECTIVE).** What character could best tell the story? Which perspective would best allow the reader to experience the story?

7. **MAP THE SCENES AND SEQUELS.** Break the plot into discrete interactions (scenes). Define each scene and identify the climax.

8. **MAKE IT REAL. MAKE IT VISUAL. (I.Y.C.S.I., Y.C.W.I!).** Know each setting as well as you know your own bedroom; know each character as well as family.

9. **HOW LATE CAN I START? HOW EARLY CAN I END?** What is the first event which the reader *must* see? Is there anything beyond the climax other than answering the story question and providing a final sequel?

10. **RECORD THE FIRST DRAFT(S).** Say it; repeat it; then record it. Then re-record it until you are satisfied with the version on tape.

11. **WRITE THE STORY.** Focus on detail, energy, emotion, word choice, and character feeling and information as you write.

Fig. 5. The *Write Right* Story Writing Progression.

1. **Plant a seed.** Use prompts, story-starter ideas, story-starter exercises, "write abouts," "what ifs," or other methods to generate a general idea, or seed, from which to begin the story.

2. **Create the main character.** Who would be most affected in a story about this seed idea? Who would have the most to lose? Who would risk the most? Who would have the most to gain? Having a character with an obvious and strongly vested interest in the outcome makes the process of creating a compelling story easier. Students should create a main character and the basic five layers of character information: core elements, sensory image, personality, activity, and history. Exercises #9, #10, #19, and #20 can assist students in creating and defining this all-important focal core of their story.

   Two additional exercises are included to assist students in the process of creating and fleshing out their main character. Exercise #24, "Be Your Character" (p. 158), encourages them to fully visualize the sensory, physical layer of their character. Exercise #25, "The Character Game" (p. 160), is a powerful and flexible tool for helping students develop any and all of the necessary layers of character information. Both of these exercises help students effectively develop their main character before the overpowering drive to create plot paralyzes further character development.

   Exercise #26, "One-on-One-on-One-on-One" (p. 164) is particularly effective for helping student writers develop their characters and the story that surrounds them. This exercise is one of the two most powerful and effective story-development exercises I have ever encountered (the second is Exercise #31, "The 30-Second Story," introduced later). It has proven itself to be consistently effective for teaching students exactly what attracts a listener or reader to a story, and how to organize and present story material to achieve this attraction.

   Exercise #26 can be used to help student writers focus on

   - their core character and story information;
   - what makes this character sufficiently interesting and worthy of a story (the unique aspects of the five layers of character information);
   - the other major story character—the antagonist; and
   - what happens in the story—its plot.

   Students should be allowed to take notes after this exercise to record new ideas for their character, as well as interesting and effective ideas for story structure and phraseology they heard from other students, that they want to incorporate into their story.

   This step is not the end of character development. Throughout most of the remaining steps, students will regularly return to their characters and character information. The creation of an effective story, though, must begin with character.

3. **Define a theme and a story question.** We haven't discussed these two story concepts yet. Both are tools to help writers structure a story and decide what should, and should not, be included within it.

   What is a story question? A story question is that question that hooks the reader, draws them into the story, and keeps them there until the end. It is the unanswered question that surrounds the entire story. With a good story, students often say that they "have to find out what happens," that they "need to know how it comes out." Really, they are saying that they understand the story question and need to have it answered. For their own story, students must ensure that readers will understand the story question and need to have it answered.

Generally, a story question is the goal of the main character expressed in the form of a question: "Once there was a girl named Susan who wanted an ice cream cone." Susan is the main character. Eating an ice cream cone is her goal. The story question is, "Will Susan get her ice cream cone?" If a reader decides and continues to read this story, it will be to learn whether or not Susan gets her ice cream cone, to answer this story question. Will the main character achieve their goal?

The story question creates suspense. The reader is literally suspended between question and answer. What makes this suspension gripping and powerful is the amount of tension associated with the question. Tension is a feeling of anxiety and discomfort within the reader. When a reader experiences urgent tension, they become highly motivated to relieve it. If the tension comes from a story, the way to relieve this tension is to read the story, hoping that the writer will answer the story question and relieve the burden. Writers struggle to create tension so that readers will *need* to read their story—through to the ending—to relieve it. Grade-school students routinely substitute the word *exciting* for *suspense* and *tension*. However, without tension and suspense, there would be no excitement.

What heightens the tension? Risk and danger. Tension is heightened when readers care about a character, and when they

a. believe it is likely this character will fail to achieve their goal, and
b. perceive that this character must face great risk and danger in trying to achieve their goal.

The greater the consequences of failure, the greater the probability of failure, the greater the necessity of trying, the greater the danger of trying, the greater the tension. This is why risk and danger are part of the core character information. They are the primary source of story tension.

Why bother to specify an exact story question? Because this question is the only tool available to the writer for creating story-long suspense and tension. This question is what the story is all about for its characters. What the main character wants to do or achieve, their goal, is part of the core information because it creates the story question.

What is theme? Theme is the subject or topic of the story. A theme is often an emotional or behavioral concept such as greed, generosity, disobedience, acceptance, revenge, and so on. Themes may also be subjects, such as Colonial America, the Civil War, time, mathematics, or the typical daily life of a police officer.

Though many writers mix story question and theme together, they are separate, and they serve separate functions. The story question defines a goal for the main character and creates suspenseful questions for the reader. The main character focuses on resolving the story question. The theme exists solely for the benefit of, and use by, the reader. Theme tells the reader what human concerns the story will concern, and how to interpret the character and the story question. Yet the story characters need not acknowledge or even understand the theme.

Two examples will clarify the concept of theme. We will use the story question presented above—"Once there was a girl named Susan who wanted an ice cream cone." Now we will add a theme. For the first example, I'll use greed as a story theme:

Once there was a selfish little girl named Susan who wanted an ice cream cone. She wanted to be the first and only person to get a luscious cone. She refused to share her ice cream and would throw a tantrum whenever she saw anyone else eating ice cream. "It should all be mine, mine, mine!" And right now, her taste buds were rumbling with a gnawing hunger for a triple-scoop, Rocky Road ice cream cone!

Same story question: Will Susan get her ice cream cone? With a clearly defined theme of greed, though, the reader will view Susan very differently, and will evaluate every story event differently. It isn't necessary for Susan to realize that she is being greedy and selfish. She doesn't need to be concerned with the concept of greed. The reader knows, and will follow this theme throughout the story to learn whether selfish girls still get their ice cream cones.

For the second example, I'll use the same story question, but use it to explore a theme of generosity:

Once there was a girl named Susan who lived at the edge of the poorest neighborhood of the whole city. Susan loved ice cream and, more than anything, she wanted a triple-scoop, Rocky Road cone. But every time her mother bought a cone for her, Susan saw the desperately poor children who needed it more than she did. She would give them the ice cream. Every time she had 75¢ to buy a cone, she saw children who needed that 75¢ just to stay alive. And she would give them the money. So Susan never got an ice cream cone of her own, even though she wanted one so very much.

Same story question, different theme. The theme changes the way a reader evaluates and views the character and her goal. Other examples of theme include: "Romeo and Juliet"—personal love versus family hatred; "Peter Rabbit"—disobedience; "Jack and the Bean Stalk"—faith in the future, that fortunes will improve; "Goldilocks and the Three Bears"—well, I'm still not sure what Goldi is all about.

If readers are to involve themselves enough to read an entire story, the story theme must be relevant and interesting to them. The story question must seem real to the story characters and create suspense and tension for readers. The time to create these elements is now, at the beginning of the story-drafting progression.

Many teachers use a "One-on-One-on-One-on-One" exercise in which students use their one-minute time slots to describe the main character, story question, theme, and sources of tension. If students can identify these critical story elements before they begin to write, and can convince other students that their character, story question, theme, and sources of tension will create a wonderful story, then they probably will create a wonderful story.

4. **Plan story structure**. Before students begin to write, they should use the theme, story question, and core character information to plan the major events that will happen in the story.

    From the main character's goal, choose an exact story ending. From a list of possible obstacles, choose those few that will actually be used in the story. Maximize the amount of risk and danger that can be associated with each obstacle. Determine the order in which obstacles will be faced and overcome.

    Students are now creating a plot for their stories. To have a reader understand and follow a story, the writer leads them along a specific, carefully constructed pathway. This path is the story's plot. It is the ordered sequence of events that will happen in the story.

However, before your students dreamily, wildly plot story events, they must remember that each event must relate to the main character's struggles to overcome the obstacles they face. They must remember that each event must be consistent with the main character's five layers of character information. This information can always be changed as new ideas refocus the story and expand the student's image of story characters. The student must ensure, though, that every action in the story is consistent with the character information they have created. Otherwise, the story will never seem real and plausible to the reader.

5. **Define necessary supporting characters.** Next, students should consider who else *must* be in the story to ensure that the main character faces the obstacles, overcomes them, and achieves (or fails to achieve) their goal. Student writers should complete character profiles for each of these supporting characters.

The most important of these supporting characters is the antagonist. The antagonist, the embodiment of the greatest obstacle the main character must face, is just as important as the main character. The more "worthy" the antagonist is as an insurmountable, invincible force, the more readers will care about the main character and about the story.

The antagonist should have their own goals and motives, which should give the antagonist good reason to become a major obstacle for the main character. Have students do a "One-on-One-on-One-on-One" exercise in which they describe their antagonist, the antagonist's goals and motives, and the risk and danger the antagonist presents for the main character. Students should try to create an antagonist that is more dangerous and more invincible than anyone else's antagonist.

6. **Who tells the story? (viewpoint and perspective).** Students should examine their options for viewpoint and perspective to find the combination that will be the most powerful and gripping and still allow them to tell the complete story. Who can best tell this story? With whom will the reader most want to identify? Whose viewpoint will create the most interesting story? Whose viewpoint will be most effective in telling the story? What perspective will be most effective in telling this story?

7. **Map the scenes and sequels.** This is a refinement of step 4. It may be skipped for younger grades, but is a powerful planning tool for older students.

First, we need to define these two terms. Everyone has watched enough television and movies to have a general idea of what a scene is. In general, a scene changes when there is a shift in time, a shift in setting, or a major shift in characters present. A scene constitutes a finite block of action in the story, a complete interaction among characters, an event.

Just like a complete story, each scene

- has a scene question,
- focuses on character conflict and struggle, and
- builds to a scene climax.

Story characters come together, something happens, and the event is resolved. This sequence constitutes a scene, or one block of story action. Then the reader is ready to proceed to the next event.

Students should take their general story outline from step 4 and lay it out on index cards, one scene per card. These scene cards are a step-by-step guide to the flow of their story, as if, flagstone by flagstone, they are laying out the path a reader must walk to reach the story's conclusion. The more detailed and specific they are, the easier it will be to write the story. Film makers call this process "story boarding."

Number and name each scene. The format I use for these scene cards is shown in figure 6. After naming each scene, I state the purpose of that scene, or what necessary part of the story will happen in that scene. As shown, I also list the

- location, or setting, of the scene,
- the story characters present in the scene,
- the scene question and conflict,
- how the scene concludes, or is resolved, and
- a one-sentence summary of the scene.

Additional information will be placed into the boxes at the bottom and upper right of the scene cards during editing, when the cards will be used to evaluate the success of each scene and to guide scene revision.

Listing scenes on index cards makes it is easy to test the effect of shuffling and rearranging scenes to tell the story in a different order. It also makes it easy to evaluate the effect of eliminating individual scenes.

What is a sequel? We generally think of a sequel as being something that follows after, or a continuation of, a previous story. A movie has a sequel when the same characters are used in a subsequent film. In writing, a sequel has a more specific meaning and purpose.

Stories are about characters. It is the stresses upon, and the reactions of, characters that readers really care about. A scene is a block of action. Following action, readers need to know how the main character reflects upon and internally reacts to this action. This brief moment of reflection is a sequel. Scenes tell the reader what happens in a story. Sequels tell the reader what this action means to the main character. Scenes are the "what"; sequels are the "so what."

The concept of allowing the main character to reflect upon previous actions and interactions is not new. Sequels appear in almost every successful story. However, character reflections are rare in student stories, which makes readers feel excluded from the character's thoughts and feelings and distanced from the character and the story.

The best solution to this problem is to have students formally design a sequel to each scene. On the back of each scene card, they should answer the following three questions about the events of that scene.

At the end of this scene:

1.   How does my main character feel about what happened?
2.   What does this scene mean to the character?
3.   What does this scene make the character want to do next?

Write Right!
Start with Story*telling*

SCENE CARDS

Prepare a scene card for every scene in your story. Do this after you have defined and developed the story theme, story characters, associated obstacles, and have talked your way through the story, and before you begin to write the first, rough draft.

# ———— NAME:————————————			
Purpose:			
Characters:			
Setting:			
Scene Question:			
Conflict & Struggle:			
Scene Resolution:			
Scene Summary:			
Action Level	Tension Level	Humor Level	Emotion Level

On the back side of each card describe that scene's sequel. Use character terms for this description: how is the character feeling? How have the events of this scene changed the way they think? The way they view other characters and the story? The way they view themselves? How has this scene changed their outlook and their planned future actions?

Fig. 6. Scene Cards.

The answers are the basis for creating a sequel to the scene.

Sequels are a bridge of internal character thought (expressed within the constraints of viewpoint and perspective) that carries the reader from scene to scene, showing them why each scene happens and what it means to the main character. Examples will be helpful:

Scene #1: *Timmy is riding his bike and being chased by a big dog. Frightened, Timmy cries and kicks at the dog, who jumps and nips at his leg as he pedals toward home.*

Sequel #1: *Still trembling and frightened in his room, Timmy decides that he hates dogs and never again wants to be near one.*

Scene #2: *Timmy's parents bring home a roly-poly puppy as a family pet. Timmy refuses to hold or touch it. His parents try to force the dog upon him. His older brother laughs because Timmy is so afraid.*

Sequel #2: *Timmy decides that his family is mean and that they hate him. He decides to run away and find a nicer family.*

Scene #3: *The next morning, while everyone else is still sleeping, Timmy packs his backpack, grabs some cookies, and sneaks out of the house. He hikes into the hills outside of town, heading toward Donut Falls, one of his favorite places for family outings. It begins to rain. Timmy seeks shelter in an abandoned miner's cabin. The rotten wood of the floor collapses under Timmy's weight. He falls and becomes trapped under the beams and floorboards that fall on top of him.*

Sequel #3: *Instead of panicking, Timmy concludes that this experience will somehow help him find his new family. Only a nice family would come hiking up here and rescue a trapped boy. He lies back, cramped but confident that a nice family will soon come along, rescue him, and love him forever.*

Scene #4: *Timmy hears scuffling and scratching on the cabin floor above him. He calls out, "Hello! I'm stuck down here. Come and get me." The shaggy head of a large dog pokes over the edge of the hole Timmy fell through. The dog hops down and sits beside Timmy. It stares at him, tongue sliding in and out over long, yellow teeth as it breathes. The dog begins to bark.*

Sequel #4: *Timmy is sure he is about to be eaten. His only chance of being rescued by his future family is to fend off this fiend until they arrive to rescue him.*

Scene #5: *Weakly, Timmy swats at the huge dog. The dog cocks its head and wags its tail slowly, gazing at trapped Timmy. Then it continues to bark. The noise echoes through the crawl space under the cabin and hurts Timmy's ears. A long snake slithers across the rocks and dirt, coils near Timmy, and hisses. The dog attacks and drives the snake away, barking savagely.*

Sequel #5: *Timmy believes that the dog is just playing with his catch before devouring Timmy, and that it drove the snake away because it didn't want to share its meal. Timmy grows weak with fear and begins to lose hope that his new family will arrive in time. He begins to cry.*

Scene #6: *The search-and-rescue team arrives, having followed the call of their trained rescue dog to the old cabin. Timmy is freed and reunited with his family.*

You probably want to know how Timmy reacts to this reunion with family and puppy, and realize that a wide range of reactions are plausible. He might decide that not all dogs are bad, that he shouldn't have run away, and that his real family does love him. Or, he might remember the terror of waiting to be eaten, realize that he still hates all dogs, and curse the rescue team for snatching him out of the cabin when he was sure his new family was just about to come along and save him.

The point is, you really want to know. Following the internal sequels of this character has suspended you between question and answer. You feel the risk to, and tension in, this poor child. The story is working. You *want* to continue reading and learn what happens. Does Timmy become an animal-hating serial killer or a kindly veterinarian? Does he run away and join a street gang, or stay at home and care for his aging parents in their golden years? What you have learned about this character in the sequels makes you care enough to want to know more.

Sequels allow us inside a character to understand them better and feel closer to their unique thought processes. Timmy's interpretations are never certain, so his reactions are always in doubt. At each sequel, we learn more about how Timmy's mind works. As readers, we hope at every sequel that Timmy will interpret the action and then internally react the way we want him to, but this outcome is always in doubt. The more doubtful it is, the greater the risk to the character—and the more we want to know what happens.

All students can use sequels successfully. They all naturally think and live in a world of action and reflection. As with so many aspects of successful creative writing, students need practice to make a habit of including character reflections in their story planning. Exercise #27, "The Scene-and-Sequel Game" (p. 167), is designed to help students focus on and investigate the potential and power of sequels. Try this exercise with your class. It is the kind of game that student writers love to play, and they will pour great energy into it. It can also reshape the way students approach stories, reinforcing the central importance of character.

8. **Make it real. Make it visual. (I. Y. C. S. I., Y. C. W. I.)** Use oral exercises and games to help students make each character and each scene real and vivid, in multisensory detail, in their mind. (If You Can't See It, You Can't Write It.) Their image of each character should be as clear and detailed as an image of a family member. Their image of each scene should be as clear and detailed as an image of their own bedroom.

Exercise #28, "The Scene Game" (p. 170), is a flexible and effective game to help students improve and expand their images of the scenes of their story. The small groups for this game may focus on any important scenes of each students' story. Every student and every story benefit from any question asked of any student. The goal is to have students talk and think about their stories until these stories have blossomed into a set of vivid, detailed images. "One-on-One-on-One-on-One" exercises are also effective for improving mental detail.

9. **How late can I begin? How early can I end?** The typical tendency of most writers is to begin telling a story too early in its plot, and end it too late. We want to tell the reader the history and background that precedes the story. We want them to understand the characters and settings. What we tend to do, though, is bore the reader and burden the story with information that means nothing to the reader until they understand who and what the story is about.

    Students should begin telling their story as late as possible, and then fill in necessary background information as the story progresses. Eliminate every story event up to the first event a reader *must* see to understand the story. This is the scene where the story should begin. Students should study their scene cards and ask themselves, What can I eliminate? What *must* I include? Can I shift background information into later scenes, or into flashback scenes?

    The same cutting process should be performed for the end of the story: How soon can I stop and still be sure that the reader will understand the ending? Are there scenes or information that I can eliminate from the end? Are there scenes after the climax other than a final sequel? Are they really necessary? Will the story be better if I eliminate them?

10. **Record the first draft.** Now is the time for students to give shape to their budding story. Students should use a tape recorder to record the first several drafts of the story. Students might record their drafts in class in small groups at a reading station, or (at their leisure) at home. Their goal in these oral drafts is not precision. It is not wording. It is not an attempt at precision. All they need do is pour their thoughts, their energy, their passion into the tape recorder. It doesn't matter if they jump backward and forward through the story, or if they skip portions of the story. These recordings are not performances. Students can pause the recording and stop for a moment to collect their thoughts. Bit by bit, scene by scene, they should try to record all the excitement and drama they have envisioned for their story.

    Students should focus on the characters and their own excitement as they record each scene of the story, pretending that they are telling the story to a friend. They should make these first recordings funny, make them wild. They should let their passions flow and their blood boil. This is a time for energy and excitement.

    After they have recorded the story, they should listen to it and decide what they like and what they don't like about this version of the story. After reviewing notes, character profiles, and scene cards, they should record additional drafts, continuing until they are satisfied.

11. **Write the story.** It's finally time to write. If students have recorded several versions of their story on tape, then this step actually becomes the first round of editing. Students should listen to their story and make notes about how they want to change or improve it when they put it on paper. Students should listen to a few sentences, or one scene, and stop the tape. As they listen, they should think of different, more powerful verbs that might be used; about details that might be included; and about important character information and the use of dialog. After they listen to these same few sentences again, concentrating on the changes they plan to make. Finally, they write.

    Then they proceed to the next few sentences, to the next scene. They shouldn't reread or edit their brief blocks of text. They shouldn't worry about overall story continuity, pace, or flow. They should focus on writing each block of text as best they can. There will be plenty of time later to fit together all the pieces.

If students haven't recorded their first draft on tape, the guidelines for writing the first draft should match those discussed in step 10. Don't have students agonize about detail and simile; about spelling and sentence structure; about tension, pace, and word choice. Writing the first draft should be energizing, exciting. Students should let their passions flow onto the page, should pour energy into the story *now*. There will be plenty of time later for precision. Students who write their first draft rather than recording it on tape will find that they must do more revising later than those who did record their first draft on tape.

Creativity: Who Has It?

The *Write Right* progression of story writing assumes that each student writer possesses a sizable amount of creativity. All first- and second-graders feel that they are creative. By fifth-grade, though, I have observed that many students have begun to doubt their creative abilities. By middle school, many (if not most) are convinced that they don't have a creative bone in their body.

This is nonsense. If you are a living, breathing human being, you create. Period. The real problem is controlling and focusing a rampantly creative imagination. I believe that it is impossible for a human being *not to* create, just as it is impossible for a human being *not to* think. The problem is that, by convincing themselves that they aren't creative, many students stop trying to *express* their creativity. They stop searching for creative outlets.

At the root of this problem is the definition of the word *creativity*. Dictionaries typically define creativity as the ability to bring something into existence, to transcend traditional views or modes of thinking. Many in our culture have slipped a "quality" qualifier into their personal definition of creativity. For them, something they bring into existence is creative only if it's of exceptionally high quality, only if it's of professional caliber. Creativity has no relation to quality. Quality comes with time, focused practice, and sustained effort. Almost nobody is "exceptionally good" at some activity the first few times they try it. Creativity has relation only to the act of creating.

I view creativity differently. I believe that creativity is the natural result of two qualities: the willingness to look foolish, and the persistence to look foolish over and over again. Creativity, itself, is a natural human force. Only pride and ego keep us from unleashing our natural creativity. Painters paint terribly when they first begin, beginning writers write terribly, and beginning sculptors slip and crack their hunk of marble in half. No dancer ever looked artistic the first time they tried a plié at the dance bar. No cellist ever sounded gifted while still trying to learn the scales.

So many people try something once and quit, saying "Yuck! That was terrible and embarrassing. I won't try *that* again!" They never find an outlet for the creative fire burning deep inside. Yet this fire continues to burn. It never dies. Many senior citizens begin painting and writing in their seventies. These are people who never thought they had creativity. They finally overcame their lifelong embarrassment to look foolish, were finally ready to let their creativity flow—and flow it does!

Natural human creativity develops with time: time to train the fingers, feet, and brain to perform what the creative imagination envisions and dreams. The creativity is always there. The rest of the body just needs time to learn how to release it undamaged.

Remind students of Exercise #23, "Guided Visioning" (p. 155), if they doubt their creative abilities. With just a few suggestive words from you and a glance at their own hand, they each created the characters for a story. From their visualization of the inanimate objects in one room of their house, they again each created the characters for a story. They *are* creative.

Right Brain, Left Brain

We are all creative. However, a writer cannot create character and story automatically, on demand, every time they snap their fingers. Like a muscle, creativity must be stretched and exercised.

Most people are aware that different parts of the brain control different physical, sensory, and thought activities. The brain is divided into two hemispheres. The right side of the brain is the residence of creativity. The left side is the residence of logic.

I believe that story-writing creativity is more complex than most people think it to be. A smooth, logical plot line is just as creative as a unique and interesting character. Creating stories requires all the mental power a writer can muster.

It is useful to examine the contribution of each side of the brain to the creation of a story. Exercise #29, "Interrupter" (p. 172), is designed to facilitate this exploration. It is a wonderful, high-energy story game. At its conclusion, students realize that they have created two different sets of stories. One set is right-brain dominant. These stories are riotously fun, silly, meaningless, filled with laughter, and loud. The second set is left-brain dominant. These stories have some semblance of story form, as we have defined it—plausible characters, plot, purpose, cause-and-effect relationships between scenes—and are much quieter and not nearly as much fun to create or listen to as right-brain stories.

We think, analyze, organize, and summarize with our left brain. For a story, the left brain is in charge of order, logic, plot, structure, and plausibility. We feel, invent, and create with our right brain. For a story, the right brain is in charge of characterization, humor, energy, passion, whim, and inventiveness.

Kindergartners tell rambling right-brain stories. You soon want to scream, "What's the point?!" It never occurs to them that there should be a point. Their stories are just for fun. Self-conscious ninth-graders tell rigid, logical stories. You soon want to scream, "Put some life in it! You're boring me to death!"

To create a story that works, a writer must engage both sides of their brain for contributions. One side cannot create a story without the other. *Write Right* predrafting activities are designed to alternately engage both sides of the brain in the process of story creation. First drafts are for passion and energy. They are right-brain dominant. Revisions are for precision. They are left-brain dominant.

Each person, each writer, is more comfortable working with one hemisphere than with the other. This is partly a function of age. Younger students tend to have a right-brain orientation. Sometime around the fourth to sixth grades, most students flip to a left-brain orientation, which they will maintain for the rest of their lives. However, this orientation is also partly a function of individual personality. Each writer is responsible for bringing both sides to the story. Each writer must assess their personal tendencies, strengths, and weaknesses, and allow time to develop their weaker side and its part of the story as they plan, draft, and edit their work.

Practice Makes Perfect

Effective writing is a learned skill. Like any other skill, practice is what develops and hones ability. Writing exercises and practice writings should be a significant part of any student writing program. Remember, though, that the purpose of a writing exercise should be to practice *writing*, not to practice story creation. Writing skills refer to the mechanics of writing. Practice writings should focus on these skills, especially word choice, clarity and economy, thought organization, effective description and detail, and thought expression. Developing these skills will help students express and communicate a story once they have created it.

Practice writings, then, should focus on practicing the act of writing, and on the process of effectively expressing an idea in writing. Practice writings should not focus on the formation of ideas. Use the following rules to govern student practice writings:

1. **Always keep your pen moving (or your fingers, when using a keyboard).** Write furiously and continuously. Don't pause to think, assess, or plan. Let the ideas flow freely from mind to paper. Write continuously throughout the allotted time.

2. **Be specific.** Strive toward more specific descriptions of characters, traits, actions, reactions, emotions, things, places. Be specific in your writing. Be specific in your thinking.

3. **Don't analyze.** Let your writing flow unimpeded. Don't stop and reread. Don't edit. Don't even stop to plan the future direction of your writing. Focus only on the sentence at hand, only on the word at hand, and keep writing.

4. **Don't worry about grammar, spelling, and punctuation.** Don't stop to correct subject-verb mismatches, sentence fragments, misspellings, forgotten periods. Keep writing. There will be plenty of time to correct mistakes later, but there won't be time later to write so freely.

5. **You have permission to write the worst junk in the world.** Every writer writes terrible junk sometimes. When it seems to be your turn to write it, just write it, shrug, and forget it. If you worry about writing awful stories, you are likely to miss the opportunity to write delightfully wonderful ones. Feel free to write both. Then save the good and toss the bad.

6. **Go for the jugular.** Practice writings are a time to write aggressively and honestly. Don't try to be kind and polite, and don't try to write toward cooperative, stress-less situations. Steer practice writings toward strong emotions and raw conflict. Remember, stories are about characters in struggle, about characters in conflict, facing risk and danger. If you practice focusing on strong emotions and the power of conflict in your writing, you will be much better equipped to write successful stories.

7. **Never apologize for your practice writings.** Never feel guilty. It's only a rushed rough draft, and everyone knows that. Don't belittle your work—others may find value and enjoyment in it, even if you don't. A practice writing can never be a failure.

Use a simple, timed format for practice writings. A suggested format and its various options, as well as suggested topics for practice writings, are presented in Exercise #30, "Practice Writings" (p. 174). The elements to focus on during a timed practice writing are free-flowing ideas; energy and passion; emotional content and effect; originality; vivid description and detail; lean, efficient writing; and rich, multisensory images. Practice writings can and should be tailored to match the particular problems your students face, and the skills they most need to develop.

An additional exercise designed to develop story-writing skills is Exercise #31, "The 30-Second Story" (p. 177). It is the second of the two most powerful and effective story-development exercises I have encountered (the other is Exercise #26, "One-on-One-on-One-on-One," introduced previously). The value of this exercise is twofold. First, it reinforces the importance of basic story structure and core character elements. Second, the Special Requirements for a given session focus students' attention on one specific aspect of story writing, and on how this aspect contributes to the overall story. Any and every aspect of story writing can be the focus of a "30-Second Story." I suggest you use this powerful tool often to help your students develop their story-writing insight and skills.

Part III

Rough to Ready

From Draft to Story

Your students followed every step of the *Write Right* progression presented in Part II. They completed every preplanning and drafting activity. Yet their story still didn't work the way either they or you wanted and hoped it would. What went wrong? Nothing. Stories never come out right the first time.

The job of predrafting and drafting is to ensure that a writer has a story worth telling, a story that possesses the emotion, passion, and energy it needs and the reader deserves. Now it's time to polish this story and make it shine. A car doesn't shine after being designed, tested, built, sanded, and painted—even if these tasks are done correctly. It won't shine until it has been waxed and buffed. Waxing isn't creative. It's methodical, systematic work. So is revising, or editing, a story.

Students typically hate to edit their stories. Their excitement and energy for the story were poured into the draft and have now faded. They want to be finished with the story and do something new. I don't believe that this strong reaction means they don't care whether their story is good. I don't even believe that it means they are unwilling to revise their story. I believe that the real culprit is that they don't know *how* to edit successfully, and that they have never had positive, successful editing experiences. They reread their story, recognize and are aghast at the myriad deficiencies, and stare in frustration, not knowing how to fix it.

Story editing isn't like doing math. There isn't a single correct solution, a single simple formula for revising a story. There isn't a single standard procedure to follow. Still, there isn't a single correct way to *write* a story either. Once a writer understands the principles that make a story work, writing becomes easier, and the writer becomes more successful at writing. Once a writer understands how to effectively use basic editing tools, editing becomes easier, and the writer becomes more successful at editing.

Editing isn't difficult work. It can appear overwhelming, though, if the writer doesn't follow a proven system, a methodical progression for approaching the task. The trick is to do the editing one step at a time, rather than all at once. The real trick, though, is knowing which step to do first, so that editing won't require continual backtracking, and so that editing won't cause the writer to cut words and sentences they have just carefully edited to perfection.

The purpose of editing is to ensure that the words of the story deliver the ideas, effects, and meanings intended by the writer. There are so many story elements to review during the editing process that it is impossible to consider them all at once. Successful story editors address individual elements one at a time. This is easier and more efficient. I have divided these elements into three groups: those that relate to the story as a whole, those that relate to individual scenes, and those that relate to specific word choices.

It is not essential that a writer assess every element of every story. Usually, only a small number of story elements account for most of the problems. I have included a comprehensive list of editing tasks, not to overwhelm teachers and students and make editing seem like an endless chore, but rather so that teachers can direct individual students to edit the elements most germane to their story. Teachers can further focus a student's editing efforts on only those elements that are most appropriate for their age and writing ability.

Does the Story Deliver?

Successful editing begins not with corrections but with an evaluation of the entire story. The writer can then correct story-wide problems and systematically correct smaller and smaller elements of that story—scenes, paragraphs, sentences, and words.

First, have students set their story aside for a while (I try to set my stories aside for at least a week). No one can evaluate the words they have just written. The writer won't see the words on the page, but rather the ideas and images they held in their mind when they wrote. These images are always perfect. To evaluate the written words, the writer must wait for these images to fade.

Separate story writing and story editing into two separate projects. Have students write a story and hand it in. Weeks later, hand back the stories and lead students through the process of evaluation and revision. Students now need to evaluate their writing, to ensure that the story keeps its promises and delivers the power and delight they intended. Using a careful editing process, it is time to make the story as good as it can be.

Evaluating the Story

A writer's first and best evaluative tool is to read the story aloud. This is not some quiet mumbling that the writer can barely hear. No. The story must be read as if the writer were reading it to an audience. It must be read with all the expression and energy the writer would give the story if they were reading it on-stage at a Young Authors award ceremony.

The writer benefits from listening to their words as they speak them, as well as from acknowledging the emotions they feel while reading the story. The writer should mark each section they feel like rushing through to reach an upcoming exciting part of the story. These are sections that need revision. The writer should mark the parts that excite them. These are sections that work well as written. The writer should note the emotions they feel as they read each scene. Are these the emotions that the writer wanted readers to feel? If so, terrific. If not, it means that character reactions and descriptions in these parts of the story need revision.

Does the dialog sound real and interesting? Will a reader recognize and want to pursue the story question? The writer must listen to the words they have written and consider what they like about them and what they wish were different. A writer's feelings and reactions while reading their story aloud will tell them exactly how well each part of the story works.

Students should have others read their story and then ask these readers specific questions to determine whether the various story elements affect readers the way the student intended. The specific questions to ask depend on the story. Here are a few suggestions:

- What do you think this story is about?
- What do you think is the best single part or aspect of this story?
- What is your favorite aspect of this story?
- Who is your favorite character? Why?
- What is your favorite scene? Why?
- What is your image of the main character? What are their wants, goals, needs, fears, and problems?
- What would you change if you had to? (The student won't necessarily make these changes, but readers typically identify the parts they like least as being parts that they would change.)
- What would you cut if you had to cut the length of this story by 20 percent?
- What new information and scenes would you add to this story if you had to?
- What scene or aspect of this story in your opinion worked best?
- Where is this story most exciting?
- In what two places do you think this story should be more exciting?

The writer must compare readers' answers to the answers they had expected and hoped to hear. Does the story deliver what the writer intended? The information gathered from reading a story aloud and from questioning others who read it will give the writer an excellent indication of which story aspects work well and which require revision.

However, this information from readers may not tell the writer *how* to fix the problems. Often, readers will say that the story lacks excitement and tension, that the story doesn't really seem to be about anything, or that specific scenes are boring. How can the writer find and fix specific story elements based on such general comments? Sometimes a writer can fix a boring scene by changing only a few lines. Sometimes they must completely rewrite the scene. Sometimes they must cut the scene and rewrite the story to allow for its omission. How does the writer know which to do? The answer is to evaluate each of the major story elements one at a time to determine if they carry their own weight. Fixing individual story elements is easy.

Primary-grade students may altogether skip this oral and peer reading evaluation. Though it is a powerful evaluative tool, they typically aren't ready to use it. It can become a confusing burden rather than an aid.

Finding the Story's Shape

Have students map the scenes of their story on scene cards (if they did not do so during story planning—see step 7 of "A Better Recipe" in Part II). Have them evaluate and rate each scene for five criteria—mood, action, tension, humor, and emotion—as follows:

1. In the box at the upper right of the card, have them draw a stick-figure face whose expression best represents the overall mood, or feeling, of the scene.

2. Have them rate the scene's level, or amount, of action, tension, humor, and emotion on a scale of 1 to 10 in the four boxes at the bottom of the card. A rating of 10 means nonstop, heart-pounding action; gut-wrenching tension; hilarious buffoonery; or profound character emotion. A rating of 1 means that there is no tension, it's not funny, or that there is no specific character emotion stated or implied in the scene, everyone is bland and neutral.

This evaluation does not concern the *quality* of the action, tension, humor, and emotion. It is just a measure of the amount, or intensity, of these elements in the scene. The emotion evaluated for this activity should concern the emotions expressed by and felt by the story characters. Students shouldn't consider *which* emotions are expressed and felt by the characters (this is recorded in the upper-right box as the overall mood of the scene), just the intensity of emotions.

Emphasize to your students that this evaluation is not a contest to see how high they can make the various ratings for each scene. First, inflating the rating won't help them improve the story. Second, a high rating isn't necessarily better than a low rating. The desired rating depends on where the scene falls in the story and what the writer wants to accomplish with the scene. There are times when a writer wants high levels of action, tension, humor, or emotions. There also must be times, though, when these levels are low, to allow the reader some relief. A writer can only determine whether the story flows as it should if they rate each scene honestly.

Having rated each scene, students should scan their scene cards and evaluate the flow and patterns of action, tension, humor, emotion, and mood. Is tension established early in the story? Does tension increase scene by scene toward the climax scene? Is tension at its peak during the climax? Has tension dissipated by the story's ending? This is the most common pattern for tension in a story.

If the pattern of tension is markedly different, the student must decide if this is what they intended. Too much tension too early means that the story can't build toward a climax. If there is too little tension at the beginning, the writer risks boring and losing the reader. If tension peaks before the climax, the climax will seem uninteresting and anticlimactic. If there is too little tension just before and during the climax scene, the reader won't appreciate the significance of this pivotal story event and will feel dissatisfied.

Students should evaluate their high-action scenes. Does the presence of action in these scenes increase, or at least maintain, the story tension? If not, the action might not be contributing to the story. Why is this action essential to the story? Could it be cut? Are character reactions to, and feelings about, the action included in the scene? Is the action clearly an essential part of overcoming a risky and dangerous obstacle? The general pattern should be for a rise in action to create a more important rise in tension. Action and tension should match well throughout the story. If they don't, the writer must decide if this is what they intended, or if this might be part of the reason their story isn't as powerful or interesting as they had hoped.

Students should evaluate the pattern of humor throughout their story. Certainly, humor isn't mandatory in a story. Still, it is one of the most attractive and appealing elements for a reader. Everyone wants to laugh. Humor also provides valuable relief from the tension and conflict in a story, leaving the reader refreshed and ready to appreciate character struggle anew.

Is there humor in the story? Is it concentrated in a few scenes, or spread evenly throughout the story? Having a few intensely funny scenes can be wonderfully engaging for the reader. It is generally better, though, if some humor is spread throughout most of the scenes. Small blocks of isolated, powerful humor are intrusive and feel inappropriate in an otherwise serious story. Typically, the reader will be less appreciative of the long stretches of story between these blocks of humor. A smattering of humor throughout the story helps set up the intensely funny moments. This is not a rule, but it is something worth considering.

Do successive scenes of the story have the same mood? A reader can appreciate and empathize with somber and serious moods for only a short time. A reader can remain scared for only so long. Then fright becomes boredom and the reader no longer empathizes with the frightened feelings of the characters. The same is true for the intensity of emotion from scene to scene. If every scene has an emotional rating of 10, the reader is likely to shove the story aside in need of an emotional break. Some scenes should be calmer so that readers can appreciate the gripping emotions of other scenes. Sequels are excellent spots to insert calmer moments into a story.

If a story has three sad scenes in a row, the reader will likely become numb to sadness by the third scene. Students should consider separating these scenes by inserting a scene with a substantially different mood, or increasing the amount of humor in these three scenes. The general pattern should be to regularly vary the mood, so that the reader will be able to appreciate and vicariously experience every mood of the story.

Does the mood of the scene match the emotions the main character feels in that scene? Readers usually want to empathize with the main character. To do this, what the reader feels (the mood of the scene) should match what the main character feels. If mood and character emotions don't match well from scene to scene, the writer must decide if that is what they intended. Is there a reason for the scene to have a mood different than the emotions the main character feels in that scene? If not, would the story read better and have more effect upon the reader if this scene were rewritten to match mood with the main character's emotions?

The goal of this evaluation is twofold. First, it reveals if a lack of story effectiveness can be attributed to simple problems with the flow and patterns of action, tension, humor, emotion, and mood. This is often the case. Once such problems are corrected, the story leaps to vivid life. Second, it allows the writer to judge whether the flow and patterns of these story elements match what they envisioned and intended when they drafted the story.

Evaluating Story Elements

Having looked at the shape and effectiveness of the overall story, it will now be beneficial to consider the major storywide elements, one by one. The writer needs to be satisfied with the overall flow of the story and with how each of these elements delivers its story promise.

We'll do this storywide check by asking a baker's dozen of questions that each student writer can use to assess and adjust the major elements of their story. Feel free to omit those questions that address story elements you haven't yet discussed with your students. Under each of these questions (and under the story-element topics presented in the sections "Do the Scenes Deliver?" and "Do the Words Deliver?") are substantial lists of specific questions to consider. These litanies of questions are guides to help student writers decide whether particular elements of their story need work during editing. No story will need work in all areas. Most will need work in only a few. The lists of questions are included to help student writers identify those elements of a story that most need work.

1. **Is there a story question?** Is it clearly presented? Is it presented early in the story? Is this question resolved at the end of the story, but not until the very end? Is the resolution of this question in doubt throughout the story? Does the reader feel suspended between this question and its answer throughout the story? If the story question isn't suspenseful, make sure there is a recognizable character goal, that the character really cares about this goal, and that the magnitude, the risk and danger, of story obstacles is great enough to cast the story outcome into doubt.

2. **Is there a story theme?** Is this theme relevant to the reader and the main character, and integral to the story? Is it an ongoing aspect of the story and satisfactorily explored?

3. **Is the main character compelling and interesting?** If not, check the core layer of character information and judge whether it has been adequately developed and translated onto the written page. Are there unique, relevant, and interesting details for the other layers of character information? Does the main character express interest and passion? Laughter and excitement? Do they care about anything, in general, and about their own goals in particular? Do they risk something to achieve them? Do they face (and acknowledge) danger and fear? Do they struggle? Is there something at stake when they struggle? Are their emotions and feelings included in the story? Is the reader allowed to see their internal reactions to events and how they interpret events, through sequels?

    If the answer to each of these questions is yes, then the main character is carrying their share of the weight of the story. Any problems must lie elsewhere.

4. **Does the dialog work?** Does it contain vital story information? Does it sound like real conversation? Does the dialog reveal the inner nature of the character speaking? Is the sound and wording of the dialog consistent with the personality and profile of the character? Does the dialog ramble, or is it concise and compressed? Is the dialog forceful, and does it take advantage of opportunities to emphasize conflict?

    Dialog is important to every story and, especially, to every character. Exercise #32, "The Match Game" (p. 180), is designed to help students develop their ability to write dialog consistent with the speaking tone, mood, and personality of a character. It is a fun game to play, and what they learn will help them review and edit their dialog to make it sharper and more revealing.

5. **Are the obstacles and conflict sufficiently compelling?** It is the obstacles and resulting conflict that allow the main character to rise to hero status. Are there enough obstacles to do this? Do they block the main character from reaching their goal? Are they as formidable as possible? Does the main character struggle and suffer enough to create gripping tension? Is all the potential risk and danger associated with the obstacles presented as convincingly and threateningly as possible? Combined, are the obstacles great enough to convince the reader that the main character will likely fail to reach their goal?

    If the answer to any of these questions is no, review each scene in which an obstacle is introduced or faced. Often, obstacles can be made to appear more imposing by having characters react more strongly to them. If every character is justifiably afraid of facing some obstacle, the reader will be afraid, too. If the main character doesn't break a sweat and shows no fear or concern while confronting an obstacle, the reader will be equally indifferent to this obstacle and bored by the lack of struggle against it. When the main character reacts strongly, the reader will, too.

Some scenes may need to be rewritten to better reveal to the reader just how risky and dangerous the conflicts really are. Extra scenes may need to be added just to show readers how gargantuan the obstacles, the flaws, and problems really are. The best solution depends on the story, but the goal is universal: A story should be about risky, dangerous conflict faced at overwhelming odds against unbeatable foes.

6. **Are the struggles exciting?** *Are* there struggles? Are the struggles relevant to the main character's goal? Are they dangerous to the main character? Are they risky? (Is it likely the main character will fail?) Is the main character forced to *truly* struggle, or are the obstacles overcome too easily? Are the struggles central to the progression of the story, and to its events? Stories are about conflict and struggle. Without grand struggles, there is no story.

7. **Is the antagonist a worthy opponent?** *Is* there an antagonist? Does the antagonist block the main character from reaching their goal? Has the antagonist been developed into a terrible, unbeatable adversary? Is it clear what the antagonist wants and why they want it? Is the antagonist the last obstacle to be overcome? Will the reader be convinced that the antagonist is more powerful than the main character, and that there is little hope of the main character defeating their opponent?

    The easiest way to perk up a lackluster, tensionless story is to increase the risk and danger to the main character of facing the antagonist. This may require the writer to add scenes, or further develop existing scenes, to show the reader just how dangerous the antagonist really is. This may require the writer to rewrite other characters' reactions to, and feelings about, the antagonist. This may require the writer to increase the conflict between the main character and the antagonist. Regardless, when a writer builds the power of the antagonist, they automatically build not only the power of the main character, but also suspense and tension.

8. **Is the plot effective?** Does the story flow logically from scene to scene? Is it understandable? Does the plot line, or sequence of events, effectively tell the story? Are any essential events missing? Do events occur in the most effective order? Are any events not essential to telling the story? Can they be cut? Does the order of events create an effective shape for the flow of tension and emotion throughout the story?

    One effective way to evaluate a plot line is to look for cause-and-effect relationships between the scenes. The events of one scene should set forces into motion that cause the events of future scenes. These new events become the cause of events that appear in still later scenes. Like an unbroken chain, these cause-and-effect links should flow from scene to scene.

    Exercise #33, "Cause and Effect" (p. 181), is designed to help students understand the value of the cause-and-effect linkage between scenes, and to develop their ability to control it. This exercise may be used as often as needed. It might also be used as a story-starter game.

9. **Does the climax work?** *Is* there a climax? Does the story steadily build toward the climax? Is that climax satisfying? Does the main character overcome the antagonist, or final and central obstacle (the one with greatest jeopardy), at the story's climax?

    Here are nine schemes to rejuvenate a disappointing climax and build the story into a spine-tingling thriller:

    1. Early in the story, establish the antagonist as being more powerful, threatening, and dangerous.

2.   Increase what is at stake in the confrontation between the main character and the antagonist. Instead of having a story about whether the antagonist will succeed in stealing an ice cream cone, change the antagonist's goal so that the confrontation is about whether the antagonist will succeed in taking control of an entire neighborhood of a city—or even the entire galaxy.

3.   Include the main character's reaction to, and dread in anticipation of, the confrontation with the antagonist. If the main character is terrified of the antagonist, the reader will be, too.

4.   Improve and expand the description of the struggle at the moment of climactic confrontation.

5.   Continually increase the power and danger of the antagonist as the story progresses. As the antagonist becomes more menacing and all-powerful, tension and interest are increased. Lucas used this technique to build Darth Vader in the *Star Wars* trilogy. Tolkien used it to build Sauron in the *Lord of the Rings* trilogy.

6.   Create a pause in action and emotional stress just before the climax. Insert one quiet, reflective scene just before the climax to establish a contrast to the upcoming action and emotional turmoil. Remind the reader of the frailty or flaws of the main character and of what is at stake in the upcoming confrontation. This scene with opposite values of action and emotion makes the climax action and emotion more powerful.

7.   Use foreshadowing to help the reader anticipate the upcoming confrontation. Foreshadowing is the placing of hints, or guideposts, early in a story about important events to come.

For example, early in a story, the main character is told, "You won't have too much trouble sneaking into the wizard's castle to recover the stolen crown—as long as you're out of there before dark. Whatever you do, *don't* get caught in the wizard's castle after nightfall!" Every reader now knows that the climax will be a confrontation with the wizard in his castle *after dark*. How do readers know this? The writer used foreshadowing to suggest the most dangerous climax possible.

Search for risk and danger that can be used to foreshadow the climax and increase reader tension as it approaches.

8.   Don't end the climax scene too soon. Readers have been waiting all story long for this moment. Give the reader a chance to revel in the wonder and glory of this moment. Include not only the actions of all major characters, including the antagonist, but also their reactions to the outcome of this most important conflict.

9.   Use scene cards to reshuffle scenes and reshape the action and tension in the early scenes of the story. Action and tension should begin at low levels and build slowly and steadily toward the climax.

10.   **Is the ending satisfying and apparent?** If the ending answers a story question for which the resolution has been in doubt, it will feel satisfying to the reader. Does the ending clarify the theme? Does it conclude something about the theme? Is the reader left with a final reflection (sequel) from the main character?

Is the ending logical and yet surprising? If readers know all along, with no uncertainty or doubt, exactly how a story will end, there will be no suspense and tension. There will be no reason to continue reading the story. *Something* must be in doubt. There must be some element of impending surprise maintained throughout the story and revealed at the ending.

Still, the ending must be logical. It must follow from the events of the story. The plot must lead toward this conclusion. Once a reader has read the ending, they should be able to recall the story and say, "Ah, yes. Of course. I should have known all along." The writer must keep the reader in doubt, in suspense, so that they must read the ending to be sure.

If the ending seems flat and insufficient, check first the goal, the story question, and related suspense and tension. Clarify the story question and place its resolution in greater doubt. Next, ensure that the final sequel satisfies the goals and needs of the main character. Next, rewrite the opening paragraphs to better set up the ending. Finally, ensure that the ending is believable and plausible.

11.   **Are the perspective and viewpoint ideal?** Is the story adequately told through the chosen perspective and viewpoint, or do they force the exclusion of some critical information? Are the perspective and viewpoint used consistently throughout the story?

Changing either perspective or viewpoint usually requires completely rewriting a story. However, if the writer suddenly realizes that the tale could be much better told through some other character's eyes, the effort is often worthwhile.

12.   **Is the writer's voice appropriate for the story?** We have not yet discussed voice. It is an advanced writing concept. Still, voice can affect the readability and success of a story.

There are two separate, writing-related meanings for this term. The first, which is the more important for student writers, refers to the tone and style with which a story is written. Tone and style create the mood, feeling, or impression of a story.

Different stories should have different voices, even if written by the same writer. The voice of the writing should match the content of the story. It is most important for period pieces, or for stories about a unique environment with a unique dialect, which carry much of the richness and flavor of the story. Just as dialog must match the character to sound real and convincing, so must the language of a story match the subject, time period, and setting of a story to sound real and convincing.

If a story is about two rough-and-tumble cowpokes on a Western prairie, the language and structure of the story should reflect the harsh, tough environment and mentality of the characters. If a story is about Colonial America, the wording, the thoughts and speech of characters, and the description of scenes should reflect this period.

The second meaning for *voice* refers to a natural style of writing that each writer settles into over time, to a writer's unique way of organizing language and story. Students need not concern themselves with this second meaning. This voice develops slowly over years of writing.

13.   **Do the tension and suspense propel the reader through the story?** By now, every student knows that tension is a critical ingredient of every successful story stew. Does tension increase toward the climax? Is it relieved by the climax? Is it created early in the story by the suspense of the story question?

For tension to exist, a character must care about some goal and be willing to risk something important while attempting to overcome whatever obstacles stand in their way. The goal, struggle, and risk and danger must be real to the character and relevant to the reader. If tension is lacking, check these story elements first.

There are additional places to develop tension. It can be increased by emphasizing the limitations of the main character. If a writer doesn't want to, or can't make the antagonist more powerful and more dangerous, the same effect is achieved by reminding the reader of how frail and inadequate for the challenge the main character is.

Readers develop their feelings for a story through the feelings and reactions of the various characters. Do the characters feel the tension and anxiety? Are they nervous, unsure? Do they show it and say it? If they do, the reader will feel the tension more keenly.

Tension is born of conflict. Conflict is implied by struggle, obstacles, risk, and danger. Increase the conflict between story characters (even friends or partners) and the tension is increased. Conflict can (and some would say *should*) exist in every interaction between story characters. Don't automatically confine the characters to being cooperative and passive. They can be demanding and pushy. It's genuine for them to want what they want and not be willing to settle for less.

Writers tend to steer conversations and stories around seemingly trivial character discrepancies and arguments. Search each scene for even minor opportunities to increase real and potential conflict for the main character, thus increasing tension. Conflict isn't just fist fighting. When some character grumbles and sneers just enough, so that the reader suspects they might not cooperate with the main character next time, tension is still increased.

Finally, the use of epiphany and irony can increase reader tension. These elements are discussed and demonstrated later.

Students will gain a detailed and accurate sense of the strengths and weaknesses of their story by asking and answering these 13 questions. They won't yet have evaluated individual scenes and sentences. These assessments are done during the following rounds of editing. Students will be sure, though, that they have an effective overall story presented in the correct sequence.

Do the Scenes Deliver?

Your students followed every step of A Better Recipe to produce a completed first draft. They have just spent days evaluating and reworking the major story elements. Yet their story *still* doesn't have the excitement and power they had hoped it would. What did they do wrong? Probably nothing.

It's just time to shift to the next step in the editing process, time to look within story scenes to judge their effectiveness. Scenes are the building blocks of a story. Each scene must work as a separate unit, like a solid cement block, before it can be cemented with other scenes to form a story wall. One or two weak blocks can cause an entire wall to collapse. Each individual scene must do its job.

A scene is like a mini-story. It is a finite block of action, or character interaction. Each scene has a scene question, which is answered at the scene's ending. There are character-based goals for a scene. Each scene has obstacles that block the scene goal. There is conflict, tension, suspense, and resolution within each scene. The writer must treat each scene as an individual unit. The scene must have a purpose. Some conflict or struggle must be undertaken and resolved within each scene. The scene must reach some conclusion that moves the story forward.

Scenes are like the separate subsystems of a car—the engine, transmission, steering, cooling, fuel-delivery, electronics, and electrical systems. The overall goal is to make the car move. No one subsystem does that. Each subsystem does only a particular task of the overall job. The car moves only when each subsystem does its unique task and also meshes with the other subsystems to work as a whole.

Scenes must fulfill similar requirements. So far in editing, we have focused on the overall story and have adjusted scenes only as needed to make the major story elements more effective. Now it is time for writers to ask themselves a litany of questions to determine whether individual scenes work as separate units. We will revisit some previously discussed story elements, but with a new focus upon scenes.

1. **The opening scene.** No scene is more important than the opening scene. If a reader doesn't like this scene, they will not read further to see others. Does the story begin when story events are already in progress, launching the reader into the middle of the action? If the opening paragraphs describe background events and occur before the story events begin, can these paragraphs be cut so that the story does begin in the middle of the action?

    Does the story begin at the best place to intrigue the reader, stimulating curiosity and suspense? Could the story begin later? Does the opening scene hook the reader and make them *need* to see how the story ends? Does it create unanswered questions that make a reader want to continue reading?

    Does the opening scene create an accurate impression of the overall tone and mood of the story? Is it visually appealing? Does it create a sense of the setting for the story? Does it introduce the main character and their goal? (This isn't essential, but a good idea in a short story.) Does it build tension and hint at upcoming struggle? Does it introduce the story theme? Does it set up the final scene? Does it foreshadow the climax? (Again, not essential, but it's an engaging bonus.)

    This is a substantial job for one scene to do, which is why the opening scene is typically rewritten more than any other. There is no firm rule listing what must appear in the opening scene of a story. If the opening scene grabs the reader's interest and draws them into the story, it has fulfilled its most important task. A writer's job, though, is to hold a reader's interest throughout the *entire* story. The experiences of countless writers over the years have shown that this is easier to do if the elements mentioned above are also presented in the opening scene.

    The keys to a successful opening scene (one that locks a reader into a story and makes them *need* to read it to the ending) are to focus on the first impression of the main character, to establish the importance of their goal, and to establish, or at least foreshadow, the great conflict and struggle that lie between the main character and their goal.

2. **The final scene.** The final scene is everything beyond the climax scene. The question a writer must ask about their story material is, How much of the information included after the climax scene is really necessary? After the climax scene and the defeat of the final obstacle, there isn't much the reader will care about. Tension and suspense have dissipated. The struggles have concluded. Thus, the story has ended.

    There are two things a reader craves from the final scene. The first is a final sequel. That is, they want a chance to see how the main character internally reacts to the climax, to learn what this character now feels and thinks (concerning topics such as the theme) and how this character now views him- or herself. Does the final scene contain this sequel information?

The second is a definite answer to the story question. The desire to answer this question has carried the reader through the entire story. Now they want to know, What's the answer? Does the character achieve their goal? If this answer is not presented in the final scene, the writer must be sure they *want* the story question left lingering to nag the reader—because nag it will.

Does the final scene also tie up any loose ends created during the story? If not, the writer must decide if it's acceptable to leave a few unresolved threads hanging in the reader's mind. If there is any other information in the final scene, the writer must ensure that it is absolutely necessary. What if it were cut? Would the story really suffer?

3. **The climax scene.** First, make sure there is a climax scene. It normally is the final action sequence of the story. Action and tension reach their highest levels in this scene. The most dangerous of all obstacles is confronted and dealt with in this scene. Is there such a scene in the story? Does it occur just before the ending of the story? If not, why not?

In the previous section, I discussed ways to increase the importance and significance of the climax, most of which involve adjusting other scenes in the story. In the rush to share the excitement and action of the climax, the writer must also ensure that the climax is an effective scene.

In the grip of climactic action, writers often forget to consider setting, character, and detail. Is the physical setting of this scene well enough established so that the reader can clearly visualize it? Is there too much description, slowing the pace of this highly charged scene? Does the scene include character reactions? Is the crucial action of the scene clearly presented and described? Is the resolution of the action clear to the reader?

To heighten the reader's tension and excitement, writers typically want to make the climax a fast-paced scene, or one that reads quickly. To do this, writers often rely on shorter sentences that are simple, direct, and forceful. Have students do a quick experiment to check this.

Have each student chose an exciting, gripping scene from a story or book they have recently read. Have them calculate the average number of words per sentence for this scene (total scene words divided by the number of sentences). Have them do the same for some other scene in the same story that isn't exciting.

They'll find that average sentence length is markedly shorter during the exciting scene. They'll also find that there are markedly fewer compound and complex sentences in the exciting scene. To check this, have them count the commas and connectors (*and, or, but, both . . . and, either . . . or*, etc.). They'll find far fewer during scenes of gripping action.

Now have students assess their own climax scene. Have they taken advantage of using short, simple sentences to quicken the pace and increase the tension of this critical scene? Also, does the resolution of this scene feel satisfying and jubilant to the reader? This is the main character's grand triumph (unless the story is about the character's failure to reach their goal, in which case the reader usually feels compassion and concern).

4. **Story budget.** Having evaluated three specific and important scenes, it is now time to reexamine all the scenes. The writer's goal should be to find the weakest scenes, characters, and events in the story. One way to do this is to put the story on a tight story budget. Have students pretend that they are a Hollywood movie producer who wants to make a movie of their story but needs to shoot the movie at minimal cost.

Each new setting, like a movie set, is very expensive. Each action and special-effects sequence costs big bucks. Each character, like a movie star, needs to be paid. Can the writer reduce their story budget?

Can several different scenes occur in the same setting? This would save the extra words necessary to describe a new setting. Can any action sequences be eliminated or simplified without decreasing story tension? Is each character really necessary? Necessary enough that the writer can afford to pay them from a tight budget? Can several supporting characters be combined into a single character, or altogether eliminated and replaced by narration? The words necessary to describe a new character, as well as the reader energy necessary to remember an extra face, will be saved.

Many student writers are reluctant to cut scenes, settings, action sequences, and supporting characters from their story. Remind your students that their goal is to tell a story as efficiently and effectively as possible. The simpler these story elements are, the more effective the story will be. Students should trim excess wherever possible.

5. **Scene budgets.** Have students continue to pretend they are the producer of a movie version of their story. The movie is overbudget and, if they don't cut some scenes, it will never be completed. Have students find two scenes they would cut if they *had* to cut something.

Students should look long and hard at their two chosen scenes. Why did they choose these scenes? Are they necessary? Could the story survive without them? If so, maybe they should be cut. If not, why were they chosen? Are they weak? Do they kill story tension? Are they awkward?

These two scenes (if they shouldn't be altogether cut) are the first candidates for re-writing. Is there a scene question for each? Is the resolution of this question in doubt throughout the scene? Is there conflict in the scene? Is the scene ending flat and lackluster? Are the transitions confusing? (Transitions are discussed shortly.) Overall, what about these scenes is troubling? Reviving such dead scenes will allow the tension and suspense to flow more forcefully throughout the entire story.

6. **Sequels.** To become involved in a story, the reader needs to feel that they understand and empathize with the main character. Sequels and character reactions are two powerful ways to achieve this feeling of reader intimacy and understanding. We have already checked the story for the presence of character reactions. Now it is time to examine sequels.

Are there sequels to the major scenes of the story? Does each sequel flow logically from the previous scene? Does it reveal how the main character feels about and interprets the previous scene? Do the events of the next scene flow logically from the main character's resolution in the sequel?

If sequels do their job, the reader is kept in constant empathy with the thoughts and feelings of the main character. If the writer suspects that this is not the case in their story, the place to look is the sequels.

7. **Balance.** Story balance is a general and qualitative concept: The overall story will be more effective if no one part is more prominent than the whole. Check for balance among scenes. Action, length, humor, dialog, tension, emotion, and description should not be forced evenly into every scene, but neither should any of these elements be concentrated unduly into one scene.

If one scene is much longer than any other, try to split it into two scenes. If one scene has all the action, consider reorganizing the story to spread out that action. There may be good reason to concentrate one or more of these story elements into a particular scene. In successful stories, though, it is more common for them to be spread throughout the story. There should be balance among all story elements—between description and action, between narrative and dialog, between character and action, between action and reflection, among the various available senses addressed in story description and detail.

"Perfect" balance is neither necessary nor even desirable. However, the writer should have good reason for any imbalance they create. If a story seems awkward, if it doesn't flow smoothly, balancing the elements and scenes might solve the problem. The ultimate guide in making these balance decisions is to ask, What will be best for the story?

8. **Cause and effect.** This is a plot check. Just as scenes create sequels and sequels lead character and reader into the next scene, so too must the events in one scene cause the events in later scenes. Is there a logical progression from scene to scene? If a particular scene is removed, do other scenes still make sense and tell the story? If they do, then why is that particular scene necessary? Could it be cut? Is there any part of the plot that doesn't logically follow from previous events? Does the flow of the story make sense?

9. **Tension and suspense.** Just as a story must create tension and suspense that holds the reader until the ending, each scene must create its own tension and suspense that are resolved at the scene closing. Does each scene have a scene question for which the resolution is in doubt? That is, is there something that *must* happen during the scene that, as the scene opens, the reader thinks may likely *not* happen? Is something significant at risk in the outcome of the scene question?

Does tension build throughout the course of the scene toward the scene climax? Is there enough conflict and confrontation in the scene to create both tension and a scene climax? It is just as essential to create tension within a scene as it is to create storywide tension. However, there is a risk. Scene tension is relieved at the end of the scene when the scene question is answered, just as story tension is relieved at the end of the story when the story question is answered. If too much tension is relieved at the end of a scene, the reader might feel relieved enough to put down the story.

This risk is especially great in scenes with high levels of tension and action. The writer must ensure that story tension will still carry the reader beyond the end of such scenes. Once the writer ensures that tension develops in each scene, they must evaluate scene closings.

10. **Scene closings.** Scene closings are to scenes what story endings are to stories. The problem, though, is that tension, character emotion, and action all naturally sink to low levels at the end of each scene, or block of action. The lower these levels sink, the more difficult it is to rebuild them for the next scene. This makes scene closings critically important. They must create a satisfying, tension-relieving conclusion and, at the same time, reestablish storywide tensions, fears, and doubts for the reader, to prevent suspense and tension from sinking too low.

How does a writer perform this balancing act? It is easier than students might think. R. L. Stine, in his Goosebumps series, is a master at ending each chapter, or scene, by creating new tension and suspense. There are more than 500 chapter endings in this series. All are worth studying.

Here are eight techniques that can help prevent "story droop" at the end of a scene:

1. Remind the main character (and the reader) of the greater obstacles that must still be confronted.

2. Focus the final thought of the scene on the frailty (flaws) and losses of the main character.

3. Increase risk as the scene closes. Show how the scene's resolution creates more obstacles, more risk and danger, for the main character.

4. Introduce a new source of tension (Stine's favorite technique) in the last lines of the scene. Have something happen as the scene closes that creates a problem for the main character.

5. Reveal an epiphany or irony (discussed shortly) that increases risk and danger for the main character.

6. Foreshadow future problems and dangers.

7. Include a strong display of emotion by one or more character as the scene closes.

8. Quickly lead the reader into a sequel focusing on the character's dilemmas.

Tension and suspense should be major concerns for every writer. They must be built and tended like campfires. Though a scene is ending, tension and suspense must not be allowed to burn out.

11. **Transitions.** A scene ends and another begins. The concept is simple. Yet there may be great leaps, in distance and through time, between two adjacent lines of text—the end of one scene and the beginning of the next. There may be shifts in perspective and viewpoint between scenes. How is the reader to know? What prevents a reader from becoming confused?

The answer is transitions. Transitions are the lines of text that lead the reader out of one scene and assuredly into the next. Are the transitions clear? Concise? Brief? Are they consistent with the tone and mood of the story? Do they kill the energy and pace of the story?

12. **Epiphany and irony.** An epiphany is a sudden realization by a character, a flash of insight. Epiphanies are common in stories. However, student writers often overlook them and fail to develop them into a powerful story element.

What does an epiphany look like?

Bill has developed a new kind of computer program and wants to open a company. He gets his good friend, Tony, to help him, confiding in Tony every step of the way. Countless problems and setbacks arise to slow the opening of this company and the release of Bill's new program. Bill suddenly realizes that Tony is causing the problems, not helping Bill try to solve them. Tony is working for a competitor and is trying to keep Bill from completing his program so that the other company can release their version first.

Bill's insight is an epiphany. It is a powerful moment in the story. The more Bill trusts Tony and shares secrets with him, the more damaging to Bill's future this betrayed trust is, the more powerful the epiphany becomes. An epiphany occurs when both reader and character suddenly realize the truth, and that they have misunderstood and misinterpreted story events.

There are three parts to an epiphany: the setup, the trigger, and the moment of epiphany. The setup allows the character to misunderstand a situation, another character, or an event. The character then acts on their misunderstanding. This action must be harmful to the character, and must create jeopardy for them. Often, as with Bill and Tony, the misunderstanding is the exact opposite of the truth. The trigger is some specific event or evidence that reveals to the character their erroneous thinking. The moment of epiphany, or moment of insight, is the moment the character realizes the truth.

To make an epiphany more powerful and effective, build the misunderstanding, the setup. The more secrets and information Bill shares with Tony, the more he trusts Tony and follows his advice, the greater the impact of the epiphany will be. Use the misunderstanding to create greater and greater jeopardy for the main character, until the truth is finally revealed at the moment of epiphany.

A writer can also add tension and suspense by delaying the character's moment of epiphany after the trigger. Bill finds the evidence that proves Tony is a traitor, but Bill doesn't realize the truth as quickly as does the reader. For a while, he continues to treat Tony as a trusted friend. The reader will be transfixed, aghast by the enormity of Bill's misunderstanding, and wondering if Bill will ever figure it out.

An epiphany can be used as a story-planning tool. A story can be built around an epiphany. More commonly, though, the writer realizes during review and editing that they have an epiphany in their story, and then revises the story to take advantage of this powerful element.

Dramatic irony is a close cousin of epiphany. The major difference is that an irony does not require any character realization. An irony is an event that proves to be the reverse of what was expected. Readers love ironic twists.

What would the Bill-and-Tony story look like with an irony?

Tony tries throughout the story to destroy Bill's program and company. In the end, though, Tony's efforts accidentally uncovered the one fatal flaw in Bill's computer program. Bill perfected his program and became rich and successful.

Now, that's ironic!

An irony also has three parts. First, the character misinterprets a situation, another character, or an event. Second, the character acts on this misinterpretation. Third, the character experiences an unexpected consequence or outcome.

Usually, but not always, the reader knows about the setup for the irony. They are allowed to know that the character is misinterpreting something. The final outcome of the irony may be what the reader expected, or it may be something even they didn't expect. This outcome, though, must be plausible and logical once the reader knows all the facts.

Many stories have the potential for a great ironic twist. Often, this potential remains undeveloped. Have students search their stories for the seeds of epiphanies and ironies. If a student finds one in their story, they should immediately examine earlier scenes to find opportunities to build the setup. Next (for an epiphany), they should develop and emphasize the trigger, an important story moment. Finally, they should develop and emphasize the character's realization of the truth (the moment of epiphany), or the unexpected outcome (the ironic twist).

13. **Foreshadowing.** Foreshadowing is a writing technique for hinting to the reader, or providing them with clues about upcoming events. Foreshadowing builds tension by allowing the reader to more accurately anticipate some future climactic event.

For example, just before a knight slays a small dragon, it hisses, "You can kill me, but my brother is 10 times my size, breathes white-hot fire, and cannot be hurt by metal swords." The dragon didn't need to tell the knight this. Had the dragon died in silence, story events would not have been affected. The dragon's final statement is foreshadowing. It allows the reader to anticipate a confrontation with that bigger, rougher, tougher dragon and begin to worry about it. It builds tension.

We have seen that foreshadowing is one way to reestablish tension at the end of a scene. The death of this small dragon would surely occur after an action- and tension-filled battle, and would surely occur at the end of a scene. The dying dragon's words of foreshadowing reestablish story tension and drive the reader into the next scene.

Student writers should not attempt to foreshadow more than two future events in a story (one event is preferable). The reader will become confused if foreshadowing clues require them to think about too many future events. Still, foreshadowing is a powerful technique for directing the reader's attention to upcoming climactic events and giving them plenty of time to worry about the outcome of these events.

Do the Words Deliver?

The story works. The scenes work individually and collectively. Yet the story is still boring. What did students do wrong? Probably nothing.

There is still one more level of editing to perform. Photographers don't take pictures of an object. They photograph *light*. Writers don't write stories. They write *words*. Before editing and revision can be complete, writers must examine the words and sentences they have constructed to judge whether they effectively and efficiently communicate the story to the reader. The time to do this check is after the writer has organized the story and its scenes into final form.

Here are 16 word-related areas to check. Most are new areas that student writers have not concerned themselves with during previous editing work. The rest are major story elements, revisited at a minute level.

1. **Sentences.** Sentences are the basic building blocks of all narrative. Every story is a long string of sentences. If these sentences are all alike in construction, the reader will become as bored and bleary-eyed as they would from listening to a preacher drone endlessly in the same tone and with the same pace. Just as speakers must vary tone and pace, so writers must vary sentence length and structure.

Does sentence length vary throughout the scenes and story? Is the construction varied (simple, compound, complex, etc.)? Are the sentences shorter and more direct during exciting action sequences? (This is one easy way to build tension and increase the pace of the story during these scenes.)

How many active and passive sentences are in the story? In a passive sentence, the subject is being acted upon. ("The book was dropped on the table by John.") In an active sentence, the subject does the acting. ("John dropped the book on the table.") Active sentences carry more energy and immediacy than passive sentences. Too many passive sentences make a scene seem flat and lifeless. Auxiliary forms of the verb *be* (*is*, *was*, *are*, *were*, *will be*, *has been*, etc.) appear in passive sentences. Too many such words might indicate too many passive sentences, which might be the reason a scene isn't working. Unless the writer has a good reason for using passive sentences, active sentences are preferable.

Are the sentences clear and concise? Or are some sentences bloated with nonessential words and information? Exercise #34, "The Sentence Game" (p. 184), is a fun test of your students' ability to detect such common sentence problems. It features a series of comparisons between two sentences. After using this exercise, create a paragraph full of sentence flaws and have your students identify the problems without the benefit of a multiple-choice comparison.

2. **Verbs.** Verbs carry the motion and action of a story. Verbs connect the individual images into a single, flowing narrative. Verbs also can be a form of detail. Strong, active verbs provide precise descriptions of actions and movements, creating important visual detail.

    Have students ignore the overall story, its meaning, and its sentences and examine only the verbs they have used:

    - Are they strong, descriptive, forceful verbs that carry an exact image of the action and (if a character is the subject) an exact image of the character's emotional state while acting?
    - Are there any passive verbs and verbs of state that can be replaced by active, action verbs?
    - Do the verbs alone paint an accurate picture of the flow of the story?
    - Can the reader understand what is happening from reading only the verbs?

    It is often effective (and fun) to extend the range of verbs outside their normal context, to create a uniquely detailed image for the reader. Instead of writing, "He combed his hair with a comb" (common and uninteresting), write, "He *raked* his hair with the comb." The image is much stronger. If students search for opportunities to creatively extend the range of ordinary verbs, they can create extraordinarily vivid images.

    Exercise #35, "He Entered the Room" (p. 188), is a powerful demonstration of the visual power of verbs. This is a fun exercise for students. At the same time, it encourages them to use strong, precise verbs to describe the action in the scenes of their stories.

3. **Adverbs.** The infamous adverb modifies a verb and usually ends with *-ly*. Some writers believe that they should be altogether eliminated. I disagree. Adverbs can play a role in creating accurate, detailed images of motion, movement, and action. The problem is that they tend to be overused. The real culprit is weak, vague verbs, which require the support of adverbs to prop them up and communicate a vivid image. Strong, precise verbs usually do not.

    Here is an example: "The king *walked angrily* into his chambers and *sat heavily* upon the gilded throne." Note the two verbs: *walked* and *sat*. Both are weak and vague, and both require adverbs, *angrily* and *heavily*, to create a vivid image of the action. Here is the same sentence with stronger verbs: "The king *stormed* into his chambers and *slumped* upon the gilded throne." Adverbs are no longer needed. The verbs *stormed* and *slumped* themselves create a vivid image.

    Have students mark each adverb in their story. For each, they should check the verb it modifies. Is there a stronger verb that would eliminate the need for an adverb? Strong action verbs create a more exciting and interesting story than do weak verbs preceding or trailing strings of adverb modifiers.

4. **Detail.** Detail creates reality. We have addressed this previously. Now it is time for a final detail check. First, is there enough detail to accurately convey multisensory images of the places, characters, and events of the story? Are there characters or scenes that are not adequately described?

Second, is the detail effective? Does it uniquely describe the places, characters, and events? Are names named wherever possible? Are there interesting, graphic details that create specific, vivid images? Does the detail describe those qualities and characteristics that distinguish the thing being described from other things of the same type? Does the detail provide insights into character while describing places and events?

Exercise #36, "The Scene Game II" (p. 189), can help students assess the effectiveness of their chosen detail. It only requires 30 minutes, and generates vivid evidence for each student as to whether or not their detail effectively describes each scene.

Third, are there places with too much detail? Does the reader receive more information than they need to create a mental movie of the story? Is there redundant detail? Can some of the detail be cut without weakening the images of the story?

Fourth, is the detail in the correct places? Do readers receive detail when they need to form images of important story elements? Does detail encumber major action sequences? Can this detail be moved to other scenes, where it won't dilute the power of intense action?

Finally, does the story effectively use all the available forms of detail? Are the nouns specific? Are the verbs strong, precise action verbs? Are modifiers used sparingly and effectively? To better acquaint students with the role of nouns, verbs, and modifiers in creating detailed images, try Exercise #37, "Where Images Come From" (p. 190). This exercise allows students to compare the images they create when listening to three versions of a paragraph—one without nouns, one without verbs, and one without modifiers. The result is that they will better appreciate and understand the role of each of these parts of speech in creating story details.

5. **Multisensory detail.** Stories are more powerful and gripping when story detail describes what all five of the reader's senses would record if they where present in the middle of the action. Student writers tend to rely almost exclusively on the sense of sight. They report what things look like. Readers also want to imagine what places smell like, sound like, feel like, and taste like.

Have students count how many details they provide for each sense. They should then evaluate overall image and detail density (number of details per page, or per 100 words), as well as detail density for each of the five senses.

6. **Simile and metaphor.** Similes and metaphors are powerful forms of detail. A simile is an equivalence between two otherwise dissimilar things. Similes use the words *like*, *as*, or *as if* to make this comparison. (His arms were *like* tree trunks. His mouth was as big *as* a house. A metaphor directly ascribes or assigns the properties or attributes of one thing to another. (His arms *were* tree trunks. His mouth *was* an open door that no one could shut.) Similes are more common. Metaphors, typically, are more powerful.

Similes and metaphors work only if the subject of comparison invokes a common, concrete image for the reader. "He whined like the gyro-stabilizer on a retro-sequencer" probably means nothing to a reader. Who knows what a gyro-stabilizer on a retro-sequencer is? Who knows if it really does whine?

The writer must carefully assess the remaining stereotypical references in their story. Is there another way to present the same story information with fresh, unique images? Are the stereotypes necessary? If they are, and if the writer is certain that they do not have negative connotations, use them. Otherwise, replace them with other detailed description.

9. **Repetition.** Repetition has gained undeserved notoriety over the last decade. In the rush for brevity, modern fiction has looked at *all* repeated lines and words as easy fodder for the red pencil. Some repetition deserves to be cut. However, some forms of repetition create powerful immediacy in a story. They are prominently used in many excellent and successful stories, and they deserve consideration by student writers.

How is repetition detrimental to a story? Needless repetition slows the pace of a story, wastes words, bloats the text, and irritates a reader by forcing them to read what they already know. If a reader grumbles, "Yeah, yeah. I *know* this. Get on with the story," the writer has repeated information that shouldn't have been repeated. The most common forms of needless repetition are excess detail; deadwood words; multiple examples of the same character trait, emotion, or action; multiple characters who fill the same role; and characters' interpretations that state what the reader already knows.

How is repetition helpful? Intentional repetition can focus the reader's attention, reinforce their understanding, create humor, allow anticipation of upcoming events and signal major story events. What is typically repeated? Character reactions, character habits and unique lines of dialog, character names, transitions into scenes that create humor, and key story lines.

There are as many varieties of repetition as there are stories. Search for unwanted and unnecessary repetition in every story and eliminate it. Trust that the reader will understand the writer's intentions the first time, with only one telling, one clue, one detail. Also search for opportunities to use intentional repetition. Repetition placed into a story to create humor not only deserves to be kept, but deserves to be emphasized.

10. **"Show don't tell."** The mantra and official theme song of modern fiction has become "*show*, don't tell"—but what does it mean? "Show" means that a writer should rely on the sensory detail they include in a story to literally show the reader what happens. "Don't tell" means that a writer shouldn't interpret that sensory information, but rather allow—actually force—the reader to make all interpretive inferences.

Does this mean that a writer should show everything and tell nothing? No. To the extent that "show don't tell" reminds writers to rely on unique, interesting sensory detail, it is a useful motto to adopt. Still, a writer must tell the reader *some* things in a story.

"Show don't tell" originated as a reminder not to tell the *feelings* and *emotions* of story characters, nor to draw conclusions for the reader about characters and story events, but rather to show relevant sensory detail to the reader and allow them to draw their own conclusions. (Not "Carol was mad. Bill was sad," but rather "Carol slammed her fist onto the table and shook a thick fistful of bills in the air. Bill sank to the floor in a corner of the office, wringing his hands, and began to sob." The writer must trust that the reader will correctly interpret sensory detail and conclude, "Carol was mad. Bill was sad.") When the reader is allowed to draw conclusions of their own, they become more deeply involved in the story. Also, showing provides sensory detail that telling does not.

What should a writer show? Show character reactions and emotions, character dialog, and the sensory detail of significant events and actions. What, and why, should a writer tell? Tell planned passages of narrative summary, character history, and repeated scenes or actions. Tell to vary the rhythm and pace of the story, and tell for brevity.

Notice that showing requires more words than telling. Telling is faster and more efficient. Showing provides detail and involves the reader. It is a trade off. Most of the time, showing seems to be more effective. There will be passages in a story, though, where telling is more effective. The writer must weigh these considerations and decide.

This decision, however, should be made during editing. We have already evaluated story detail. Now writers should search for passages where they have summarized, or told, character emotions and reactions, and where they have drawn conclusions about the characters and events for the reader. Can these passages be converted to sensory detail? Will the story suffer if they are? Usually, the story is significantly strengthened by this conversion process.

11. **Beats.** Search through dialog passages for too few or too many beats (see "Working with Dialog" in Part II). Does the reader get a clear image of the place, the characters, and their actions while they talk? If not, consider adding beats. Do the beats encumber the dialog and slow the pace of the story? If so, perhaps there are too many beats, or perhaps they should be gathered into a narrative paragraph just before the collected lines of dialog.

12. **Humor.** I haven't discussed humor yet. Everyone agrees that humor is good. Everyone wants to laugh. There are precious few story moments that would be harmed by the addition of appropriate humor. The question is never, *Should* the writer add humor to their story? It is always, *How* do they do it?

Writing humorously is difficult. I have read a dozen books written about the subject. They all eventually arrive at the same conclusion: Humor can't be translated into a formula. Either something is funny, or it isn't—but it's better if it is.

There are, however, story structures that lend themselves to humor. First and foremost are character reactions. Many stand-up comedians earn their living by exaggerating the way people react in various stressful situations. We have already discussed the power and necessity of character reactions in a story. If the writer exaggerates character reactions to stressful situations and repeats these reactions during a story, it is almost always funny. Character reactions are the surest place for inserting humor into a story.

Generally, exaggeration (whether over- or understatement) is funny. It is the basis for tall tales, most of which *are* funny. I will mention two other structural situations that lend themselves to humor: image reversal and perspective shift. An image reversal occurs when the reader is led to expect one thing, and the writer adds new information that reverses the reader's image. A short story I received by e-mail is a good example of image reversal:

> I went for a horseback ride yesterday, wind streaming through my hair. But my horse began to rotate, to twist so that its legs pointed straight up as it ran. Well, okay, it was really my saddle that loosened. It, and I, slowly rolled downward to the horses belly. I now bounced along upside down underneath the horse. It never slowed, charging full speed ahead. My body was thrown from my upside-down saddle. Desperately I clutched the saddle horn with one hand, one foot caught in the stirrup as I was bounced and dragged by my stampeding mount. Then, just before I blacked out, a man stepped out of the drug store and unplugged the horse.

The last line completely changes your image of the physical setting and situation. So it makes you laugh. The image reversal is funny. Have students look for this technique in books and stories they read. It requires them to structure a story, or at least a scene, to achieve the effect, but the effort is usually worthwhile.

Perspective shifts can also be funny. The Calvin and Hobbes comic strip used this ploy on a regular basis. Tell a scene from one character's viewpoint, then suddenly shift to another character's viewpoint—a character who would view the events very differently. (Parent and child viewpoints, often used in the Calvin and Hobbes series, work well for this purpose: Tell most of a scene through the eyes of a child as a desperate, exciting, death-defying adventure. Then shift to the practical, reality-based viewpoint of a parent who just wants to know why the child ruined his good pants.) If the two viewpoints are different enough, the shift from one to the other will be funny.

Have students keep humor logs or journals. Have them write down what makes them laugh, what they find humorous, from day to day. Periodically, have them look for patterns and trends. Generally, what makes them laugh will also make others laugh.

13. **Punctuation.** Two punctuation checks are worthwhile, aside from ensuring that basic punctuation is correct. First, mark every exclamation mark. Treat this form of punctuation like an exotic, pungent spice. A few grains add a delicious complexity to the flavor of the stew. If the cook uses more, though, it first destroys the basic flavor of the stew and then eventually overpowers the tastebuds of the eater, so they can't taste anything.

Exclamation marks have the same effect. A rare few are powerful. More become comical, and eventually blur all emphasis in the story. Does every exclamation mark indicate a spot of extreme emphasis? Can any be changed to simple periods? The fewer exclamation marks present in a story, the more power they have.

Second, check commas. Have students count the number of commas in a particular length of the story—400 words, for example. Students who have more than the average number for the class either are using commas incorrectly or are using too many compound and complex sentences for the good of the reader. If commas bog down the story, the reader will begin to feel like they are wading through the text. Reading will become too great an effort.

14. **Foreshadowing.** Is foreshadowing used in the story? Could it be? Is it clear? Is it accurate? Do all foreshadowed events actually occur? Does every line of foreshadowing provide new, significant information for the reader?

Search for opportunities to foreshadow upcoming climactic events. Still, the writer must trust that the reader will understand just one (or at most two) foreshadowing hints. The writer who repeatedly broadcasts what's to come will alienate the reader. The one exception is when repetition is emphasized and used for humor.

How many events are foreshadowed in the story? Does foreshadowing one event dilute the power of another? Typically, only one climactic event is foreshadowed in a short story (1,000 words or less). Stories foreshadowing two events rarely work.

15. **Force.** Stories have more impact and immediacy when forceful words are used, and when definite, specific actions occur. Don't use "big sound." It's too vague and indefinite. Don't even use "huge noise." It's still indefinite. Use "monstrous hiss." Now the reader forms a definite auditory image of the sound. "Monstrous hiss" has force, or power, because it is so specific.

Have students review first the nouns they have used. Are they definite, specific, and unique? Next, check adjectives. Are they as specific and forceful as possible? Finally, check verbs. Do they create precise and visually explicit images of the actions? Are any of the verbs tentative when they could be more forceful and definite? *Walk* is nonspecific and indefinite, even though it may be technically accurate. Rather, did the character actually *amble, stroll, plod, saunter, stride, strut, wander,* or *traipse?* These verbs are more forceful; that is, they force a more vivid and specific image into the reader's mind. Find more forceful substitutes for weak verbs.

16. **The final act.** After all other editing has been accomplished, have students count the number of words in their story, take several deep breaths for courage, and cut 15 percent of their total words.

What?! After all this? Cut more?

Yes. Cut more. We writers tend to love our words too much and leave too many of the precious darlings in our stories. Cutting 15 percent of the words forces the story onto a strict diet. It will emerge lean, tough, and powerful—a much better read for the reader.

The ultimate theme of editing is to cut, cut, cut, cut, cut, cut, cut . . . .

Many writers repeat this entire editing process many times for a single story. Having finished reworking the words and sentences, they set the story aside. Several weeks later, they begin again with the storywide questions. Often, one round of editing uncovers new problems and new opportunities to improve the story—problems and opportunities that could not have become apparent until the previous round of editing had been completed.

Figure 7 (pp. 101-3) is a checklist you and your students can use for evaluating the various elements of a story. This checklist includes revision elements for all three editing levels: story, scene, and word. Many teachers modify this list to include only those elements they have discussed and want to emphasize with their class, and use it to review, comment on, and evaluate student stories. It is also a helpful guide for students.

With practice, the editing process becomes faster, smoother, and easier. The story elements and concepts discussed in this editing guide are those that will help your students reach their fullest potential as story writers. There is no need to introduce all these elements and concepts at once at the beginning of the school year. Add them to the writing stew a few at a time, as your students' writing ability and understanding of the form and structure of a story warrant the new considerations.

Copyright

Do students really need to know about copyrights? Yes. Students routinely lose copyrights for their stories by not understanding what a copyright is and how to protect it. They don't need to be copyright experts, but a basic understanding of copyright is worthwhile.

First, what is a copyright? A copyright is a bundle of five rights that society grants to the person who creates a story (or other creative work—poem, photograph, film, song, etc.). These exclusive rights are: 1) the right to *reproduce*, or make copies, of the story; 2) the right to create *derivative works*, or to change the story; 3) the right to *perform* the story (for a live audience, in a recording studio, etc.); 4) the right to *distribute*, or sell, the story; and 5) the right to *promote* the story. No one can legally take any of these actions without the copyright holder's permission.

How does a student obtain a copyright? As soon as a story is created and fixed in permanent form (written down, recorded on audiocassette, etc.), it is automatically and instantly protected by a copyright. The act of creation creates the copyright. Every story your students write is instantly protected by a copyright. Writers may register their copyright by completing a form and sending it and a fee to the Copyright Office in Washington, D.C. This makes it easier to prove that the story is copyrighted (should this ever become necessary). Regardless, the copyright exists as soon as the story exists.

How can a student lose a copyright? This is the key question. Students unwittingly relinquish their copyrights every day. Currently, a copyright exists for the life of the copyright holder plus 50 years. A copyright can be relinquished, though, at any time. How? If the copyright holder 1) sells their copyright contractually, or 2) *knowingly releases a copy of any copyrighted material into the world without affixing a copyright notification*. In the latter case, the copyright holder has relinquished their copyright to the public, after which time anyone can copy, change, perform, distribute, and promote the story without the writer's permission.

Every time your students turn in a story without a copyright notification affixed to it, they relinquish their copyright. Usually, it doesn't matter. Usually, they hadn't intended to pursue future options for their story anyway. Usually, everyone will still acknowledge their rights to the story—but not always.

People have stolen stories from student writers. Typically, the students have no recourse because they didn't affix a copyright notification to their story. Later, someone copied and circulated their work. Then it fell into the hands of someone who recognized it as being a publishable story. . . .

Protecting a copyright is easy to do, and is a smart precaution for all student writers. How does a student give notice of their copyright? They write either of the following two phrases on the front page of their story: "Copyright [Year] [Their Name]" or "© [Year] [Their Name]." They aren't bragging. They aren't being pretentious. They are simply being a smart story writer.

Write Right!
Story Checklist

LEVEL 1

THE STORY (Do you really have a story?)

- **CHARACTERS**

  Is Main Character "real," specific & interesting?

  Clear Goal and motive?

  Obstacles real, relevant, risky, satisfying?

  Conflict & Struggle clear & compelling?

  Antagonist interesting, compelling & worthy?

  Can we see, hear, etc., each character?

  Do characters express real emotions?

- **PERSPECTIVE & VIEWPOINT**

  Consistent, appropriate?

- **THEME AND STORY QUESTION**

  Universal in their appeal?

  Maintained throughout?

  Resolved at the end?

  Powerful and interesting enough to hold a reader's interest?

- **VOICE**

  Tone and writing consistent and appropriate?

- **CHARACTER REACTIONS**

  Included?

  Interesting?

  Consistent?

- **DIALOG**

  Realistic?

  Concise?

  Move the story?

  Reveal character?

- **CLIMAX**

  Is it satisfying?

  Does the story build to a climax?

  Is the climax logically set-up?

  Is the climax anticlimactic?

- **SUSPENSE AND TENSION**

  Are they created?

  Maintained?

Fig. 7. Story-Editing Checklist.

LEVEL 2
THE SCENES (Do scenes propel & deliver the story?)

- **1ST & LAST**
  Are they necessary?
  Linked?
  Effective?
- **LOGICAL SEQUENCE**
  To scenes?
- **"SHAPE" OF SCENES**
  Do tension, action, & emotion vary and build in reasonable way?
- **SCENE QUESTIONS**
  Clear?
  Answered?
- **NECESSARY?**
  Does each scene move the story forward?
- **SCENE OUTCOMES**
  Clear?
  Consistent?
- **SCENE CONFLICT**
  Present?
  Satisfying?
- **SEQUELS**
  Do we see the scene's effect on characters?

LEVEL 3
THE WORDS (Are the words powerful descriptive, and effective?)

- **VOCABULARY**
  Varied?
  Appropriate?
  Interesting?
- **WORDING**
  Fresh?
  Interesting?
  Appropriate?
- **CONCISE**
  Cut & trim enough (You can always cut more.)
- **DETAIL**
  Are scenes, characters, and events adequately described?
  Was strong detail chosen?
  Is the detail visual and specific?
  Is detail in appropriate places?
  Is there excess detail?

Fig. 7. Story-Editing Checklist (*cont.*).

- **"SHOW DON'T TELL"**
    Does the writer show character feelings, reactions and emotions?
- **DIALOG**
    Is dialog used?
    Is dialog real and consistent?
    Does dialog reveal character and events?
    Does dialog contain essential story information?
- **VERBS**
    Strong & forceful?

LEVEL 4
THE POWERFUL EXTRAS (Does the story have 'em and does the writer use 'em?)

- **EPIPHANIES**
- **IRONIES**
- **SIMILES & METAPHORS**
- **HUMOR**
- **REPETITION**

Fig. 7. Story-Editing Checklist (*cont.*).

Part IV

Write Right Exercises

Complete directions for all exercises referenced in *Write Right* are presented in this part. Additional discussion and explanation of the individual exercises, their use, and the writing concepts they demonstrate and develop are included in Parts I–III.

Write Right Exercise #1

The Hard Part

Explore what your students think are the hardest parts of creating and writing a story.

Appropriate Grades: All
Concept

Some aspects of writing a story are harder than others. It's valuable when beginning the process of developing story-writing skills to clearly identify these aspects. The best way to address most of these problems is to develop an understanding of what really makes a story work, and what a story really is.

Time Required: 5 minutes
Goal: Identify aspects of story creation students think are the hardest.
Directions

This is a verbal exercise. Ask your class, "When you have to create and write a story, what is the hardest part for you?" As they answer, require that they be specific. You'll find that their complaints fall under several common themes:

An idea or theme to write about.

The mechanics of writing (spelling, word choice, sentence and paragraph structure, etc.).

Drawing the illustrations.

Not being boring.

Title.

Dialog.

Beginning the story.

Now ask them to discuss *why* these aspects are hard. What makes these aspects of writing harder than others (such as plot, setting, and action)? Remember that this is a preliminary exercise designed to help them begin thinking about the elements of a story. Still, it will be valuable for them to probe beyond these surface complaints and think about how a lack of vision or knowledge creates these problems.

Teaching Points to Emphasize

Note that three aspects of writing a story are almost never mentioned: creating interesting, compelling characters; determining how the story will end; and visualizing sufficiently interesting, relevant detail to make the story seem real. This is not because students believe that these aspects of story creation are easy, but because they rarely, if ever, think about them. This oversight is often the greatest single problem student writers face in their creative writing. If they were to address these three aspects (which most writers consider the real keys to story writing), most of their other problems would correct themselves.

Write Right Exercise #2

What Is a Story?

Explore what separates a story from other narrative forms and gives it such power and appeal.

Appropriate Grades: 2+

Concept

Every student has read stories, heard stories, and written stories. Yet few (if any) are able to define and describe the term *story*, nor are they able to separate story from other narrative forms. They all recognize a story when they encounter it, but they haven't thought about what uniquely defines a story. Yet this explicit understanding is at the very heart of writing a successful story. This definition is the place to begin a writing program.

Time Required: 15–30 minutes (step 4 of this exercise might be extended as homework)

Goal: Develop a class definition for a story.

Directions

This exercise consists of four steps, all of which ask the same question: What is a story? It is, in part, a precursor to Exercise #3, "Is It a Story Yet?"

Step 1

Begin with these general questions to your class: "You've all read stories, right? You've all listened to stories, right? And you've all written stories, right? So you all know what a story is, right?" Pause to let them answer yes to each question. Then ask, "So what *is* a story? What makes a story a story? What makes a story different from an article or a textbook? How do you *define* a story?"

As each student answers, establish whether their answer is a synonym for *story* ("A story is a tale, a fable, or a fairy tale."), a characteristic of a good story ("A story is fun to read." "A story is exciting."), or a possible definition. When I do this exercise with a class and hear either a synonym or a characteristic of a story, I say, "Yes, *tale* is another word for *story*. But what makes a story a story?" Or I say, "Yes, a good story is fun to listen to. But is 'fun to listen to' a *definition* of a story, or a *characteristic* of a good story?" Then I proceed to the next student.

When someone responds with a definition term, explore the limitations and applicability of that term. A student might answer, "A story is something written down in a book." You could respond, "A story could be written down. But does it have to be? Couldn't it also be verbal, told from person to person, like the stories you tell that happened to you? So a story is either written or told. This could be part of a definition."

Allow time to consider as many definitive elements as possible. List them on the chalkboard as they are mentioned. Avoid digression into lists of types of stories, and always explore the limitations of each answer. Does it define or characterize a story? Does it describe *all* stories, or only some stories? Help students differentiate definitions from descriptive characteristics.

Step 2

Now that they are thinking in definitive terms, have each student write their own definition of a story. They may use terms presented during the class discussion, as well as any others that occur to them. Allow them enough time to develop a complete definition.

Step 3

Have each student read their definition to at least three other students. After this exchange, allow students a moment to revise their definition, should they so choose.

Step 4

Have students nominate definitions (their own or others) that they particularly like, to be read aloud to the class. Have four to six students read. Make a list of the elements that the class thinks should be included in the definition of a story. Don't worry about wording or overlap among elements. The class must agree upon terms and elements, as well as aspects that should be excluded from the definition of a story.

Typically, the class will create a rambling definition, such as: "A story is something either written or told that has a plot and characters and a setting, with a beginning, a middle and an end, that tells about something that really happened or something someone made up." Their definition will probably contain unnecessary terms and verbiage. It may not even be particularly useful. You may not agree with their definition, and *Write Right* most likely will not agree with it, either. Let it stand for now, though. As your class proceeds through the next few exercises, a clearer definition of a story will emerge.

Options/Variations

As an extension, assign as homework that students revise their personal definition of a story and show, explain, or justify how this definition uniquely identifies the elements that make a story work.

Teaching Points to Emphasize

This definition should be created by the students with as little prompting as possible. After they have completed their composite definition, determine how many of the story myths (see p. 2) listed earlier are stated or implied by their wording.

Their definition will probably be plot-based. Ask students to recall stories they like and why they like them. These answers will be predominantly character-based. Ask students if this is consistent with their definition.

Write Right Exercise #3

Is It a Story Yet?

Explore how and when a narrative piece becomes a story, and the elements responsible for this conversion.

Appropriate Grades: All
Concept

Your class has struggled through forming a tentative definition of a story. However, it is likely that they formed their definition from intellect, from what they have been told, rather than by listing the characteristics that excite them and draw them into a story.

Exercise #2 asked, What is a story? You could have substituted the question, What makes a story fun? (Exercise #5 addresses this question.) *Fun* is a catchword that, for most students, includes aspects of humor, excitement, entertainment, and so on. These two questions are not independent. The elements that make a story fun are the same elements that define a story, and are the same elements that make a story so powerful.

This exercise approaches the same question with a different slant. In this way, it will help your students penetrate to the real heart and soul of a story.

Time Required: 15 minutes
Goal: Identify the key elements that uniquely define a story.
Directions

This exercise requires that you either read or tell a short story to your class. Included here is one I often use because it is short, because it strongly accents all the key story elements, because it is versatile and easy to mold to your personal style of telling a story, and because it works well.

As you tell this story, you will stop periodically to ask your class, "Is it a story yet?" Students must then defend their answers. Why is it a story? Why isn't it a story? The story is italicized to separate it from the running discussion of the exercise.

Read the first segment with a neutral tone.

Little Brian woke one morning after an all-night hard rain. He headed off to school just as the rain ended. Clouds began to drift apart. Sunbeams filtered down, splashing light on the grass and sidewalk around him.
That afternoon, Brian came home from school to find his mother waiting for him on the front porch.

Stop for discussion. Ask, "Is it a story yet? Has what I said created a story, or is something critical still missing? How many of you think it is a story? How many think it isn't?" Have students vote by a show of hands. Typically, 85–90 percent will vote no.

Ask students why they voted as they did. Begin with those who answered yes. Have them justify how this "story" fits their definition of a story. Have those who voted no justify their answer. Why isn't it a story? What critical information is missing? What information do they still need to know?

From *Write Right! Creative Writing Using Storytelling Techniques.* © 1999 Kendall Haven. Teacher Ideas Press. (800) 237-6124.

Interestingly, students will readily and accurately identify the key elements of a story during even the earliest stages of this exercise. They will do so indirectly by articulating what is missing from the story, even though they likely failed to mention any of these elements while defining a story during Exercise #2.

Finally, ask the class what this "story" is about. Have them explain and justify their answers. You will typically hear a wide variety of answers because the information defining what the story is about has not yet been included. We have been introduced to a main character, Brian, but know neither his story goal nor the obstacles that keep him from reaching this goal.

Repeat or summarize the first segment before continuing. Read the next segment with as stern and furious a voice as you can muster.

> *Her fists were jammed onto her hips. Her foot angrily tapped on the wooden floorboards of the porch. Her eyes glared down the steps Brian would have to climb up if he was ever going to make it into the house for dinner that night.*
> *"Brian! What on earth happened to you today? Your teacher called!"*

Again, stop for discussion. Repeat the questions you asked after the first segment: "Is it a story yet? Has what I said created a story, or is something critical still missing? How many of you think it is a story? How many think it isn't?" Again, have students vote by a show of hands. Typically, all students will now vote no.

Again, ask students why they voted as they did. Begin with those who answered yes. Have them justify their answer. Have those who voted no justify their answer. Why isn't it a story? What critical information is still missing? What information do they still need to know? Have them identify what important information they learned during this segment.

Again, ask the class what the "story" is about. Have them explain and justify their answers. You'll find that their answers now all concern the conflict and struggle the main character must face.

Repeat or summarize the previous segments before continuing. Read the next segment using an innocent but somewhat whiny voice for Brian, and a sternly furious voice for the mother. Brian should sound as if he were groping for an answer, as if he were making up an excuse. It is important to exaggerate Brian's overly innocent reaction, and to emphasize the mother's anger.

> *"But Maaahhhmmm [Mom]. I know she called. I was standing right beside her in the office when she did."*
> *"She was furious, Brian. She said you were an hour and a half late for school. Now why were you late?"*

Stop for discussion. Repeat the questions and have students vote by a show of hands. Typically, all students will still vote no.

Ask students why they voted as they did. Have them justify their answers. Ask those who voted no to identify what important information they learned during this segment.

You will find that everything your students want to know concerns the story characters, their actions, their motives, their plans, their reactions, and what Brian is going to *say*. Point this out to your students. After all, it is the characters who drive every story. (Note that, because you have used a furious voice for the mother, students will be more concerned with whether or not Brian will avoid being punished, and less concerned with why Brian was late for school.)

Repeat or summarize the previous segments before continuing. For the next segment, continue using an innocent but somewhat whiny voice for Brian, and a sternly furious voice for the mother. Brian's final answer should also sound concerned and sincere.

"But Maaahhhmmm. It rained last night."
"Brian, the rain ended before you left for school. Now why were you late?"
"But Maaahhhmmm. After all that rain, all the worms crawled out on the sidewalk. I was afraid the sun would dry them out and kill 'em, or that some of the mean kids would step on them and squish 'em. I had to put the worms back in the grass where they'd be safe. . . . There were a lot of worms, Mom."

Stop and repeat the vote. You'll find that many students will hesitate and that 30–50 percent will shift their vote to yes.

Ask those that changed their vote what happened in this segment to create a story. Discuss these elements that they needed to know.

Ask those who voted no what they still need to know. Almost all of their answers will concern wanting to know what the mother will do next and whether or not Brian will avoid being punished.

Say, "I'll add that part," then pour all the loving warmth and sweetness you can into the last lines.

And Brian's mother said, "Brian, I love you."
That's the story of Brian.

Your dramatic—or more correctly, melodramatic—presentation of the story is critical to its success. Brian must speak with an overly innocent voice. The mother must speak with an overly angry voice (except during her last line). The more extreme each is, the better.

Teaching Points to Emphasize

In a story, three critical elements must be identified for the reader or listener: the main character, the problem or struggle that this character faces, and the resolution to the problem. The first two define the story and the essential events of the plot. Stories are defined by the problems and struggles of characters. The third provides release from story tension and suspense and completes the story.

To better illustrate this point, tell students something to this effect: "The truth is, Brian's mother wasn't mad at him. She was worried about Brian and what might have happened to him. But if I had told you that, and *then* asked you what you wanted to know, almost all of you would have wanted to know what happened to Brian on the way to school. Why? You'd be looking for a problem. But when I made the mother angry, you didn't worry so much about what happened in the morning. You found a dandy problem right there on the front porch in the afternoon. The more angry I make her, the less you care about what happened in the morning." It's true. Readers and listeners search for a problem to use as the central focus of the story they are receiving. I have tested it with hundreds of student audiences.

There are two more points to address concerning this exercise. The first is humor. If students laughed while you told this story, it was probably when you whined, "But Maaahhhmmm." Why laugh there? Ask them. They will attribute it to the *way* you said it. They are partially correct. More importantly, though, this line is a character reaction. A stressful situation arises; the character reacts. These reactions are among a reader's or an audience's favorite parts of a story. These reactions are what they will remember best and longest about the story.

Finally, compare the key elements uncovered in this exercise—character, problem, resolution, and character reaction—to the elements students included in their definition of a story for Exercise #2. Are they the same? Similar? Different? Discuss this with your class.

Write Right Exercise #4

What Makes a Story Real?

Explore those aspects of a story that make it seem real.

Appropriate Grades: 3+

Concept

By transforming a review of what makes a story seem real into a game, students are compelled to search a story for possible clues. Without realizing it, they create a short list of elements to include in their own stories to make them seem equally real.

Time Required: 20–25 minutes

Goal: Demonstrate that specific, relevant story details create a sense of reality.

Directions

Divide the class into groups of three or four students. Assign a theme and ask students to each recall a personal (real) story related to this theme. Use simple, broad themes—something funny that happened to students, or something scary. Even a theme as broad as something that happened in their family will work well. These personal and family stories should have happened at least three years ago, and should *not* have been previously shared with other students in the class.

Have each student share with their group a basic summary of their story. Some students will want to drift into elaborate storytelling here. Don't let them. These summaries should be 20 to 30 seconds in length. Allow the groups a total of two minutes for this task.

Have each group choose what they think is the best story. They cannot combine stories to create a new story. They must choose one of the stories as told by a group member. Allow the groups 30 to 45 seconds to accomplish this task and proceed only after every group has chosen a story.

Have each member of the group learn this one story well enough so that they could tell it as if it had happened to them. This means that each group member must question the person to whom it really happened to uncover the information they will need to tell the story convincingly. If necessary, guide them in deciding what kinds of information they need to know (When and where did the story happen? Who was there? What happened? Why? How did the storyteller and others feel? Why? etc. Allow the groups two minutes to gather whatever information they need.

Students may adjust the physical reality of the story to be plausibly consistent with their own history. For example, if the story happened between the storyteller and a brother, a student who doesn't have a brother might say the story happened with a male cousin. Who would know that this isn't true?

If the story happened when the storyteller lived in Atlanta, for example, and the other students have never lived in Atlanta, they can say it happened where they were really living at the appropriate time. If Atlanta is important to the story, they might say it happened while their family was visiting someone (grandmother, friend, etc.) in Atlanta. Again, who would know that this isn't true?

Choose one group and have them line up in front of the class. Have each group member, one by one, tell the complete story, claiming as they do that it really did happen to them. Instruct each storyteller that their goal is to say and do whatever they can to convince the audience that the story really *did* happen to them. Tell the audience that their goal is to determine to whom the story really happened. Don't allow any pause for discussion between stories. As soon as the first storyteller finishes, say, "And now we will hear the story from storyteller #2."

When the group has finished (and the thunderous applause has died away), have the audience vote by a show of hands for the storyteller to whom they think the story really happened. Do not allow any discussion before this vote. All students in the audience must commit themselves and vote. Usually, the storyteller who collects the most votes is not the student to whom the story really happened.

This is a fun game, and does develop oral storytelling skills. The real value of this exercise, though, will present itself in a follow-up discussion. Ask the class, "Why did you vote the way you voted? It doesn't matter if you voted for the right person or not. I still want to know why you thought one story seemed more real than the others."

Write their responses on the chalkboard, dividing them into two groups: elements that relate to the story, and elements that relate to the way the story was told. Discuss these elements and how they made the story seem real. Emphasize the importance and power of these story elements, and encourage students to include them in their stories.

When repeating this exercise, vary the story theme. Any common student experience will work—summer vacation, a time they were scared, something that happened on a bike, disasters with a pet (theirs or someone else's), and so on.

Teaching Points to Emphasize

Everyone bases their vote on the same few reasons. It doesn't matter whether they are first-graders or teachers, fifth-graders or college seniors. Even more amazing, almost everyone mentions these reasons in the same order.

The first reason mentioned is always the *details* in the story. One storyteller included more details, so their story seemed more real. One storyteller included impossible or unlikely details, so their story seemed less real. Details create reality.

The second reason mentioned usually concerns the *way* the story was told. One storyteller overacted; one hesitated and seemed to be making up their story; one had more expression; one seemed more confident. The general impression created by the way the story was told seemed more real or less real, so the story itself seemed more real or less real.

A more complete list of reasons is included in Part II. Still, it is a very short list. Alone at the top are story details. Students must learn to create and include effective details in their stories if they want them to seem real.

Write Right Exercise #5

What Makes a Story Fun?

Explore what your students think makes a story fun to read (and fun to listen to).

Appropriate Grades: All
Concept

Everyone has a concept, an idea, of what makes a reading or listening experience enjoyable. What students think they like in stories they read is what they will try to write into their own stories. A major problem arises when the terms and the vocabulary students use to describe what draws them into stories lead them down a very unproductive (in fact, *counter*productive) path when they write. It's worth exploring what they really like and why they like it. The place to begin is with their initial impressions.

Time Required: 10–20 minutes (depending on the amount of discussion)
Goal: Realize that the enjoyable plot elements (action, fear, excitement, humor, etc.) do not exist in isolation, but only become enjoyable through their relationship to characters and character reactions.

Directions

Begin with a broad question to your class: "What makes a story fun to read?" List their answers (preferably one or two words each) on the chalkboard in a column. Accept five or six answers and then stop. The list will probably include plot elements such as *action*, *excitement*, *adventure*, *humor*, and *scariness*.

Review the list, response by response. Ask the question, "What makes [response] fun to read?" (For example, "What makes action fun to read?") Have the student who first proposed the word answer first. Your role is to push the class into examining what *really* draws them into each of these plot elements they have listed. Ask "Why?" for each answer you receive. (For example, if a student says, "Action is fun because it's exciting," respond by asking, "Why? What makes action exciting?") Have them quote specific examples and passages from stories they have read, if possible. This will make it easier for you to connect the plot element to a character, and to a character's reaction to the plot element.

Continue to probe students' answers until they either reach an impasse ("It's exciting just because it is." "But why?" "Just because it is. That's all.") or arrive at the realization that the plot element is dependent upon characters and how they react to situations involving this plot element.

Don't expect any great discoveries during this one discussion. We're just beginning the *Write Right* program. It's okay to simply leave unanswered questions for further discussion if your class doesn't understand why they enjoy these story elements. Your goal, though, should always be to lead them toward appreciating the central role of characters in a story (rather than the plot elements surrounding characters).

Options/Variations

As an extension, ask students, "What makes a story fun to *listen to*?"

Follow the above format, but expect two separate groups of elements: those that relate to the story (these should be the same plot elements listed above), and those that relate to the way the story is told. The second group will include such elements as *expression* (students' typical catchword for "emotional variation and presentation"), *vocal and physical characterization*, and *energy and enthusiasm*. This group of elements, too, in the final analysis, is related to story characters: These elements bring characters to life and show their emotional reactions.

Teaching Points to Emphasize

Two important teaching points become apparent during this exercise. First, stories are about characters. As readers, we often forget to give characters the credit for our enjoyment and attribute enjoyment to story events, or to the actions these characters perform. It is character information (goals, problems and flaws, reactions, etc.) that draws us into a story, makes it seem real, and makes it enjoyable.

Second, the same short list of elements that makes stories fun to read (or fun to listen to) also makes them seem real (see Exercise #4). This short list is headed by story details. Details create reality. They also provide the information readers need to be able to imagine a story as they read it. The better they can imagine a story, the more fun it is to read.

Write Right Exercise #6

Character Myths

Explore what really makes a character interesting.

Appropriate Grades: 3+

Concept

Creating and presenting interesting, believable characters is critical to the success of a story. However, most of us don't know what character information to create and present to accomplish this important goal. This exercise compares how we view ourselves, how we naturally approach the process of gathering and reporting information, and what information we present to create an interesting character.

Time Required: 30 minutes (including discussion)

Goal: Show students what kinds of information make a character interesting, and how this information differs from what we naturally tend to gather and report.

Directions

Step 1

Have each student list five things about themselves that they think others would want to know. Allow the class three or four minutes to accomplish this task. Avoid giving examples or more specific direction, if possible. The goal is not to have them produce information based on your modeling, but to have them report the information that naturally occurs to them. Have students set these lists aside when they have finished.

Step 2

Pair the students. Within a three-minute time limit, have each student interview their partner to learn about their life (history, goals, family, hobbies, etc.). The interviewee may only provide information specifically requested by the interviewer. Instruct students not to answer general statements masquerading as questions, such as "Tell me about yourself," or "Tell me what you have done." The interviewer must request specific information to receive an answer.

Step 3

Have eight to ten students introduce their partner to the class, as if this person were new and unknown to the class, and as if this person were not present during the introduction. Through this introduction, the student's only goal is to make this person appear as interesting as possible. However, don't tell students about this requirement before they begin. Force them to improvise.

The student may not request more information from the person they are introducing. They must use information they already know to present an interesting, intriguing "character." However, they may invent information to accomplish this goal. Allow 45 to 60 seconds for each introduction.

Step 4

Discuss the information (real and fictional) that was reported. Which introductions accomplished their goal of being interesting? What kinds of information were most intriguing? Most revealing? What made students want to learn more about this "new" person? What made them laugh?

How does the information reported in the introductions compare to the information requested during the interviews (step 2)? How does the information reported in the introductions compare to the information students listed about themselves (information they thought others would want to know—step1)? What kinds of information from step 1 and step 2 were not used in the introductions? Why not? What we really want to know about a person (or character) often does not match what we think we are supposed to want to hear or report.

Options/Variations

On subsequent uses of this exercise, you might require that students not invent information, but use only information they collected during the interview, to make the person appear as interesting as possible. The presentation requirements are the same, but students are limited in the information they can use. This will require them to rely more on the five layers of character information that make any character interesting.

You might also vary the topic to focus on story elements rather than strictly character elements. Instead of a general introduction, have the student describe the person's best (or worst) vacation, holiday, or birthday. Now, they must consider what makes both a character and a story interesting.

Additionally, some teachers have each student conclude their introduction by listing what they wish they had asked during the interview and then explaining how they would have used that extra information. These "wish lists" will reinforce student learning about what really creates an interesting character.

Teaching Points to Emphasize

Typically, the presentations become progressively wilder, funnier, more fictionalized, and more interesting. They tend to become outrageous. Why? Because students intuitively realize that what they've learned through the interview isn't very interesting, and because they don't know how to reshape this information into an introduction that is. As a result, they drift toward slapstick humor and outrageous exaggeration. Still, every student in the class is fascinating. The interviewer, though, didn't ask for and uncover interesting information.

To complete this exercise successfully, students must understand the core elements of a character, aspects that grab our attention and draw us into the character's story. Review and discuss the five layers of character information, especially the core layer, with your class. They have just experienced the importance of character information in creating an interesting story. Which introductions and what information were most interesting? Most intriguing? Most memorable?

Also, review interview skills with your students. The information they obtained was only as useful as the questions they asked. Good interview skills are critical to many kinds of writing.

From *Write Right! Creative Writing Using Storytelling Techniques.* © 1999 Kendall Haven. Teacher Ideas Press. (800) 237-6124.

Write Right Exercise #7

Campmate

Compare what students think they want to know about a character with what really interests them most.

Appropriate Grades: 3+

Concept

Every student has faced situations in which they were thrust together with someone new. Every student can imagine being confronted by such an event. This is a perfect opportunity for further exploring what we need to know to make a character seem real, what draws us to them, and what makes them interesting.

Time Required: 15 minutes

Goal: Illustrate the kinds of character information we really want to know and the critical kinds we typically overlook.

Directions

In this exercise, you will have students imagine a situation in which they will need to learn about a new peer, and then record the information they say they want to know about this person. Pose this scenario and question to your class: "You will be stuck for a week at camp with a bunkmate [or campmate]. What would you want to know about them before you arrive at camp?" (If you are working with high school students, pose this scenario and question instead: "You are being set up on a blind date. What do you want to know about this person?")

List on the chalkboard all information students want to know. You will create a long list. Every element of information will fall within one of four categories: the character's **sensory image**, or what your senses would directly record; the **personality** of the character, or how they relate to and interact with the world; the **activity** of the character, or what they do; and the **history** of the character, or what they have done.

When I conduct this exercise, I create four columns on the board (one for each of these four outer layers of character information) and write elements of information in the appropriate column. However, I don't label these columns until after I have stopped accepting new elements of information, so as not to influence the kinds of information students want to know about the person.

Your job during the exercise should be to control and manage the flood of ideas as every student thinks of some new kind of information to add to the growing list, and to probe for a greater variety of information during lulls ("Is there anything else that would be nice to know?" "What else would your parents want to know?" etc.).

Upon completion, discuss the lists and show that all desired information falls into the four categories. Students' requests for information show that each of these layers is an important part of building a complete and believable character.

Also point out that no one mentioned wanting to know any *core* character information. It is possible that they will, but no one ever has when I have conducted this exercise. Most likely, none of the students will have mentioned wanting to know basic character motives (hopes, dreams, fears, passions, etc.). However, this core information that we tend to overlook is necessary to create interesting, powerful, captivating characters.

Teaching Points to Emphasize

These are the outer four of the five layers of character information. In real life, these four layers of information are as deep into another being as we typically probe. In a story, though, there is a fifth, deeper layer we tend to overlook, yet which forms the real allure of a story character—the **core elements**. The outer four layers make the character seem real; they show us what the character does and why they do it. It is the character's core elements, though, that pull the reader into a story and hold them there.

Write Right Exercise #8

React to This!

Explore how character reactions are created and used to enhance a story.

Appropriate Grades: 3+
Concept

Character reactions are one of the core elements of a character, but students struggle to create them. The problem is that students aren't accustomed to consciously recording other people's reactions, even though they happen all around us every day. They need an exercise, a game, a hunt to become more aware of the reactions they subconsciously record each day.

Time Required: 20 minutes for Part 1, 50 minutes for Part 2 follow-up discussion.
Goal: Demonstrate typical character reactions and develop an understanding of what they are and how to create and use them.
Directions

This exercise is conducted in two parts. Part 1 is a class demonstration and discussion to help students become more aware of what reactions look like and when they take place. Part 2 is a multiple-day, small-group activity to search for specific kinds of reactions.

Part 1

Begin this exercise with a general discussion of reactions. Differentiate reaction from action. Reactions are subconscious, automatic, reflex, emotional responses to a stressful situation. Every human continuously reacts. See Part II of this book for a discussion about the power, use, and value of character reactions.

Ask the class to tell you what character reactions look like. They will most likely be too unsure of the images that come to mind to hazard a guess in front of their peers.

Select one student and have them stand in front of the class. Sternly, forcefully, and quickly tell them that when you say "Go!" they will have five seconds and only five seconds to [ask them to answer a question you are sure they can't answer]. As soon as you've asked the question, shout "Go!" and, holding up your watch, stare expectantly at the student. Then don't move for *ten* seconds.

By bringing one student to the front of the class, using forceful words, and asking an impossible question, you create a stressful situation. By standing still and staring at the student for ten seconds, you give them plenty of time to feel this stress and to *react*.

Everyone in class will laugh. Ask them why they laughed. The conversation will proceed something like this:

"Because it was funny."
"What was funny?"
"Her face. She just stood there getting embarrassed."
"What do you call what she did?"

Keep prodding them until someone realizes that they just witnessed, enjoyed, and laughed at a *reaction.*

Tell the class that you need three volunteers and that those you select will receive automatic A's on their next two tests. Then thoughtfully scan the room as if trying to decide who to choose. Hands will fly. Students will beg and plead, dropping to their knees to plaintively crawl toward you. Several will use truly outrageous antics to be noticed and selected. Others will begin to chuckle. They are chuckling at the *reactions* of their classmates.

Finally, choose three overactors and tell them to come stand in front of the class. Carefully note what they do, how they react to being selected. As they reach the front of the room, mimic—but *exaggerate*—their reaction. The class will roar.

Tell the volunteers that you lied and that they really won't receive automatic A's for volunteering—you just wanted to see their reaction to being selected. Carefully watch their reaction to this announcement. Again, mimic, but exaggerate, their physical, facial, and vocal reaction. The class will roar.

Ask the class why they laughed. Again, use their answers to reveal the value of reactions. Character reactions are always mesmerizing and entertaining. When exaggerated, they are funny.

Angrily tell the class that you are tired of all the noise and that the next student to make a sound will be sent to the principal's office. Then sternly, slowly march up and down the rows of desks, glaring at the students. Pause at one desk, frowning down at its occupant. For five seconds, simply stand and stare at the student. I guarantee that this student will react. They'll flush beet-red. They'll grimace. They'll giggle. They'll sheepishly glance up at you out of the corner of one eye. They'll react, and everyone else will struggle not to giggle.

Ask them why they laughed and again emphasize reactions. Create a stressful situation and the target of that stress will react. It's human nature.

The teacher's role in part 1 is critical. You must create the stress needed to trigger strong reactions. You must then allow the chosen students time to wallow in that stress and react. Too much stress will keep the class from enjoying the victim's reaction. Too little stress will keep the victim from reacting strongly enough to provide a useful demonstration.

Part 2

After the Part 1 in-class demonstration of what some character reactions look like, and of how attracted we are to them, it's time for students to find reaction outside the classroom. Divide the class into groups of two or three students. Allow each group several minutes to make two lists of two items each. For the first list, they should write down two situations that they think would be likely to create interesting reactions. Let them struggle with this list for a while, without offering suggestions. For the second list, they should write down two emotional reactions that they want to find and observe.

The first list might include such situations as a driver honking their car at a child who's standing in the street but doesn't see the car; a favorite basketball team scoring a basket; a big dog jumping at someone and barking; or a book slipping from a shelf and crashing to the floor. The second list might include such emotional states as boredom, sadness, embarrassment, surprise, fear, shock, happiness, relief, pleasure, disgust, or delight.

Have each group read their lists. If any of the situations are impossible or unlikely for students to find (or re-create), have students use more common situations. If more than two groups list the same situation or emotional reaction, have one of the groups use a different situation or reaction.

Allow each group several days to find as many occurrences as possible of the two situations they listed. For each, they should write a detailed description of the reaction they observed. They must also find the emotional reactions they listed and describe the situations that created them.

At the end of the allotted time period, have each group report their observations to the class. They should describe and then mimic (exaggerate) the reactions they observed for each situation. They should describe the situations that created each emotional reaction. Finally, have the class discuss which mimicked reactions were, and were not, fun to watch.

Teaching Points to Emphasize

We all love to watch others face and react to mildly stressful or embarrassing moments. These reactions are a powerful writing tool, for two reasons. First, reactions reveal a character's personality, so they are an excellent form of character detail. Second, the reactions, themselves, are delightfully fun to watch, so they add humor and interest to a story.

To create believable character reactions, the writer must first become consciously familiar with typical human reactions, so that they can decide exactly how their character should react to positive situations (when something goes right) and to negative situations (when something goes wrong). If the writer begins their story by planning obstacles, risk and danger, and conflict, stressful situations will be easier to create.

The BIG Three

Explore how the core elements of a character create the story.

Appropriate Grades: All
Concept

If students begin their stories by creating core character information, they greatly increase their chances of producing a successful story. However, this isn't a "natural" place for students to begin. They want to begin by creating plot, but this is the surest way to undermine their own story. This exercise helps them establish a new and better habit.

Time Required: 10 minutes
Goal: Demonstrate the power of beginning a story with core character information.
Directions

Have three students come to the front of the class, and announce that these three students will create a story for the class. Each student will create one of the BIG Three core character elements: identify the main character, define that character's goal, and create problems and flaws for that character. However, the specific wording you use in soliciting these elements is important.

The goal of this exercise is to demonstrate that core character information always defines a story. Reinforce this concept regularly. I present here the wording that works best for me in soliciting the BIG Three.

To the first student: *The other two students are going to make up a story. All you have to do is make up that first, most important, bit of information they need, which is . . .* [Here I pause to let student and class consider what information should be created first.] *. . . the character. Every story needs to start with who the story is going to be about. This character you're going to make up can be, but doesn't have to be, a human being. It does have to be a fictional, never-before-made-up character. It could be an animal—a dog, a frog, an elephant, a snake, a snail, or a mosquito. It could be a bush or a tree. It doesn't even have to be alive. It could be a cloud, a chair, or your shoelace. You can have the other two students make up a story about anything—but it does have to be about a brand-new fictional character. What do you want them to make up a story about?*

The first student now creates a character first impression: the species, name, age, and just enough physical information so that everyone envisions the same image of the character. You can veto any character you don't like. I always veto aliens because they require too much background information for everyone to understand their species, their world, and their basic life patterns and needs. Repeat and summarize whatever information the first student creates. (For example, "Once, there was a young, floppy-eared rabbit named Seymore.")

From *Write Right! Creative Writing Using Storytelling Techniques.* © 1999 Kendall Haven. Teacher Ideas Press. (800) 237-6124.

To the second student: *Now the second bit of core character information. In this story, what did* [Name] *want either to do or to get? It doesn't have to be anything that would make sense for a [species] to want to do or get.* [Name] *could want to do anything. What do you want* [Name] *to want to do or get in this story?*

Your wording here is important. If you ask for the character's *goal* (what you really want), you'll receive nothing but a blank stare. Ask for what the character "wants to either do or get" and you'll receive an imaginative answer.

Again, summarize the information created thus far. ("Once, there was a young, floppy-eared rabbit named Seymore who wanted to eat some chocolate-chip ice cream. He was tired of carrots and lettuce. He was tired of always going to the salad bar. He wanted dessert. He wanted some ice cream!")

To the third student: *Now the third bit of core character information. Why hasn't* [Name] *gotten* [goal]*? What's keeping* [Name] *from getting* [goal]*? Something must be, or* [Name] *would already have it. So what's keeping* [Name] *from getting* [goal]*?*

You are now asking for obstacles, either external problems or internal flaws. This wording will spark the student's creativity. Asking for *obstacles* typically won't.

Allow the student to create three or four potential obstacles. Stop the student anytime they drift into creating a plot sequence (a series of events that happen in the story). You want to know only the potential obstacles, not how they will fit into the story.

Again, summarize the information. ("Once, there was a young, floppy-eared rabbit named Seymore who wanted to eat some chocolate-chip ice cream. He was tired of carrots and lettuce. He was tired of always going to the salad bar. He wanted dessert. He wanted some ice cream! *But*, Seymore had no money to buy ice cream. And his mother said he couldn't have any because it was bad for him and would rot his teeth. Besides, the owner of the ice cream store hated rabbits and would shoot any rabbit that came near his store. But Seymore *really* wanted some ice cream.")

Now, turn to the class and ask, "How is this story going to end? What's the last thing that will happen at the end of this story?" They will answer that the ending occurs when the character achieves their goal. ("It ends when Seymore gets some ice cream.") Likely, they will try to include the plot sequence that explains *how* the character will achieve their goal. Cut short such discussion. You want to know only what happens at the *very* end of the story.

Tell the class that this is only one of two possible endings for the story. Ask students if they know what the other ending is. The other ending, of course, is that the character will never achieve their goal. ("Seymore *never* gets any ice cream.") It usually takes a while for students to realize this option. If any student suggests that the story will end when the character dies (as fourth-, fifth-, and sixth-grade boys surely will), ask whether the character will *still* want to achieve their goal, even after death. This will force their answer back into one of the two possible endings for the story. This discussion will help students understand that the main character's goal defines the story's end and creates structure for the story.

As a class, discuss other possible obstacles, both internal and external, for this story. Stop anyone who begins presenting a plot scenario. They should only be allowed to suggest other obstacles that could keep the character from achieving their goal.

As a class, discuss which obstacles will create a better story. Invariably, it will be those obstacles that create the greatest risk and danger for the character. Risk and danger create the suspense and tension every story needs to propel the reader through it, to the exciting climax.

Ask if any students think they know how the story will unfold. Many will say that they do. Don't allow them to begin telling their version of the story. Rather, ask them *why* they think they know how the story will unfold. The discussion will lead them back to the chosen obstacles. Obstacles create plot and create the all-important risk and danger the main character must face.

During this exercise, your job should be to keep the story moving and to prevent students from interjecting plot. Plot should not be mentioned or discussed during this exercise. However, once these basic character elements have been created, every student intuitively "knows" what must happen in the story.

Options/Variations

For third grade and up, add a fourth student. After the first three have created their contributions, this student must define the personality of the main character. For most students, this is the most difficult of these four pieces of character information to create.

To simplify this task, ask the student to identify how the main character reacts (physically) in two general situations—when something goes right, and when something (anything) goes wrong. They must be specific in their description of the physical reactions of the character. Typically, they answer with an emotional state. ("Seymore feels sad.") This won't work. Readers need sensory information. Different characters do different things when they are sad. What does Seymore the rabbit do and say when he's sad? Often, students will still need prompting and suggestions to help them clearly define a character's physical response to positive and negative situations. As they invent character reactions, exaggerate them as a demonstration of the potential for humor of exaggerated reactions.

Teaching Points to Emphasize

This exercise powerfully demonstrates the true heart of every story—core character information. The character's first impression provides a rough sensory image of the character and usually hints at that character's personality. The character goal creates story structure and direction. It defines the ending. It creates purpose and significance for all events and interactions in the story. Either they help the character achieve a goal, or they hinder this process.

Obstacles create conflict. Conflict leads to struggle. Struggle, the actions a character makes to overcome obstacles, defines plot. Creating character, goal, and obstacles creates the basic plot. All elements of core character information except the crucible are accounted for in three simple bits of made up information.

Finally, character reactions provide interpretation of story events. They create energy and humor. They draw readers and listeners into the story. They also provide insight into personality and sensory image, two additional layers of character information.

Review Exercise #3 ("Is It a Story Yet?") with your class. Character, goal, obstacles (which define conflict), and reactions (which define personality) are essential starting points for the creation of a story.

Once your students become accustomed to beginning stories with core character information, they'll realize that this approach is easier and far more effective than more traditional (plot-based) approaches. It's a simple, four-step habit—character, goal, obstacles, and reaction. The more often they practice it, the more automatic it becomes.

From *Write Right! Creative Writing Using Storytelling Techniques*. © 1999 Kendall Haven. Teacher Ideas Press. (800) 237-6124.

Write Right Exercise #10

Character Creation

Demonstrate that stories can be successfully created through character information alone, without directly considering plot.

Appropriate Grades: 2+
Concept

Plot exists to allow characters to confront the obstacles and struggles before them. Most students create stories by trying to create plot first. However, this is the surest and easiest way to complicate the process. This exercise demonstrates how character information alone, by articulating the struggles a character must face and the background of these struggles, defines a story.

Time Required: 15–25 minutes
Goal: Demonstrate that character information and background define a story and establish its plot.
Directions

Tell your class that they will collectively make up a story. Ask them to invent a new fictional character. Accept three or four suggestions for the general first-impression identity of this character. Have the class vote to select one. Ask them what this character wants to do or obtain in this story. Accept three or four suggestions, vetoing any you think are inappropriate, and have the class vote to select one.

Now ask *why* this character wants this goal. No matter how they answer, keep asking why. If they justify the goal with a feeling ("She likes it."), ask why. If they justify the goal with a state of affairs ("He doesn't have any friends."), ask why. If they justify the goal with some past action ("She wants it because someone else cheated her."), ask student to identify who did the action, why they did it, and how the main character felt about it. Continue responding to each answer by asking why.

Answers will be shouted at you from all corners of the room. Each student will quickly develop a clear sense of how they want to structure this story. You should respond to and put to class vote only those answers you think are appropriate. Continue to build the history of this character until you are satisfied that a clear picture of the story has emerged.

Though fun and productive, this exercise involves much work for the teacher. As moderator, story coordinator, and scribe, you must stay alert. Without you, the process can fizzle. Direct and control the class's creative efforts by asking them appropriate "why" questions and by selecting only plausible suggestions to incorporate into the story. Let your own curiosity about the emerging character and their history be your guide in directing student efforts. Focus on character goals, motives, feelings, and reactions to each of the past events students uncover.

Teaching Points to Emphasize

As you push the class into creating a clear picture of the character, their personality, their relationships, and their history (what has happened in the past to bring this character to their present situation and goal), you will find that the story's plot presents itself. Directly focusing on the plot and events will not be necessary.

Not every student will envision exactly the same plot. Yet they will each clearly envision the same detailed outline of the story. Emphasize that information about the character's goals, personality, and history is what creates this picture. The plot of the story is subservient to, and dependent upon, this information.

Description and Detail

Explore the difference between description and detail.

Appropriate Grades: 2+
Concept

It is valuable for students to develop a clear, concrete understanding of what description and detail are, and how they differ. This exercise is designed to focus their attention on the relationship between these two important elements of writing.

Time Required: 20 minutes
Goal: Clearly differentiate description from detail.
Directions

Have each student select an object in the room and study it for one minute. They should study its size, shape, texture, appearance, function, sturdiness, and so on. Have them write as complete a description of that object as possible in two minutes. They should search for every way possible to describe the object—its function, appearance, likenesses, and various parts—that they can think of, including the use of metaphor and simile.

This is a description. Now have them search through their description for two *details* that they think best communicate the essence of the object and the impression they want the reader to remember. These are details. Details are description, but not all description is effective detail.

Have several students read their description and then state the details they selected to represent their description. Have listeners evaluate the description and then debate how well the selected details communicate an image of the object.

Finally, have your students each write one paragraph explaining why description and detail are necessary in a story, and what they contribute to a story. Have them discuss their individual explanations and arrive at a consensual explanation. The class explanation should include two concepts: detail is the one element in a story that creates believable physical reality, and detail makes a story accessible to a reader. Details make it possible for a reader to envision the scenes, actions, and characters in a story.

Teaching Points to Emphasize

Two points should be emphasized in this exercise. First, details are a specific subset of description. Description is what a writer includes in a story to define the objects, actions, and characters, and to create vivid, specific, accurate images of them for the reader. Details are those specific bits of description that accurately and efficiently convey a physical sense of the thing being described and also provide some insight into the entire scene or characters surrounding the thing being described. Detail is more powerful than description because it performs this job more quickly and efficiently.

Second, there are many forms that effective description and detail can take. Verbs, nouns, modifiers, similes, metaphors, and phrases can all be used as story detail. A writer's job is to seize every opportunity to make words act both as detail and as the basic building blocks of the story.

From *Write Right! Creative Writing Using Storytelling Techniques.* © 1999 Kendall Haven. Teacher Ideas Press. (800) 237-6124.

Write Right Exercise #12

Detail Alert!

Explore what descriptive detail looks like and sounds like in typical story context.

Appropriate Grades: 2+.

Concept

The most common teacher criticism of student creative writing is that it lacks description and detail. What is description? What is detail? Detail is a subset of description. What does effective detail look like and sound like? This quick exercise is a good way to begin a discussion.

Time Required: 10–20 minutes.

Goal: Develop an understanding of effective detail and how a writer uses and creates it.

Directions

Select a short passage of a story that features abundant description and detail, yet still has a strong sense of action. You will read three versions of this passage to your class: the first with minimal, weak detail; the second with better, but still general, detail; and the third with the specific, dynamic detail of the actual passage. You will need to create the first two versions of the passage.

Tell the class that you will read a passage and that you want them to listen for and remember all the detail they hear. I provide here three versions of a passage from my book *The Wrong Side of a Neighborhood Witch*, but any powerful passage will do.

The first reading (minimal, weak detail):

> *I ran between two dumpsters and down the alley. "Run faster," I said. I heard Charlie Fancher's car. They were getting close. Ritchie Farnsworth ran beside me.*

Ask the class to identify and evaluate all the detail in the passage. Write their answers in a column on the left side of the chalkboard for later reference. The nouns and pronouns in this version create images, but they do so only in a vague and general way. They create images, but imprecise ones. The verbs describe action, but they are weak, general (*ran, run, said, heard,* and *were getting*) and don't create sharp, vivid images. There are few sensory specifics and, thus, little reader interest in the passage.

The second reading (with better, but still general, detail):

> *I ran between two dirty dumpsters behind the Fulton deli and sprinted down the alley behind. I smelled sour milk and saw broken asphalt and weeds. I breathed hard and could barely talk. "Run . . . run . . . faster!"*
> *I heard the rumble of Charlie Fancher's car. They were getting closer. Ritchie Farnsworth ran beside me. He has lots of freckles, red hair, and long arms and legs.*

Again, poll the class to identify the detail added to this version. Write their comments in a second column on the chalkboard. There is more sensory information, but none of the detail is effective enough to create vivid images of the action, setting, and characters. Note the use of nonspecific and general words and descriptors (*dirty*, *weeds*, *lots*, *long*, etc.). The resulting description doesn't paint a strong picture of either character or emotional state.

The third and final reading (the actual text of the book—description containing specific, dynamic detail):

> *I zig-zagged between two slime-stained dumpsters out back of the Fulton deli and sprinted hard down the ragged alley behind. The sour reek of long-curdled milk blasted into my nose. My tennis shoes flashed over rough, broken asphalt and spiny weeds. My heaving chest ramrodded thick, humid air into my lungs like a churning steam engine. I could only hiss one word per breath. "Run! . . . Run . . . faster!"*
> *I heard the threatening, muffler-less rumble of Charley Fancher's super-charged Chevie. They were getting closer, like a shark cruising down the bloody trail of a wounded seal.*
> *Gangly Ritchie Farnsworth galloped beside me. A whole world of freckles under a floppy, carrot-top bush of hair, Farnsie's arms and legs always seemed three sizes too long for his body. He lopped when he ran like a scurrying daddy longlegs spider.*

Have students identify the added detail. Write their comments in a third column. Also, have them evaluate the added detail for effect on their images of this scene.

What has happened to the detail? First, it has become specific instead of vague and general (*zig-zagged*, *ramrodded*, *hiss*, *galloped*, etc.). Second, it now identifies unique rather than common characteristics (*super-charged Chevie* instead of *car*, *a whole world of freckles* instead of *lots of freckles*). Third, it presents sensory information about the physical setting, action, and characters in a way that helps the reader understand each character's emotional state and personality. The reader begins to feel that they "know" these characters, based on the way this scene is described. Fourth, much of the description has been shifted to simile and metaphor (*a floppy, carrot-top bush of hair*; *like a shark cruising down the bloody trail of a wounded seal*; *like a scurrying daddy longlegs spider*; etc.).

Ask your students to decide which version they like best. Why? Which version creates more vivid, more colorful images of the scene. Which version is more interesting? Which version makes them want to hear more of the story? Why?

Options/Variations

Some teachers conduct this exercise using passages from their students' writing. In this way, the exercise may be used repeatedly as part of editing and assessment efforts.

From *Write Right! Creative Writing Using Storytelling Techniques*. © 1999 Kendall Haven. Teacher Ideas Press. (800) 237-6124.

Teaching Points to Emphasize

During all exercise discussions, have your class be specific and detailed in their answers, observations, and comments. We are prone to wave a vague and general hand over the terms *description* and *detail* and proceed without having developed a clear understanding of these two important elements of effective writing.

Detailed description (description with specific, dynamic details) is one of the most powerful and important tools a writer has. It refines the writer's images of a scene, makes these images seem real to the reader, and encourages the reader to create equally detailed images for other aspects of a scene. However, detailed description doesn't just happen. Writers must search for it, refine it, both during story creation and during story editing.

Write Right Exercise #13

The Detail Game

Explore the creation of effective, descriptive detail.

Appropriate Grades: All
Concept

It's difficult enough to write a basic story line without considering the necessities of description and detail. When students explore effective description and detail through games (or practice writings), they develop their skill at creating it for stories.

Time Required: 10 minutes
Goal: Develop the ability to identify and create effective, imaginative, descriptive detail.
Directions

Divide the class into two teams. This game will be a contest between these two teams. Have one student (the Contestant) from one team step out of sight of the other students. Give the Contestant an object that they must describe well enough so that their team members can guess what it is. Begin with simple objects, such as a book, a pencil, an eraser, a paper clip, an orange, a cardboard box, a glass, or a paper cup. Even simple objects are difficult to describe.

During the game, the Contestant may not name the object directly, nor may they use a synonym for it. They must *physically describe* the object, not classify it. They may not use hierarchical categories. If the object is a pencil, for example, they may not say "a #2" or "a writing implement." If the object is an orange, they may not say "fruit." If the object is a brick, they may not say "construction material." Classification categories either contain, or are contained in, the name of the object; they are not descriptions.

What are they allowed to say? Details. For a pencil: "Long, yellow, hexagonal. Pink rubber at one end. Pointed black lead at the other." For an orange: "Spherical; the size of your fist. Bumpy skin. Skin tastes bitter. Inside it's sweet and juicy. Smells fragrant." For a brick: "Rectangular. Heavy. Barely fits in both hands. Straight sides that are all red and feel rough and crumbly. No smell and you can't eat it."

Allow the Contestant a very limited time (five to ten seconds) to create their description before they begin. Limit the number of guesses by the team to avoid haphazard guesses of anything that might fit the first descriptive clue. Three or four guesses should be plenty for correctly guessing each object.

If the Contestant gives an illegal clue (saying, for example, that an orange is "an orange fruit"), they forfeit their turn. Their team receives no points, (or the maximum points possible, for a game in which low score wins) and the game moves to the next Contestant from the opposing team.

After each round, you may want to pause and discuss as a class what other details the Contestant might have used. What details would have more quickly led the team to a correct guess? Students gain valuable insight from such discussion.

The game element comes from the contest you set up between the two teams. Each Contestant has a goal. The contest is to see which team meets that goal best when it is their turn. I have seen four goals used that all work well. Advance through these four as your students are ready for them. They are listed here from easiest to most difficult.

1. **Time.** Successfully describe the object as fast as possible. Score is measured in seconds. Low score wins. Illegal clues receive a score equal to the maximum allowable time (30 seconds, for example).

2. **Efficiency.** Successfully describe the object using as few words as possible, within a fixed amount of time (30 seconds is usually adequate). A team's score is the number of words the Contestant used in their description. Low score wins.

3. **Nonvisual description.** The Contestant's description may only use senses other than sight (smell, touch, taste, and hearing). The goal may be either minimum time or minimum number of words. Score is measured in either seconds or words. Low score wins.

4. **Figurative language.** The Contestant's description may only use similes and metaphors. (For example, an orange: "Round as the earth itself. Sweet as a welcome bird's song. The color of a glowing, morning sun just peaking over the horizon.") The goal is minimum time. Score is measured in seconds. Low score wins.

Teaching Points to Emphasize

Good description creates specific, memorable, unique images for the reader. It isn't necessary for a writer to describe every aspect of an object, just those unique and key features that create a detailed image of that object. Good description should involve more than just the sense of sight. Often, detail for other senses is more powerful and informative. Have students look for opportunities to use vivid description when they write and edit. They should then create unique, specific, imaginative descriptions of these places, characters, and events.

Write Right Exercise #14

Narrative to Dialog

Explore how to use dialog to move a story forward.

Appropriate Grades: 3+

Concept

Students struggle with dialog. Their most common dialog problem is an inability to include core story information in their dialog. They are much more comfortable placing important information into narrative exposition. However, good dialog both propels the story forward and reveals character and relationships. This exercise will help students develop their ability to write meaningful, effective dialog for their stories.

Time Required: 60 minutes

Goal: Develop an improved sense of effective dialog.

Directions

The idea of this exercise is simple: Take a narrative passage from a story and assign students the job of converting it into script form. Students must include in this character dialog all story information appearing in the original passage. They must make the dialog seem like real and plausible conversation between the various story characters.

Divide the class into teams of two or three students. Each team will work together to create a script. As a class, agree upon the identity of the characters who may be used in this script. A narrator should not be allowed. All information must come from the story characters, and must be logically presented as dialog to other characters. The students' challenge will be to convert story information into dialog and keep the story moving, without making the dialog sound awkward and unrealistic. They must accomplish this task using as few words as possible.

The best passage to use will be one from a book your class has recently read. They know the characters and the sound of their voices. They know the flow of the story and the history and significance of the information in the scenes. They know the relationships among the characters. This will make it easier for them to focus on their task.

After teams have finished, have them read their scripts aloud. Discuss the following:

1. Which story elements were easy to convert into dialog? Which were difficult to convert? (Typically, action and detailed scenic description are difficult to convert. Character emotions, reactions, and interaction are easier.)

2. Which lines of dialog sound natural and real? Which sound forced and phony? Why?

If you don't have a ready passage from a recently read book, here is a fun one from my book, *Bedtime Stories*. For younger students, use only part of the passage. Even half of it will present plenty of challenge for inexperienced dialog writers. To make this dialog passage work, include two additional characters in the scene—Jimmy's twin brother, Jason, who is walking with Jimmy and a 60-year-old adult neighbor, Mrs. Ingerson, standing in her front yard. Jimmy and Jason are both 11 years old.

Just past the Ingerson's brick house, and just before the Johnson's, Jimmy spotted a flash of red amongst the crinkly, dead-brown leaves next to his left foot. With one toe he flipped aside a wide walnut leaf. Underneath lay a solid red rubber ball, a little smaller than his fist. It looked new—brand new. Not a mark on it; not a crack or wrinkle in the shiny outer coating.

Jimmy stepped back to kick the ball far down the street. But something made his hand reach down and pick it up instead.

That ball felt cold and hard as if it were made of steel instead of rubber. He tossed it from hand to hand. No, it wasn't a super ball. This thing was . . . different.

He wound up for a bounce on the sidewalk and drove the ball down. Varroooom! That ball blasted back off the cement. It scorched past Jimmy's ear and smashed up through the trees.

Jimmy snapped his head back. His mouth fell open as he squinted through glowing yellow rays of morning sun and up to his ball drifting leisurely to a stop seventy-five, maybe eighty feet in the air. It seemed to hover for a moment, surveying the landscape like a tourist before drifting lazily back to earth. "Plop," that ball dropped straight back into Jimmy's hand.

Seventy-five feet! Higher than a seven-story apartment building! What kind of a ball bounces seventy-five feet in the air? He hadn't even thrown it down that hard.

Jimmy wound up for his blistering fast ball. And, POW!, he slammed that ball into the cement with all his might. ZROOOOOMMMM! It rocketed past his cheek and raced into the sky like the sizzling streak of a laser blast.

"Look at that!" cried Jimmy, shading his eyes, as he watched the ball roar into the bright morning air. A thick fog bank sat on San Francisco. But the east side of the bay, where Alameda lay, was clear.

As the ball floated back down, Jimmy thought, How high did I bounce it? 200 feet? 250 feet? I bet 250 feet would be an Olympic record! Can a ball do that? What kind of ball is this?

Jimmy was so stunned he forgot to hold out his hand to catch the ball. At the last second the ball curved in toward Jimmy and plopped square into his left palm.

Jimmy jumped in surprise. Both hands jerked into the air. The ball dropped quietly to the ground.

"This is definitely weird," Jimmy said out loud to an empty Willow Street. He bent over to peer carefully at the ball. It looked . . . ordinary, laying in the Johnson's driveway.

Jimmy reached out a trembling hand and lifted the ball. As if it decided to act all on its own, Jimmy's right arm started into a super fast-ball windup.

Slam! The ball smashed into the sidewalk and blasted back into the sky.

"Wow!" cried Jimmy as his magic ball soared far higher than before. "That's almost high enough to hit planes taking off from Oakland airport! This is the most fun I ever had."

Each bounce roared higher into the sky. On each leisurely descent, the ball found its own way back into Jimmy's hand, whether he tried to catch it or not.

"This is great! What a ball!"

A car drove by with a 4th-grader Jimmy knew hanging out the passenger window. "You're gonna' be late," she called.

Jimmy glanced at his watch as he shook his throwing arm to loosen it up for another throw.

Oh, no! 8:28! School! He had completely forgotten about school!

He has less than two minutes to make it all the way down Encinal to the school. Nine blocks in less than two minutes!

Jimmy stuffed the ball into his backpack and blasted down the sidewalk toward school. At a desperate, all-out sprint Jimmy rounded the corner onto Encinal screaming, "Out o' my way!" as his watch ticked toward the 8:30 bell.

Teaching Points to Emphasize

Good dialog reveals character, establishes (or increases) story tension, and moves the story forward. It's best to practice fitting these elements into dialog one at a time. Not all story information can be naturally and easily conveyed through dialog. We *do* rather than *talk* in the midst of action. We don't normally describe actions or things that others present can see. We don't describe events that others present already know. In conversation, we don't talk in long dissertation. All these human tendencies make it more difficult to use dialog to describe every aspect of a story. Still, dialog must move the story forward. It must give the reader important information: character motive, intent, reaction, interpretation, and information that sets up future action.

Have students listen to tapes of good radio drama to study techniques others have used to successfully convert all story information into character dialog.

Write Right Exercise #15

Compression

Explore improved methods for presenting dialog.

Appropriate Grades: 4+
Concept

Human beings converse in short bursts, in phrases. They interrupt each other. They repeat, or echo, previous statements. They stammer and falter, struggling through long pauses to find the right words. They stop midthought. They jump from thought to thought. They often have a reason for the conversation—something they want, which they return to throughout the conversation.

This is not how most writers write dialog. Dialog typically sounds too academic and too formal. It is also often bloated with more words than necessary. This slows the pace of the story and hides the power of the necessary words. This exercise is designed to help students squeeze the greatest power from their characters' words.

Time Required: 60 minutes
Goal: Develop an improved sense of the sound and rhythm of effective dialog.
Directions

This exercise is very simple in design. Students will convert dialog, published dialog as well as their own dialog, into *compressed* dialog. This means that they will rewrite a section of dialog, either individually or in small groups, by limiting each speaker to a maximum number of words per line of dialog.

Limits per line of five, seven, or nine words are the most common in this exercise. Their first task is to read the passage and decide exactly what each character wants and needs from the conversation. Their next task is to determine the personality of each character (the way they express and conduct themselves), and the relationships between the characters. Finally, as they dissect and compress the dialog, they must carefully add beats to identify the physical reality of the scene and action, and carefully space identifiers, or character tags, throughout the conversation. (See the section "A Better Recipe" in Part II for a discussion of beats and character tags.)

An example of this compression process, using a seven-word limit, is shown in the section "Dialog" in Part II. Students should work with a passage from a familiar or recently read book before working with their own dialog. When students are finished, have them share their versions of the compressed dialog. Discuss the benefits of using compression to present a conversation, as well as the limitations of this technique. When would a story benefit from violating a compression limit?

Options/Variations

Have several students play the roles of the characters in the story and, in their own words, speak the conversation, which the class tries to compress. Discuss their oral interpretation of the scene, focusing on how characters spoke to each other, and on when short (compressed) lines were or were not more effective than uncompressed lines of dialog. When students try to write compressed dialog for their own stories, they'll have the memory of this real-life conversation to use as a model.

Some teachers have students compress a section of dialog using a nine-word limit, then further compress it using a five-word limit. Students may then compare and contrast these two compressed versions.

Teaching Points to Emphasize

All good writing presents the minimum number of words necessary to create an image of the desired mood, tone, scene, action, and characters. Dialog is a tempting place to indulge in wordiness, but the extra words usually do little except weigh down the interaction of two or more characters. Compressing each line of dialog to a few powerful, revealing words improves the story. The tools writers have to make it sound real include interruption, repetition, pauses, echoes, jumps from topic to topic, tension (or disagreement), reversals, and changes in tone and mood. Each can make dialog more powerful and effective.

Write Right Exercise #16

Where's the Camera?

Explore the various available story perspectives and their implications.

Appropriate Grades: 4+

Concept

Most students never consciously consider the perspective and viewpoint from which they write. They certainly don't consider how their choice will affect the reader. They will, though, if they play a game in which perspective and viewpoint determine their interpretation in a story.

Time Required: 25 minutes

Goal: Develop an understanding of the available story perspectives and the advantages and disadvantages of each.

Directions

This exercise is a demonstration of perspective and viewpoint. Select a well-known children's story. Any will work. I'll use "Little Red Riding Hood" for this example. Assign students to play the roles of the major characters: Granny, the wolf, the woodsman, and Little Red.

Now assign two additional key roles: the *camera* and the *narrator*. These two students will do the real work of the exercise. Finally, assign a first and a second assistant director. They will be responsible for directing changes in perspective and viewpoint to dramatize the effect of changes in these two important story elements. You will be the story director. This gives you control of starting ("Action!") and stopping ("Cut!") the exercise and also the power to decide which scenes are used in the exercise.

Review with the class the possible perspectives and the difference between perspective and viewpoint (see Part II for a discussion). Select and discuss a scene from the story; for example, the scene where Little Red and the wolf meet in the forest. Place the four characters in appropriate places in the classroom to act out this scene. (Little Red and the wolf are together in the forest. Granny is alone in her cottage. The woodsman is alone chopping on trees in another part of the forest.)

Have the first assistant director specify the perspective to be used while telling this scene. Have the second assistant director specify the viewpoint character, if appropriate. (Any of the story characters may be designated as the viewpoint character, whether or not they are directly involved in the action of the scene.)

Before beginning, the student who is the camera must move to a position appropriate to the assigned perspective and viewpoint (see Part II for a discussion of these camera placements).

Allow the narrator a moment to gather their thoughts. When you yell "Action!" the characters begin to *slowly* act out their parts of the story, under your continuous direction, *miming* their action and interactions (characters may speak very softly to each other, if it will help them act their parts). You must ensure that the actors proceed slowly enough to avoid outpacing the narrator's telling of the story.

From *Write Right! Creative Writing Using Storytelling Techniques.* © 1999 Kendall Haven. Teacher Ideas Press. (800) 237-6124.

The narrator tells the story to the class, as if they were a solo storyteller, using only concepts, information, language, and phraseology appropriate to the assigned perspective and viewpoint. That is, the narrator tells exactly what the camera sees. The camera will need to move as necessary to stay in perspective.

Whenever the first assistant director wants to, they call out a new perspective. The second assistant director then calls out a new viewpoint character. You yell "Cut!" to freeze the action while the camera scurries to the new camera position. Then you yell "Action!" and the narrator continues telling the story with concepts, information, language, and phraseology appropriate for this new perspective and viewpoint.

It will be possible to have a perspective or viewpoint, or a combination, that strays from the main action of the story. That's fine. It shows the limitations of the various perspectives and viewpoints. (For example, the directors might assign a third-person perspective, with the woodsman as viewpoint character, for the scene when Little Red meets the wolf. The narrator can't talk about this meeting because the viewpoint character isn't there. While this meeting occurs, the narrator can only talk about the forest trees, how much wood the woodsman has chopped, and so forth.)

You should not allow the first assistant director to shift perspective more often than once every 20 or 30 seconds, but encourage them to do so often enough so that the class can see and hear the effectiveness of different perspectives, and the effects of perspective shifts. Let the story proceed for four or five minutes.

Stop the story if the narrator or the camera break the rules of perspective or viewpoint. It is better to yell "Cut!" and pause to discuss the situation than to continue allowing the narrator or camera to portray incorrect information to the class. The purpose of this exercises is for the class to visually and audibly experience the effect and power of different perspectives.

The class must listen to the narrator and observe the camera closely to prepare themselves for a discussion of their performance, as well as the plusses and minuses of using the various perspectives and viewpoint, at the end of the exercise. After this discussion of narration and camera position, switch to a new crew and another story and repeat the exercise. As a final discussion, compare and contrast the success of the two crews with the various perspectives and viewpoint characters used.

Options/Variations

Some teachers periodically change narrator and camera during a story, to allow more students to experience these roles, and to relieve the burden on these two key students.

Teaching Points to Emphasize

The perspective a writer chooses dictates three major story parameters: 1) where they will place the reader within the story, 2) what information a writer is allowed to provide to the reader, and 3) how the reader will regard each character. These are very important factors in determining the success of a student's story.

Omniscient perspective is easy for the writer, but it pushes the reader farther away from the action and characters. First-person perspective is more limiting for the writer, but more exciting for the reader. Remind students to carefully consider, in the early planning stages, what perspective will be most successful for telling their story. Then they should consider which viewpoint character (if appropriate) can most effectively tell the story. Finally, they should try to see the world of the story from that perspective and viewpoint, as if they were a camera filming the story.

Write Right Exercise #17

Word by Word

Generate story seeds.

Appropriate Grades: All
Concept

The greatest of all student story-writing complaints is the trauma of deciding what to write about. Students desperately need an idea, a place to begin, a seed from which to grow their story. *Any* seed will work because the seed is not what the story is, or will be, about. It is only a starting spot from which to grow the story. There are many ways to create these story seeds. Most of them place the burden on the teacher. This exercise is a great way for students to create their own imaginative seeds.

Time Required: 5 minutes
Goal: Create imaginative, unanticipated, expansive story seeds.
Directions

This exercise is typically done with two-person teams, but first demonstrate it for the entire class with two volunteers. Have two student volunteers come to the front of the class. Have one stand on your right side, the other on your left.

Tell them that, jointly, they will create the first sentence of a new, award-winning story. Each student will create half the sentence. If either looks nervous, remind them how easy their task will be. They must each only create *half* the sentence.

Begin with either student. Ask that student to tell you only the first word in the first sentence of this story-to-be. They may try to tell you more than one word. You must stop them at one word.

Ask the other student to provide the second word of the sentence that could logically follow after the first word. Back and forth, one word at a time, the two students build a sentence. The only rule is that every added word must be grammatically and logically plausible in its spot in the sentence. A student might try to take control of the sentence by blurting out an entire phrase. If they do, disallow the entire phrase and make them provide another word.

Repeat the sentence after each new word is added, to give students a moment to think and to help everyone remember the entire sentence. Either student can end the sentence, at any time, by adding a period instead of a word—as long as it is grammatically and logically plausible to end the sentence there.

If a student can't think of a word to add to the sentence, ask the class to contribute suggestions. Accept four or five. Then have the student select a word, either a suggested word or a word they have thought of based on these suggestions.

These co-created sentences are often silly, and occasionally flat and boring (in which case, just create another sentence). Most of the time, however, they are filled with imaginative and creative ideas to use as story seeds.

Ask the class what they would do next, now that they have created the first sentence. Most will want to write the second sentence or decide what happens next. No! This sentence is only a seed, a focal point for their initial story thinking and planning. Story planning always begins with characters.

If the class were to proceed with the development of this story (not a part of this exercise), the next step would be to identify the main character of the story. This character may not appear in the first sentence. Then they would proceed through the rest of the planning progression. When they finally reached the point of actually beginning to write the story, they would return to this first sentence as the place to begin.

After the class demonstration, have two-person teams create several possible first sentences. These sentences may either be used as story seeds by these students, or, preferably, exchanged with another team to provide the seeds for some future story.

Teaching Points to Emphasize

These sentences seem to take on lives and directions of their own, creating story ideas neither student would have imagined separately. These sentences, though, are only seeds, places to begin story planning. The story really begins when the writer defines character, goal, conflict, and struggle.

Write Right Exercise #18

Love/Hate

Create effective story seeds.

Appropriate Grades: All

Concept

Creating any seed for a story is helpful. Creating a seed that encourages the writer to infuse passion into the main character is better. This is the focus of the "Love/Hate" game.

Time Required: 5 minutes

Goal: Create story seeds that both provide a sense of story structure and open an avenue for the writer's own passions to enter the story.

Directions

This is an exercise students can do on their own. First, demonstrate it several times for the class. Have students think of 1) something they hate and 2) how they wish it were different. Students must be able to specifically articulate both parts.

Have one volunteer announce what they hate and how they wish it were different. They must precisely identify both parts. Otherwise, the story seed will be vague, lack shape, and be difficult to write about. Your job is to help students be specific.

As an example, the conversation might proceed like this:

Student: *I hate my brother.*
Teacher: *What about him do you hate? Everything, or just some things?*
Student: *I hate the way he treats me.*
Teacher: *Do you hate everything about the way he treats you, or just some things?*
Student: *I hate the way he steals my stuff and gets away with it.*
Teacher: *Which do you hate more? That he steals your stuff, or that he gets away with it?*
Student: *Both.*
Teacher: *Pick one for this story.*
Student: *I hate that he steals my stuff.*
Teacher: *Great. Now, how do you wish he were different?*

Hating a brother is far too vague and general a seed to develop in one short story, and too vague for an audience to quickly empathize with or appreciate. Hating that a brother steals your stuff is easy to handle. It works because it is specific. Specific hates work far better as writing topics than vague, sweeping hates.

Now, proceed through a similar process to focus how they wish their brother were different. This often requires considerable thought. It isn't as easy as it appears. However, if the subject is something the student truly hates, they likely have already engaged in this thought process and know exactly how they wish it were different.

From *Write Right! Creative Writing Using Storytelling Techniques.* © 1999 Kendall Haven. Teacher Ideas Press. (800) 237-6124.

When the student finally arrives at a specific story seed, it might be something such as "I hate that my brother steals my things, and I wish that, whenever he did, that he'd get an uncontrollable urge to give away his own favorite things." It might be as simple as "I hate the taste of brussels sprouts and wish they tasted like chocolate," or "I hate going to school and wish we didn't have to go at all."

In this one simple step, here is what they have created for their story:

1. **The opening condition.** Stories are about character struggles—the greater the struggles, the better. To make this struggle as big as possible, the student must now exaggerate the condition they hate as the opening condition of their story.

    For the demonstration, have the student who suggested the topic think of ways to make the condition as despicable as possible. Then have the class offer other suggestions. For the previous example, the main character might come home from school to find half of their stuff missing, or, on successive days, *every one* of the main character's favorite things might turn up missing, including things the character really needs—homework or a proof of purchase for some item the character has been accused of stealing. For a character who hates brussels sprouts, the worst possible situation would be having to eat them for every meal. Have the story begin as the family moves to a brussels sprouts farm, spends all day growing sprouts, and eats them morning, noon, and night. That's despicable!

    The worse and more exaggerated that the opening conditions are, the bigger the obstacles and struggles the character must face and overcome.

2. **The ending situation.** The story ends when the main character experiences the student's wished-for scenario. This is why students must be specific in stating how they wish the thing they hate were different. What they wish for becomes the ending of their story.

3. **The main character's identity and goal.** This one simple "hate-wish" statement identifies the main character (the story character who has this wish) and the goal of that character. The student will closely identify with, and be able to clearly visualize, this character.

4. **The main character's attitudes and passions.** Finally, by knowing what the main character hates (a strong emotion), the student learns something about the attitudes, motives, and personality of this character. When the main character acts in the story, the student knows why because they know the character's feelings and goal. More importantly, the student shares the same hates, wishes, and passions with the main character. Now the student can more directly write their own feelings and energy into the story.

    "Love/Hate" is a simple technique for defining a story, but it works. The student identifies the thing they hate or love, identifies exactly how they wish it were different, and then exaggerates it to make the opening condition as despicable as possible. The key to successful use of this exercise is helping students identify tightly focused, specific hates or loves. Demonstrate the process, then have students help each other in pairs. Help them establish a habit of being specific before allowing them to individually develop their themes. No hate or love is too petty to produce a good story. Many, however, are too general and vague.

From *Write Right! Creative Writing Using Storytelling Techniques.* © 1999 Kendall Haven. Teacher Ideas Press. (800) 237-6124.

Options/Variations

As an alternative to having students think of something they hate, have them think of something they love, but can never get enough of to feel satisfied. Interestingly, students are never as enthusiastic about this theme as they are about the hate theme. Still, with thought, they can identify an appropriate topic. The story now tracks a character's journey from never getting *any* of this thing they love, to getting as much of it as they want. Roald Dahl's *Charlie and the Chocolate Factory* is a classic example of this story structure.

Teaching Points to Emphasize

"Love/Hate" provides powerful story seeds because it provides more than just the starting idea. This technique provides an opening condition, the ending situation, the main character, their goal, and information about their personality. Still, this is only a seed. The writer must develop the rest of the core character information, thus defining the plot, before beginning to write.

Emphasize that readers care more about characters who care about something. The more they care, the more passion they feel and show, the more readers care about them and their story.

Write Right Exercise #19

Getting Into Trouble

Identify and begin to develop strong, interesting characters as story seeds.

Appropriate Grades: 3+
Concept

Stories are about the conflicts and struggles of characters. The more risky and dangerous these struggles are, the better readers like the story. A helpful way to begin the process of building a story, then, is to identify obstacles and risk and danger.

Time Required: 45 minutes
Goal: Create more powerful basic story characters and structures to develop into stories.
Directions

Divide the class into teams. Three seems to be the ideal team size. (The exercise will work with teams of four, or, after it has been used a few times, with two.) Have each team create a situation: character, place, and activity ("a person selling shoes in a small-town general store," "a bear climbing a tree to get honey"). The more specific the details of the situation, the easier this exercise will be.

Teams should now develop this situation into a story by answering the following three questions. Have teams trade situations before each question (for each question, a team should work with a new situation) so that students will better restrict themselves to answering the specific question instead of focusing on creating plot, as is their natural tendency.

1. What could go wrong in this situation? The new team should collectively make a list of at least six things (or fewer, if you are working with younger students) that could go wrong in this situation. Then they should choose the three that they think create the biggest character obstacles. Some teachers have teams read their situation, complete list, and short list to the class for approval before continuing.

2. Who could get into the most trouble? Given the general situation and group of three things that could go wrong (obstacles), the new team should now identify the character who has the potential to get into the most trouble, within the limitations of the emerging story structure. This might not be the character identified in the original situation. There may be many other characters who could be placed at greater risk and danger, given the obstacles the previous team selected.

3. What could the main character want that would get them into the most trouble? For the main character identified in step 2, the new team should now create a goal. What goal will force the character to get into the most trouble, given the nature of the three obstacles? How will these three obstacles prevent the character from obtaining this goal?

Now the teams have identified a character, a goal, and obstacles for each situation. These story characters and situations will be easy to work with and write about. They are effective, powerful story seeds. The exercise can end with team presentations to the class, or can be used to generate individual story-writing assignments for every student in the class.

Options/Variations

Some teachers choose to model this process as a class before forming student teams. Have a volunteer create a situation. Then, lead the class through the three exercise questions as a model for teams to follow later.

Teaching Points to Emphasize

Story characters who don't have a vested interest in the story outcome are boring. Those who never risk anything (internally or externally) are equally boring. Successful stories are not created from these characters.

Any goal or obstacle becomes fascinating and gripping if enough risk and danger is associated with it. By beginning with obstacles and their associated risk and danger, each team automatically creates a character in the midst of struggle. Good stories are about character struggles.

Notice that answering the question "What could go wrong in this situation?" actually requires the team to specify, or at least imply, a goal for the character provided by the situation. The subsequent questions either refine this goal, or replace it with one that will allow the writer to create even bigger obstacles for the character.

Write Right Exercise #20

Who Could Struggle Most?

Explore an effective way to create strong story seeds.

Appropriate Grades: 3+

Concept

Stories are about character struggles. A helpful way to begin creating a story, then, is to create a struggle. One way to locate struggles is to find the character who could suffer most, or have the most to lose. This character will likely be the character who struggles most, to avoid this suffering and loss.

Time Required: 10 minutes

Goal: Identifying strong story situations and seeds.

Directions

Students can use this technique in small groups, but first demonstrate it for the class. The goal is to slowly build information around a story situation until a good story seed emerges.

Ask the class to name and describe a location. If you receive more than one good suggestion, have the class vote to choose one. Ask, "Who could struggle most in this location?" Anyone who answers must support their nominee by explaining exactly why this character will, or could, struggle most. Typically, though, no one will be able to present a workable character at this stage. The story information is still too vague.

Ask the class to name an activity that could happen at this location. Again, vote to arrive at one activity. Ask, "Who could struggle most at or around this activity, in this location?" If the class agrees that one of the nominees is a good character for a story, they have accomplished their goal. The seed has been identified. This character is the story's main character, and the obstacles they must overcome are the cause of their struggle.

If a good idea has not yet emerged, ask the class to name a character who could arrive at this location. Ask, "Who could struggle most at or around this activity, in this location, when or because this character has arrived?" Students always erupt with character nominations at this stage. Have each student justify their nominee, explaining their character's potential for suffering, loss, and struggle. Finally, have the class vote to choose the best main character.

There is one more element and question that you can add to this series if a story seed has not emerged: Ask the class to name the emotional state of the character who has arrived. Then ask, "Who could struggle most at or around this activity, in this location, when or because this character, who has this emotional state, has arrived?"

Teaching Points to Emphasize

This is an exercise for creating a story seed, not a complete story. The result is an idea to focus the process of story creation. Students know the main character and a set of obstacles. However, they do not know the main character's goal. Nor have they searched for other, even bigger obstacles to block this character from reaching this goal.

This exercise works because struggle is at the heart of every story. No character struggles without a reason. A character struggles because they want or need something that they don't have, or to avoid losing something precious that they already have. Searching for the character who could struggle most identifies the character who has the most to lose (or gain). This character will help students create a successful story.

Write Right Exercise #21

Picture Personality

Explore character elements as story seeds.

Appropriate Grades: 2+.

Concept

A picture of a character's face is a powerful cue for creating the character elements behind that visual image. A picture may not always be worth a thousand words, but a picture can certainly spark the ideas *for* a thousand words.

Time Required: 15 minutes

Goal: Create character elements from pictures of a character's face.

Directions

This group exercise works well with an entire class or half a class. In preparation, you must find and cut out about 20 half- to whole-page photos of interesting faces. *Life* and old *Look* magazines are excellent sources. The photos must be close to life-size.

Have a volunteer come to the front of the class, randomly select one of the photos (it doesn't matter if the photographed person is a different sex than the student), and study the face for 10 to 15 seconds to imagine a character, personality, and voice to go with the face. Have the student turn the picture around, so that the class can see the face, and hold it as a mask in front of their own face. Then the student, playing the role of their character, performs a self-introduction using the imagined character's voice, vocal intonations, and speech patterns.

The student should address the following seven elements of character information: name, age, job, family, what they do for fun, what they are afraid of, and something they now need or want. Of course, all this information is made up, or imagined, based on the appearance of the face in the picture. Still, it should be presented as if it were completely factual and autobiographical.

Allow the class a chance to ask questions of this character, based on the information provided. The student answers, still in character. After three or four questions, stop the exercise and have the class comment on the characterization, and on the character, created by this student. These comments should focus on aspects of the vocal characterization and character information that were interesting, enjoyable, and believable when compared to the picture.

Have a second volunteer use the same picture to create a new, unique character. This allows the class a chance to see two interpretations of the same visual image. Then proceed to another student, who randomly selects another picture from the stack and begins a new round.

Teaching Points to Emphasize

This exercise involves extrapolating or inferring substantial blocks of character information from the appearance of the face. This is something we do all the time. We see a person and envision their entire life. We hear a voice and do the same.

The human face is very expressive. It tends to accurately represent much of the emotional information hidden beneath the surface. As students become more comfortable with the process of relating facial expression and characteristics to internal emotions, moods, and attitudes, they will learn to rely more on describing shifts in facial expression and characteristics to represent deeper emotional shifts in their characters.

This exercise produces story seeds, not stories. From these character images, though, complete character profiles and stories can be built.

Write Right Exercise #22

Write Abouts

Explore the class's experiences to find story seeds.

Appropriate Grades: All

Concept

Events and situations that your students have experienced, or thought about, create stronger stories that are easier to write, even if students completely fictionalize the event or situation. The problem is that most students overlook their own experiences, memories, and ideas when creating a story. They won't, though, if they formalize them in a class list.

Time Required: 25 minutes

Goal: Begin a list of age-appropriate story seeds based on the experiences of the class.

Directions

The goal of this exercise is to create a log of the hopes, dreams, fears, and common experiences of your students. This list then becomes a list of potential seeds to use when they begin the story-writing process. This exercise may be done individually, but it is more effective if the list is compiled collectively. Comments from one student trigger memories in others that they would have otherwise overlooked.

If you lead and monitor the discussion, have one student act as class scribe to record the list. Feel free to customize this list of topics below, and to add topics that are better suited to the age and concerns of your students. Read the topics to the class, one at a time, and have the class discuss each for a few minutes while you collect their responses.

- Five things that happened to me, or to other family members, on family trips.
- Five major family events I've witnessed (weddings, funerals, graduations, etc.) What happened that wasn't supposed to?
- The first time I rode a bike.
- The first time I got lost.
- The first time I was home alone.
- Family things I thought were funny.
- Five books I've read and liked. What do I remember? What did I like about them? How could I create a similar story?
- I thought it was funny when . . . . (something got spilled or misplaced, someone got locked in or out).
- My first school memory.
- Secrets my grandparents told me, about the times before I was born.
- The thing I remember most about _____ grade.
- Five things I'm afraid of—critters that scare me.

From *Write Right! Creative Writing Using Storytelling Techniques.* © 1999 Kendall Haven. Teacher Ideas Press. (800) 237-6124.

What happened when I met one (or more) of these critters?

- Three things I wish I could do.
- It was a disaster when I tried to . . . .
- What I remember about the first time I tried to cook.
- The first dish I successfully cooked.
- The closest I ever came to running away was when . . . .
- If I had one wish . . . .
- My most memorable Halloween moment.
- The person who saved me was _____. How did they do it?
- The best thing I ever got away with—at home, at school.
- What if . . . ? (Make a list of 20 "what ifs"—for example, What if chairs could walk and talk, but never did it when a person was present?)

You will collect a long list of specific incidents. These specific incidents can be condensed into single phrases and generalized to form a list of story seeds that will keep your students writing all year.

Teaching Points to Emphasize

Our own experiences are a treasury of story ideas. The best way to use them is to let them act as story seeds. However, these are only seeds, places to begin. Student will become so excited by their plot ideas that they want to jump directly from seed to story writing. However, a number of steps must occur before a planted seed will sprout into a workable story that is ready to write.

Write Right Exercise #23

Guided Visioning

Explore yet another method for generating story seeds.

Appropriate Grades: 3+.

Concept

Every human mind bristles with story ideas. Generating ideas is not the problem. The problem is sifting through the noise and clutter of a thousand competing ideas, finding one, and focusing on it long enough to allow it to emerge as a story idea.

Time Required: 5–15 minutes

Goal: Develop powerful story seeds, and character relationships and attitudes to develop these seeds.

Directions

If students focus on a familiar setting or situation for a few minutes, story ideas will emerge. It's always difficult for them to do this alone. It's easier if someone guides them through these familiar settings and situations. Here are two guided-visioning scripts that consistently produce good story seeds:

1. **"Look at Your Hand"**

Have your students study their right hand for 15 seconds, noting the marks, lines, hairs, wrinkles, scars, and calluses. Have them close their eyes and picture their right hand in as much detail as they can recall. Have them visualize their fingernails; the dirt under them; the cuticles; the nicks, burns, and cuts; their knuckles; the veins; and every twist and turn of their hand. (Mention these details slowly, allowing students enough time to create an accurate image of their hand.)

Have them open their eyes and study their hand to note the marks and aspects they forgot. Allow them another fifteen seconds, have them close their eyes again, and continue guiding their visioning in a slow, even voice. At this point, I say:

"Picture your right hand again, but in more detail this time. Note every hair, line, and contour. Picture the way light and shadow play across the surface of your hand. As you study your right hand in your mind's eye, you see that your hand is holding another hand. Look at that hand you hold for a moment. Now look up the wrist and arm of that other hand. Look up to the face that goes with that hand. Whose face is it? What expression is on that face? Why? Why are they holding your hand? What happened just before they began to hold your hand? How do you feel while holding this person's hand?"

I usually pause here for four or five seconds before having students open their eyes. Then I allow them a minute to take notes about their images and the associated character information. In particular, they should note each character's emotional state. Emotions lead to motive, which leads to goal. This is the seed for a story. Then I have students share what they imagined. This helps students expand the range of possibilities they might consider when trying to invent seeds for future stories.

2.   "Going Home"

A similar exercise that students always enjoy, and that tends to develop more powerful story ideas, is "Going Home." Have students close their eyes and try to remember all the images that rush through their minds during the exercise. Speaking slowly to allow them enough time to visualize each new element, I say words to this effect:

"Picture yourself leaving school and getting picked up by bus or car. Picture yourself riding home. You walk to the house or apartment where you live and enter through the door you always use.

"As you step inside that door, you drop your bookbag and jacket. Then you pause for a moment, looking around the house, enjoying the familiar sounds and smells. You leave that first room or entryway and step into a second room.

"You stop right in the middle of this familiar room and slowly gaze around the room at each of the objects, the things, in this room. As your gaze drifts from object to object, you find that one object more than any other holds your attention. You are drawn to that one object. You stare at that object, studying it closely.

"As you study that object, you realize that you are not yourself studying that object. You are that object, gazing out at the rest of the room. As this object, glance at the objects around you. Which do you feel superior to? Which are you afraid of? Why? Which things in the room are your allies? Your enemies? Why?

"What do you want to have happen most? What do you need to have happen? Why? What are you most afraid will happen, and why? What dangers lie in this room for you? What dangers lie outside the room? Why? Are there any objects in the room you are jealous of? Which ones and why? Do other objects have reason to be jealous of you? Why? Does that worry you?

"What have you done with the other objects in this room before? Which events turned out well? Which didn't? Why? Do you know the history of the other objects around you? Do they know yours? Are you hiding any secrets from the rest of the room? Why? Do you know any of their secrets? How does that make you feel?

"As you gaze around the room, you realize that you are not that object, but a human being standing in the room staring at that object. Then you realize that you are not standing in that room at all. You are sitting in a classroom. As you realize this, with a deep sigh, open your eyes."

I now allow students time to take notes about their images. In particular, they should note the relationships, motives, and attitudes of the various characters they have imagined.

I am always amazed by the genius and power of the stories created through these two easy visioning exercises. The goal is to mentally put yourself in the place of another character and let your imagination envision the world through their eyes. With practice, students can use this technique on their own to create story ideas.

Teaching Points to Emphasize

The product of this exercise is a story seed, not a story. The value of this exercise is that it produces a seed *plus* characters, their attitudes, their motives, their personalities, and their relationships. This information greatly accelerates and simplifies the story-creation process.

From story seed, the writer must shift to character. They must identify the main character, their goal, obstacles that prevent them from reaching their goal, and the risk and danger associated with each obstacle.

Write Right Exercise #24

Be Your Character

Explore the characters that inhabit a story.

Appropriate Grades: All
Concept

We rarely spend enough time imagining the level and complexity of detail that will give our characters the power they could and should have. It is especially difficult for students to imagine a rich and vivid character. This will be easier for them if they incorporate physical movement into their character-development process.

Time Required: Varies (depending on the format selected)
Goal: Create a detailed image of a story character through performed characterization.
Directions

For this exercise, every student must be currently involved in the process of creating a story, and they must have the main character well in mind. However, this exercise should be used before any story writing has begun. It has been successfully used in three different formats:

1. **The Informal Format**

    Students are allowed one minute to concentrate on their main character. They should try to imagine the character's appearance, attitude, expressions, mannerisms, posture, walk, voice (sound and vocal patterns), and phraseology. They may take notes if desired. This work should be done individually. Students then stand and, in full physical and vocal characterization as their character, introduce themselves (as their character) and state two sentences about this character and their story.

    There are two important considerations for this format. First, the emphasis is not on anatomical correctness, but on correctness and completeness of personality and attitude. If the character is a dog, the student does not need to drop to all fours and bark. However, they do need to decide how this character would act if it were in the classroom and then personify the character's actions and reactions. Is this dog friendly, gruff, suspicious, afraid, alert, lazy, feisty, or arrogant? Would it bite the class members, snarl at them, ignore them, tremble in a corner, or yap for attention?

    Second, this is not an acting exercise. It is a character-development exercise. *How well* the student physically imitates the character is not important. That they consider the personality and all vocal and physical aspects of the character and try to bring them to life in their presentation *is* important. The goal is to develop more complete images of the character.

    No one considers how their character scratches an itch, or what they do with their elbows, until required to physically do it. When playing the role of the character, a writer is forced to consider these unexplored aspects of the character. Often, the writer finds (creates) interesting and valuable mannerisms.

After everyone has stood and introduced themselves, hold a three- or four-minute "character reception" during which the students must circulate through the room in full characterization and interact with other characters as their character would. Adding physical movement and improvisational reactions, and seeing how other students present their characters, help the student further develop their image of their character.

Finally, allow students time to take notes about what they learned and saw during the exercise.

2. The Formal Format

Play "The Character Game" (Exercise #25), with full vocal and physical characterizations.

3. The Homework Format

This exercise may be assigned as individual homework. It is usually completed in two steps. First, the student practices their characterization alone. Second, the student adopts the complete characterization and interacts with family or in public. This exercise will only work if it is accomplished with, and in front of, other people.

Based on the comments I have received from teachers and parents, the grocery store is the best place for practicing characterizations. Have students go grocery shopping with a parent. They begin at one end of the store, becoming one story character as they walk the first aisle. As they change aisle, they change characters, from one end of the store to the other.

Options/Variations

There are two common variations to the rules of this exercise. First, you may direct students to develop characters other than the main character. It is often more valuable to develop the antagonist than the protagonist, or main character. Have students develop both protagonist and antagonist to ensure that both are unique and separate from each other.

Second, you may direct students to over-exaggerate the personality and all vocal and physical aspects of their characters. Students may tend to inhibit themselves when doing characterizations. They will learn more about a character's eccentricities and quirks when they use exaggeration. Exaggerations are also more fun for other students to watch.

Teaching Points to Emphasize

Good characters are a composite of many types of information including direct sensory data (what they look like, what their voice sounds like, how they move, how they talk, etc.), their habits and quirks, their likes and dislikes, their attitudes and personality, their thoughts, their fears and hopes, their goals and problems, and their history.

The goal of this exercise is not to develop acting ability. Rather, students should use performed characterization as a vehicle to help them develop a stronger image of their character, and to develop this character in more detail. Also, anatomical correctness in characterizations should not be the focus. Students don't need to *be* a duck, a tree, or a bear. Rather, they should represent the personality, attitude, and manner (the essence) of this duck, tree, or bear.

Write Right Exercise #25

The Character Game

Explore specific aspects of character through feedback and suggestions from a small group.

Appropriate Grades: 3+
Concept

Having to formally present a character to a group of peers, and receiving feedback and suggestions from that group, greatly improves a student writer's images of that character. Using a group to help the writer consider seemingly nonessential (even seemingly irrelevant) aspects of a character often reveals rich character details and mannerisms that become valuable to the story. In addition, watching one writer struggle with a character encourages all other students in the group to similarly develop their characters.

Time Required: 30 minutes
Goal: Use small groups to improve the clarity and appeal of story characters.
Directions

This is a character-development exercise designed to assist students in forming a more detailed image of their main character. It is best completed in two steps. Step 1 is an intellectual analysis. Step 2 is a physical characterization. Performing both steps more ensures the development of a more consistent, complete image of the character.

Step 1

Divide the class into groups of four or five students. Have the groups sit in chairs in a circle. In each group, one student at a time is chosen to be the speaker. This student tells the group about their main character for one minute. Their goal is to create as interesting and complete an image of this character as possible in the allotted time. Have students include answers to the following six questions in their one-minute introduction. These questions help students decide what to say about their character and stimulate better questions from the group.

1. What is the goal of this character? What flaws, problems, and risk and danger does this character face in this story?
2. What are the unique and interesting aspects of this character's physical being and personality? What are their hopes and fears?
3. How does this character want the story to end, and why?
4. How does this character feel about the story's antagonist, and why?
5. Why does the writer like this character?
6. Why does the writer think we should care about this character. What will make them interesting and unique to a reader?

From *Write Right! Creative Writing Using Storytelling Techniques.* © 1999 Kendall Haven. Teacher Ideas Press. (800) 237-6124.

The group now has two minutes to ask questions about this character, about any aspect of the five layers of character information, or about any of the statements the student made during the introduction. The group's goal in asking these questions is twofold. First, they should investigate anything about this character that isn't clear to them. If it isn't clear to them, it probably isn't clear to the writer, and so it won't be clear to the reader. Second, they should probe the speaker for any undefined or ambiguous aspects of this character.

Questions about any aspect of the character are legitimate and valuable:

"Where was this character born?"

"What are this character's favorite and least favorite foods?"

"What color are their eyes?"

"What was this character's favorite thing to do when they were half their present age?"

"What is this character afraid of?"

"What sports is this character good at and bad at?"

"Do they like to comb their hair?"

"How many friends does this character have, and why?"

All character questions are fair game.

The speaker must answer all questions, even if they need to make up an answer. However, encourage them to ask the group for ideas and opinions about any aspect of the character they are struggling to envision. This is an opportunity for the writer to seek peer ideas and help in developing and defining their character. After this two-minute period of questioning and discussion, the group selects the next speaker.

Step 2

Students remain in their original group and circle for step 2. One student at a time is chosen to be the performer. This student steps outside the circle, *becomes* their main character (adopts full physical and vocal characterization), and reenters the circle as their character. They walk as the character would walk, sit as the character would sit, perform a self-introduction (in character), and tell about their story (still in character) for 30 to 45 seconds. Emphasis should be placed, first, on presenting the character's personality, attitudes, and mannerisms through physical characterization, and, second, on revealing the character's goals, fears, problems, desires, and personality through word choice and phraseology. To do this, have students use the following six questions as a guide for their introductions:

1. What do you want, why do you want it, and why don't you already have it?

2. What are your favorite activities? Your least favorite?

3. Which of the other characters in this story do you like? Which do you respect? Are there any you despise?

4. Why should this story be about you?

5. What do you want to happen to the antagonist at the end of the story?

6. What one action are you most proud of? What one action are you most ashamed of?

From *Write Right! Creative Writing Using Storytelling Techniques.* © 1999 Kendall Haven. Teacher Ideas Press. (800) 237-6124.

The group now has two minutes to pepper this character with questions. All questions must be directed to the character in the second person, as if the character and not the performer were sitting in front of them. The questions may be about the character (their history, their attitudes, their fears and desires, their likes and dislikes, etc.), or about any statements made by the character. The group's goal is to probe for inconsistencies in the characterization and for undefined aspects of the character. In other words, their goal is to stump the character with their questions. The performer must stay in character during this entire process.

After the two-minute period of questioning, the performer leaves the circle, still in character. Once outside the circle, they drop the characterization and then return to the group as the next performer leaves to become a new character in the circle.

Options/Variations

Three common options are used for this exercise. First, apply this exercise to the antagonist instead of to the main character. Students must answer the same lists of questions. Antagonists, too, should have wants, goals, and obstacles. When these elements are developed, the story gains power and appeal.

Second, have students exaggerate their vocal and physical characterizations in step 2. They may tend to inhibit themselves when doing characterizations, especially with mannerisms and quirks. Directing students to exaggerate their characters encourages them to act silly and goofy during the exercise, freeing them to more fully explore the physical presentation of their character. They will "get into" character more quickly and learn more about them.

Third, use the exercise to help students develop a clear distinction between their main character and antagonist. For a story to work, the reader must be able to clearly distinguish one from the other. This means that the writer, too, must clearly see the differences between these two characters. Have students act out a conversation between the main character and the antagonist. They should act out both sides of the conversation, jumping back and forth between these two characters.

Have students use some interaction between these two characters that will occur in their story, but they should improvise the actual dialog they say during the exercise. It will appear frantic and unnatural as they jump back and forth between two completely different physical and vocal characterizations. However, the goal is not to develop polished story delivery, but to develop more vivid and complete images of these two key characters.

The student should briefly introduce the scene and the significance of this moment in their story, pause to gather their thoughts and imagine these two characters, and then launch into their production of protagonist versus antagonist. It usually helps them get into character if you instruct them to exaggerate for the sake of the group.

The group's goal is to ensure that these two characters talk and act differently, and that the student maintains two consistent characterizations. After the student completes a 30–45 second interaction, the group should comment about the two characters. The student may ask the group questions about their characters, and may ask for suggestions and ideas for developing these two characters.

Teaching Points to Emphasize

Successful story writing depends on creating a complete and detailed image of each major story character. Strong images include not only the present physical appearance and circumstances of a character, but also their history, their memories, their attitudes, their beliefs, and their mannerisms. Peers help us expand our creative processes to produce stronger, richer, more interesting characters.

Another valuable aspect of group work is that every group member benefits from each question asked, even if they aren't the current speaker. They will consider the answer to every question as if it had been asked about their own character. Thus, each student receives a full 30 minutes of character development.

The goal of this exercise is not to develop acting ability. Rather, students should use performed characterization as a vehicle to help them develop a stronger image of their character, and to develop this character in more detail. Also, anatomical correctness in characterizations should not be the focus. Students don't need to *be* a duck, a tree, or a bear. Rather, they should represent the personality, attitude, and manner (the essence) of this duck, tree, or bear.

Write Right Exercise #26

One-on-One-on-One-on-One

Explore effective basic story structure and any assigned aspect or element of a story in progress.

Appropriate Grades: 3+
Concept

We refine story elements best with feedback. Most writers, however, work in isolation, devoid of outside help. What could be more constructive, then, than having the opportunity to tell a story, using a particular structure and presentation; receiving instantaneous, detailed feedback while telling it; and having the opportunity to revise the story and immediately retell it? A "One-on-One-on-One-on-One" exercise provides just such an occasion.

Time Required: 15 minutes
Goal: Develop an intuitive understanding of successful story structure.
Directions

This is one of the two most powerful and effective story-development exercises I have ever encountered (the other is Exercise #31). It's easy to use, and it never fails to improve both the story at hand and the student's understanding of the form and structure of a story. It is an oral exercise.

First, assign a story topic. If this exercise and topic are being used as part of the development of an existing story, no advance notice is necessary. Announce the topic and begin the exercise. Typically, these topics relate to specific aspects of a story you want your students to further develop (e.g., tell a story about the main character, about the character's struggles and problems, about the antagonist, or about the story line itself).

If this exercise is being used to develop student awareness of how to shape, organize, and deliver effective stories, announce the topic several days before the exercise. You can use fictional topics with this exercise, but it is better to begin with factual events students recall from their own lives. Keep the topics simple and personal, so that the stories will be easy to recall and remember while students tell and then revise their story.

Any topic common to student experience will work: something that happened during summer vacation, a time when you got in trouble, something that happened on a bike, something that happened on the school playground, someone who gave you something very special, someone who has been especially important to you, any topic on your list from "Write Abouts" (Exercise #22). All will work well for a "One-on-One-on-One-on-One" exercise. Tell the class that, in a few days, they will tell a one-minute story related to this topic.

One day before the exercise, tell the class an improvisation story related to this topic. Don't make this a rehearsed and polished telling. It's helpful if they see you struggle to order your thoughts and words. This is, after all, exactly what will happen to them tomorrow.

For the exercise, have students pair themselves with a classmate. All telling will be done one on one. Each pair sits facing each other, knee to knee and eye to eye, with no desks or tables between them. They should quickly decide who will be "student #1" and who will be "student #2." As a general instruction to the class, direct student #1 to begin telling their story to student #2. Student #2 must listen only. There should be no interruptions, questions, or comments from listeners. Their feedback will be nonverbal.

Time the story, shouting "Stop!" after one minute. Immediately, direct student #2 to begin telling their story to student #1. To avoid having to yell, some teachers use a coach's whistle for start and stop signals. Don't allow any time for discussion between stories. Make these transitions as rapidly as possible.

After student #2 finishes their minute of telling, have everyone switch partners. Allow no time for discussion or comments. As soon as students are settled into their new pairs, repeat the exercise. Finally, have them switch partners and repeat the exercise for a third time.

Many teachers vary the time limit for each telling in two ways. First, there is nothing magical about one minute for the duration of each telling. For younger students, some teachers reduce the time limit to 30 or 40 seconds, and then slowly increase it toward one minute over the course of the school year.

Second, many teachers trim a few seconds off the first round of tellings, and increase the time limit by a few seconds for the third round of tellings, without announcing it to the class. Tell students that each round will be a one-minute telling. Then actually stop them at 50 or 55 seconds for the first round and at 70 seconds for the third round. Stories grow with practice. Students will need more time to tell the same story during the third round.

In less than 15 minutes, a vast amount of telling, assessment, and critical listening have taken place. Each student has told a short story; seen in the face of their listener whether or not it worked effectively; restructured, reworded, and revised this story twice based on the feedback they received, and based on their own impressions of the story; and tested the effectiveness of each of these revised versions through their second and third tellings. While listening, students provide instantaneous, nonverbal feedback, through facial and body reactions, for the teller to use. They are also mentally revising their own story, and are sifting through the structure and wording of the story they are listening to for any ideas and phraseology they can borrow and incorporate into their own story.

Every student can do a "One-on-One-on-One-on-One" exercise. No one is embarrassed or forced to struggle in front of the class. This exercise greatly enhances confidence and enthusiasm. It builds a strong sense of effective story structure, pacing, and delivery. It gives students a chance to explore variations and options in the way they structure story material.

Options/Variations

Assigning a clear, manageable, specific topic is critical to the success of this exercise. Four topics are particularly successful if this exercise is used as part of the story development process:

1. **The main character.** Who is this character, and what makes them so fascinating and worthy of a story? This allows students to employ all layers of character description, and all facets of core character information, to present an intriguing, compelling character for their story.

2. **Struggles and conflicts.** What are they, and what makes the struggles and conflicts, problems and flaws, and associated risk and danger formidable enough to engross the listener (or reader)?

3. **Story line.** How should the storyteller order and pace the events of their story to successfully guide the listener (or reader) through it?

4. **The antagonist.** What makes this character such an imposing and formidable adversary for the main character? The antagonist is the embodiment of the obstacles the main character must face. The more powerful the antagonist, the more risk and danger associated with confronting the antagonist, the better listeners (or readers) will like the main character, and the story.

After using this exercise several times, many teachers follow it with an evaluation period. Quick written critiques work better than class discussions. Have students make journal entries answering two groups of questions:

First,

- How did my story change over the three tellings, and why?
- Did my story improve over the three tellings? Why or why not?
- How would I reorganize this material if I were to tell it again?

Second, of the three stories I heard,

- Which did I most enjoy, and why?
- Which scene can I most vividly remember, and why?
- What did the teller do that made me remember it?
- When did I laugh? What did the teller say that made me laugh?
- When was I most bored, and why?
- What did the teller say that made me so bored?

These evaluations help students remember what they have learned about their story, and about stories in general. Students can also use them as reference lists to focus their writing. What worked *on* the student, will work *for* that student. What bored them, will bore others. You might keep these critiques on file and use them to check each student's progress in writing.

Teaching Points to Emphasize

During a "One-on-One-on-One-on-One" exercise, every student works continuously on their story while continuously assisting others with their work. While a student isn't telling their story, they accomplish three important tasks. First, they provide instantaneous, explicit, nonverbal feedback to the teller. Because they are sitting face to face with the teller, the teller can't avoid seeing and interpreting it. Second, they review and restructure their own story for the next telling. Third, they sift through the structure, phraseology, and wording of the teller's story for anything they can borrow and incorporate into their own story.

This exercise is also an excellent opportunity to review what makes a story work—characters, goals, conflicts, struggles, obstacles, risk and danger, character reactions, and detail. The variety of ways to organize and present these elements is infinite. Yet every successful story incorporates all of them.

From *Write Right! Creative Writing Using Storytelling Techniques.* © 1999 Kendall Haven. Teacher Ideas Press. (800) 237-6124.

Write Right Exercise #27

The Scene-and-Sequel Game

Explore the interdependency of scenes and sequels.

Appropriate Grades: 4+
Concept

Student stories tend to jump from action to action, from event to event. Overlooked are the critical character reactions and reflections concerning these various events. Though this information can be woven into the fabric of the story in a variety of ways, one consistently effective system (which has an added benefit of emphasizing the necessity of tracking character reactions and reflections) is the scene-and-sequel system. This exercise is a fun demonstration of this system.

Time Required: 15 minutes
Goal: Understand the role and function of sequels.
Directions

This exercise demonstrates the power and allure of sequels by making a game of the process of inserting sequels into a story line. First, discuss with class the concept of scenes and sequels (see the section "A Better Recipe" in Part II), and provide some examples from existing stories. I have included my own examples here.

This exercise is a demonstration game played as a class. Assign one student to play the role of Mr. Sequel. Initially, you may want to assume this role. Have a volunteer make up a character and initial core character information.

Once there was a young brown bear named Squirt who wanted some honey. But he was very small. So the other bears shoved him aside when they found a honey comb and wouldn't let him have any. Even worse, Squirt couldn't climb trees, and so couldn't get his own honey from a beehive. But Squirt really wanted some honey.

This paragraph contains a first impression, a goal, and two obstacles.

Have a second volunteer create a scene—that is, an event or interaction involving this main character and the specified goal and obstacles.

One day Squirt saw a fat bee buzzing through the meadow and decided to follow it back to its hive. Maybe he'd find a way to get their honey.
But the bee angrily turned on Squirt. "Don't you follow me! I know you just want to steal our honey. But you can't have any. And if you try to get some, a thousand bees will sting and bite you and make you so miserable you'll wish you never heard of honey!" And the bee flew off.

Have Mr. Sequel step out of the room. Have several new volunteers guess what might happen next, that is, at the events of the next scene. (If *you* are playing the role of Mr. Sequel, don't leave the room.)

Guess #1: The bear swats and kills the bee.

Guess #2: The bear says he's not afraid of a bee and follows the bee home and pushes over the tree to get at the hive and the honey.

Guess #3: The bear is terrified and runs away to eat grubs.

Have Mr. Sequel return to the room. Ask Mr. Sequel to provide a sequel for the first scene. (Word this request something like this: "How did Squirt feel, and what did he think, after the first scene?")

Squirt realized how mean and unfair it was for bears to steal honey from hard-working bees. He wanted honey, but realized he couldn't steal it anymore. If he was going to get some honey, he'd have to find a way to get it fairly.

This is a sequel. Nothing has physically happened in this sequel. Nothing should, except for the character reflecting on the previous scene, internalizing it, and deciding what the action and interaction of the scene mean to them.

If Mr. Sequel includes any major actions taken by the main character, or any interactions with other characters, stop the sequel and correct this incursion of scene into sequel. Review with the class the difference between scene and sequel and the purpose of each.

Now have the class compare their guesses to what actually will happen in this story, based on the sequel. This is the point of the exercise. The reason you send Mr. Sequel out of the room is so that the nature of the sequel Mr. Sequel invents won't be influenced by other student's guesses about the action of the next scene. Sequels lead us from scene to scene by showing us how the main character interprets the previous scene and plans for the next.

Have a volunteer now create the next scene, based on the first scene and its sequel.

Squirt went to the grocery store and asked for a job to earn the money to buy his honey. He volunteered to be a stock boy, a cashier, even a sweeper.
But the store owner said he didn't trust bears, and besides, health codes said bears weren't allowed in grocery stores because of all the moldy bear hair.
The owner said, "Go away!" and slammed the door in Squirt's face.

Note that a scene should have a purpose, some conflict or problem that is addressed, a character interaction, and a conclusion to that action or interaction.

Again, have Mr. Sequel leave the room while several other students guess what might happen next. Mr. Sequel then returns and reveals the next sequel (how Squirt feels about this previous interaction and what Mr. Sequel thinks it means to and for Squirt).

Continue in this manner through four or five scenes, until students create the ending of the story and a final sequel. Afterward, hold a final class discussion about the role and importance of sequels, and about how the information presented in sequels helps us understand and empathize with the main character.

During the exercise, your job is to ensure that students present complete and valid scenes (but only one scene at a time); that all scenes are consistent with core story and character information, and consistent with past scenes and sequels; and that Mr. Sequel provides a plausible sequel for each scene. Some teachers have students watch for, and point out, any improprieties in either the scenes or the sequels supplied by other students.

Options/Variations

Many teachers play the role of Mr. Sequel for the first use of this exercise, to ensure that sequels are used correctly. Before assigning this important task to students, you may want to model effective sequels yourself. Some teachers rotate the role of Mr. Sequel after each scene, allowing one student to provide only one sequel, thus allowing more students the opportunity to try to create a sequel.

Teaching Points to Emphasize

The information in sequels in essential to our understanding of both character and story. We want to view all scenes through the eyes of the main character, but can only do this when we understand their interpretation of, and internal reaction to, the events of the story. This is a sequel.

Sequels are the intersection of the events of the previous scenes and the personality of the main character. Sequels reveal how the character reflects upon and understands the events and action of a story. Sequels help the reader understand and empathize with the character. If action is the "what" of a story, then sequels are the "so what."

The Scene Game

Explore the multisensory details available in each scene.

Appropriate Grades: 3+

Concept

We rarely take the time to carefully visualize each scene of our story. Until a student can make a habit of envisioning expansive, detailed images of each scene, it's helpful to receive guide assistance from other students.

Time Required: 20 minutes

Goal: Develop more detailed images of story scenes, and demonstrate the value of this increased detail.

Directions

This exercise is designed for use just before beginning the actual writing of a story. Students should already have the story idea in mind, and should have already developed the characters, the ending, and the general plot sequence.

Divide the class into groups of five students. A six-student group will also work, but larger groups are unwieldy. A four-person group is passable, but smaller groups won't generate the needed barrage of ideas.

Rules for "The Scene Game" are similar to those for "The Character Game" (Exercise #25). One student in each group is the speaker. This student has 30 seconds to describe to the group an important scene in the story they are planning to write. This description should identify who is present and the general action of the scene, but should concentrate on identifying the setting, the physical scene itself.

The group now has two minutes to ask any question about this physical setting. The group acts like suspicious police officers interrogating a suspect. No question is too trivial. Their goal is to either catch the speaker in a contradiction in the information they provide, or to ask questions that momentarily stump this student, questions that cause the student to think of aspects of the scene they had never considered.

The speaker must answer every question, even if they need to make up an answer. They may not answer "I don't know" or "It doesn't matter." They aren't committed to this answer, of course, and may change it later when they write the story. Still, being forced to answer all questions will expand their image of each story scene.

The group should be encouraged to explore all five senses during this questioning, and encouraged to search for possible inconsistencies or gaps in the writer's story. After two minutes of questioning, the group selects the next speaker.

You should circulate among the groups as you time each questioning period. Look for groups who are struggling to invent tough, probing questions, or groups who are floundering, unable to think of questions at all. Help them by interjecting one or two obscure questions about background sounds; where the shadows fall; what color the curtains are, and whether there is any dust on them; the humidity; or some other such topic. This modeling will encourage the group to follow suit with more effective and beneficial questions of their own.

Teaching Points to Emphasize

Writers never think of all the aspects of a scene, even though they visualize it in as much detail as they can. Peers can help widen the writer's horizon and encourage them to think about aspects of a scene, and the story, that they hadn't considered. Every writer needs this help. The tougher the questions the group asks, the more clearly the writer must envision their scene.

During this exercise, all group members benefit from each question asked, even if they aren't the current speaker. They will consider the answer to every question as if it had been asked about their own story.

After this exercise, ask your students if they see the scenes of their stories in more detail. Do they see them more clearly? More detail means that the story will be easier to write, and that it will seem more real to the reader.

Interrupter

Explore how and what the left and right sides of the brain contribute to story creation.

Appropriate Grades: 3+
Concept

Kindergartners create rambling stories that go nowhere but are filled with infectious, enticing energy and passion. Middle school students write with plot-conscious precision, but tend toward emotionless tedium. We need both elements in our stories—logical plot flow and infectious energy—but they come from different sides of the brain. Here's a fun exercise to demonstrate this distinction and to help spark students' creativity.

Time Required: 15 minutes
Goal: Demonstrate the contribution of each side of the brain to story creation.
Directions

Every student in the class needs a partner. Partners must sit as close together as possible because this exercise will become raucously noisy. Partners will need to be able to hear each other. Partners should decide who will be "student #1" and who will be "student #2." Student #1 is designated as the Storyteller. Their job is to improvisationally create and tell a one-minute, fictional story.

Student #2 is designated not as the listener, but as the Interrupter. The Interrupter's job is to regularly interrupt the Storyteller by blurting out any random word that crosses their mind. It's better if the word has absolutely no connection to the story being told.

The Storyteller must incorporate each word into the next sentence of their story. The Storyteller may not refuse a word or pretend not to hear it. They must listen for, accept, and use every word the Interrupter blurts out.

The Interrupter must interrupt at regular, frequent intervals. As a general guide, as soon as the Storyteller has completed the sentence incorporating the previous word into the story, the Interrupter should blurt out another word.

What does it sound like? Here is a short, typical sample of this joint creative process:

Storyteller: *A cat leapt onto the alley fence.*
Interrupter: *Pajamas.*
Storyteller: *A man wearing pajamas yelled at the cat from an upstairs window—*
Interrupter: *Peanut butter.*
Storyteller: *—to go eat some peanut butter instead of howling.*
Interrupter: *Shark.*
Storyteller: *But the cat couldn't because a shark was guarding the grocery store.*

Time these stories for one minute. There will be lots of noise and laughter. These stories are outrageously fun, so stopping them will require an attention-getting noisemaker. A coach's whistle has always been my favorite.

From *Write Right! Creative Writing Using Storytelling Techniques.* © 1999 Kendall Haven. Teacher Ideas Press. (800) 237-6124.

Have partners reverse rolls and begin a completely new story. Again, time this new story for one minute. Afterward, lead a brief discussion about students' reactions to this experience. Which was harder, telling or interrupting? Which was more fun? (Typically, a class will be divided almost evenly in their answers to these two questions.) Were the stories fun? (The answer is always Yes.) Did they create any good stories they want to share with the class? (The answer is typically No.) Did their stories have strong characters and goals? (No.) Powerful obstacles and antagonists? (No.) But were they fun? (Yes!)

Announce that you want to repeat the exercise but think that you need to adjust one little rule. The Storyteller's job will remain exactly the same. The Interrupter will interrupt at the same rate. However, instead of interrupting with some fiendishly random word, the Interrupter *must*, at every interruption, provide the Storyteller with the "perfect word for them to use to keep the story going where it's going and make it better." Because the Storyteller must create all the other words, and the Interrupter must only create one word for every sentence or two, that one word should be the perfect word to make a truly great story.

The Storyteller still may not reject any word the Interrupter provides. The Interrupter may not pass, saying either that they couldn't think of a word, or that the Storyteller didn't need their help. The Interrupter must do their part and interrupt at the same rate. All that has changed is the Interrupter's goal in selecting words with which to interrupt the story.

Do two one-minute stories so that each partner can experience both roles. You will immediately notice that the room is quieter during this second round. Repeat the previous discussion and compare this exercise to the first exercise. Was it easier or more difficult to be the Storyteller this time? Was it easier or more difficult to be the Interrupter? Were the stories more or less fun? (Less, typically.) Did they have a more understandable plot structure? (Yes, typically.) Were the characters better defined? (Yes, typically.) Were the stories better? (A mixed answer is typical. Being fun is part of what makes a story good.)

Teaching Points to Emphasize

Now to the point of the exercise: What you and your students have just demonstrated is the difference between left-brain and right-brain thinking. The first story was pure right-brain fun. Everyone intuitively understands that the story will be a nonsense story. Their job is to add as much fun, farce, and enthusiasm to it as possible.

Because of the rule change, everyone feels responsible for creating a "real story" during the second round. Often, the interrupted words are no better, and no more helpful than they were in the first round. Now, however, everyone treats them differently. This feeling of responsibility shifts students' thinking to logical, analytical, left-brain thinking. Everyone thinks in terms of plot flow, cause-effect sequencing, rational plausibility, and logical structure. Fun is forgotten.

For a story to work, it needs contributions from both sides of the brain. Every writer is more comfortable working with one side of their brain than the other. Incorporating the side you are less comfortable with is the trick.

The left side provides order, logic, plot, structure, plausibility. The right side provides energy, passion, humor, fancy, exaggeration. The left side creates core character information. The right side creates characterization. The left side tells us *what*. The right side tells us *how*. Writers need to successfully involve both sides in their stories.

Write Right Exercise #30

Practice Writings

Explore effective, successful writing styles.

Appropriate Grades: 2+
Concept

Writing is a skill. Effective writing requires practice, as does any other skill. Usually, the content to be written, not the writing itself, is the writer's focus. Sometimes it is beneficial to concentrate on the writing, not the content being written. This is a practice writing.

The writing-related skills that are best addressed through practice writings are word choice, clarity and economy, thought organization, effective description and detail, and thought expression. Grammar, spelling, and punctuation are better developed using other techniques.

Time Required: Varies (depending on the specific writing assignment, and on follow-up sharing or discussion time)

Goal: Develop more effective and successful writing styles, and an awareness of natural writing strengths, tendencies, and weaknesses.

Directions

Timed practice writings follow a four-step process:

Step 1

Assign a writing topic. Even though the focus will be on the act and style of writing, students still need something to write about. They need a place to begin their writing. Use any system, idea, or list you have created or developed through earlier exercises to create a story seed or theme.

Remember, practice writings are not *story* writing, just writings. The theme can be more general than would be appropriate for a story. Many teachers have found success with themes such as "I remember. . . ," "On a dark and stormy night. . . ," "What I liked about my old . . . [home, bike, friends, room, yard, neighborhood, etc.]," "Things I've already forgotten," or an emotionally charged topics such as "I was afraid when. . . ," "A time I got lost. . . ," or "I think the scariest things in the world are. . . ." Or, try some of the more creative story-seed exercises, such as "Word by Word" (Exercise #17) or "Love/Hate" (Exercise #18) to create a place to begin a practice writing.

Step 2

Optionally, have students do an oral prewriting activity. Practice writings, in general, do not require content development and forethought. Part of their value and benefit lies in the ideas that emerge as the writing progresses. Still, there will be times when you think the class would benefit from a chance to *quickly* talk through their writing topic. Try a short "One-on-One-on-One-on-One" activity (Exercise #26), or an abbreviated "Scene Game" (Exercise #28) to develop student thoughts on the chosen topic.

Step 3

Assign the time allotted for the exercise and begin. Ten minutes is an ample amount of time for older students; often, teachers allot less time so that it will be possible for a number of students to read their work during a class period. Five minutes usually works well for younger students. There is nothing magical about either length of time. Adjust the requirement to suit your students' needs.

Everyone must write continuously for the entire time allotted. They may not stop to organize their thoughts. It's acceptable for their writing to wander from topic to topic. If a student suddenly draws a complete mental blank, they should repeat the first phrase (the theme or topic) and continue with whatever new thoughts emerge.

Step 4

Optionally, evaluate the practice writings. Students are usually eager to hear or read what other students have written. They certainly benefit from hearing the ideas and the language others produced based on the same topic. The simplest postwriting assessment is to have students read their work aloud, either in groups or to the entire class.

Following these readings, you might have students comment about ideas, images, or wording they particularly enjoyed and found effective. Time might also be allotted for students to evaluate their own work. What worked well? Did they unleash the emotion and power of the images they saw in their mind? Did they convey the feeling they hoped to communicate? Was their writing wordy, or lean and powerful? Did they find effective detail?

Some teachers have students keep journal entries to assess the progress they make on successive practice writings. I would recommend that you have students focus these entries on their successes, so that, over time, they will see a chronology and litany of what they do well.

Options/Variations

As is true with the right-brain stories from "Interrupter" (Exercise #29), it is fun to occasionally direct practice writings toward a right-brain activity. Use "Word by Word" (Exercise #17) to have pairs of students create wild first sentences, which they should then exchange with another pair and use as the first sentence of their practice writing.

Have pairs of students periodically exchange stories during a practice writing. Each continues writing where the other stopped. For example, you might have each student begin their own story and write for 45 seconds. You yell "Switch!" Partners exchange work and have 45 seconds to read what the other student wrote and 45 seconds to add to the story. Let them switch back and forth for about 10 minutes, and let each student finish the story they started. This practice writing format is very popular with students. As with all right-brain story activities, it is fun, expansive, and filled with energy. The stories tend to be wild and funny, but also silly and meaningless.

Some teachers extend the switching concept so that no student ever works on the same story twice. After each 45-second writing period, stories are rotated around the room. Reading periods must be lengthened because each student must read through an entirely new story for each writing period.

Teaching Points to Emphasize

Writing, itself, is the final tool in the process of creating and communicating a story. The more your students practice this process, this skill, the more able they are to use it effectively in their stories. Students should study their practice writing. What do they like? What worked? They should listen to what others have written. What did they do well? Did they effectively present character emotions, conflicts, tension, description? What information did students like and need to know? What created vivid images of characters?

Writing is also a good practice for observing. If students observe closely, they'll be better able to describe in detail and create vivid images. Have students practice observing the places and people around them. How would they describe these places and people? What details would they use?

If students did the switching activity, have them discuss this. Did writing with another student help them feel creative, or was it frustrating not to have control over the entire story? Did the story develop in unexpected, interesting, or enjoyable ways?

Write Right Exercise #31

The 30-Second Story

Explore every facet of the process of creating and structuring a story.

Appropriate Grades: 3+
Concept

Having students actually write and present entire stories is very time consuming and stressful. It is a slow, labor-intensive way to develop writing skills. Often, it is far more productive to use an exercise in which the class as a whole can focus on a specific problem area (e.g., description, character development, word choice, using multiple senses, etc.), still within the context of a story. The "30-Second Story" is one of the two most powerful and effective story-development exercises I have ever encountered (the other is Exercise #26). It allows your entire class to quickly and efficiently focus on any specific story concept or technique.

Time Required: 20 minutes
Goal: Develop individual story-related skills by focusing the class's attention on this single aspect of story writing during the development of an improvisational story.
Directions

Have four students come to the front of the class. Tell them that they will make up a four-minute story, 30 seconds at a time. Though this is a verbal exercise, it focuses on aspects of story creation, structure, and development.

One student begins the story and tells it for 30 seconds. Then the second, third, and fourth students each continue telling the story for another 30 seconds. Repeat this process for the second round, but now the fourth student must end the story. Time each segment, yelling "Switch!" at the 30-second intervals. There are no pauses to think between tellings. One ends and the next begins, even if the student is in midsentence.

The General Rules keep this story from degenerating into a mindless, boring story, as most circle stories do. The Special Requirements focus the class on the particular story aspect you want them to address.

General Rules

These six rules apply every time your class uses this exercise. They should be considered a mandatory part of this exercise because they force the four tellers to create a single, unified story.

1. The first teller begins the story by providing three key story elements during their first 30-second telling: the identity of the main character, this character's goal during the story (what they want to do or obtain), and an initial setting for the story.

2. The second teller, during their first 30-second telling, must create at least one suitable obstacle that blocks the main character from achieving their goal. If the first teller provided an obstacle, the second teller provides a second obstacle.

3. Every teller must accept the first teller's main character and goal and use them as the focus and purpose of each story segment.

4. Every teller must continue the story *exactly* where the previous teller stopped, with no temporal or spatial jumps. They may not shift to other characters, other settings, or other events at the beginning of their 30-second telling.

5. Any teller may have the main character overcome an obstacle, but they must immediately pose another obstacle to take its place. There must always be at least one obstacle for the character to struggle against.

6. The fourth teller must bring the story (goal of the main character) to some resolution during their final 30-second telling.

The class should monitor and evaluate each teller's success at fulfilling the General Rules. This task helps every student recognize and appreciate the roles of goal, conflict, and struggle in basic story structure.

Special Requirements

In addition to the General Rules, you should create Special Requirements for each telling. Special Requirements apply only to the current round of the 30-second story. You select them to focus the telling on any aspect of story writing you want the class to study. After meeting these requirements under the pressure of a timed, improvised story in front of the class, students will find it easier to incorporate this aspect of story writing in the future.

Some commonly used Special Requirements are the following:

Character development. Require that each teller reveal two new pieces of significant information about the main character's history, likes, fears, physical appearance, personality, activity, and so on, during each of their two 30-second tellings.

Senses. We often describe only what we see. Richer stories result from engaging more of the reader's senses. Require that each teller include detailed sensory information for three, four, or all five senses during each 30-second telling.

Action verbs. Verbs of state do little to spark a listener's (or reader's) imagination. They do little to create vivid, detailed images. Require that each teller use no more than two verbs of state (or only one) in each telling. Have the class monitor verb usage.

Descriptive detail. We all drop modifiers and speak (or write) in simple subject-verb sentences when we're not sure what we're speaking or writing about. Hand each teller a slip of paper on which you have written the name of an object and several appropriate modifiers (e.g., "a long red string," or "an empty brown bottle"). During each of their two 30-second tellings, each teller must incorporate that object, with its modifiers, into the story. The class's job is to identify what is written on each teller's slip of paper. Each teller's job is to keep the class from successfully identifying their object. Tellers can succeed only by filling their 30-second tellings with other modifiers, thus disguising the modifiers assigned to them. Soon, incorporating descriptive modifiers will become automatic.

Scene description. Young story writers often forget that, though they can imagine each scene, readers cannot do so without descriptive help. Require that each teller spend half of their 30-second tellings describing details of the story scenes.

Similarly, characterization, simile and metaphor, word choice, irony, or any other aspect of story writing can become the Special Requirement focus of a "30-Second Story." As your students become more adept at this exercise, you can establish two or three Special Requirements for them to accomplish during each telling, in addition to fulfilling the General Rules.

After one "30-Second Story," discuss with the class as a whole each teller's success at fulfilling the General Rules and the Special Requirements. Then discuss the effective use and importance of the particular Special Requirement in story construction. Finally, have a second group of four students create a second story, fulfilling the same Special Requirements. Have the class compare and contrast the performances of these two groups, evaluating improvement in fulfilling the particular Special Requirement.

In 20 minutes, two groups can create different stories while focusing on a particular Special Requirement, and the entire class can monitor and discuss this aspect of story writing. If used only once a week, this exercise will greatly expand your class's mastery of successful story structure.

Remember that making up a story under pressure, in front of peers, is much scarier than a "One-on-One-on-One-on-One" activity (Exercise #26) and most other story-development exercises. First, introduce a "30-Second Story" exercise without Special Requirements. Then gradually build more complex requirements into the format, always keeping the tone of this exercise that of a light-hearted game.

Options/Variations

Many teachers have found that their class responds more enthusiastically when a system of award points is created for this exercise. Tellers earn points for successfully fulfilling the General Rules and the Special Requirements. Class members earn points for noting discrepancies, or for accurately monitoring particular Special Requirements. This exercise becomes a game played for points, and the class is hooked. They all want to be selected to be part of the four-teller story-creating team because tellers can earn more points. The audience studies every word, looking for a way to earn points.

Teaching Points to Emphasize

Emphasize the importance of the particular Special Requirement, as well as the central role of the General Rules in creating effective, successful stories. The General Rules represent the core layer of character information and the core of a story's structure.

Write Right Exercise #32

The Match Game

Explore the relationship between character dialog (vocal tone, vocabulary, and phraseology) and character personality, history, and attitudes.

Appropriate Grades: 4+
Concept

We learn an amazing amount about a character's personality, background, and intelligence by the way they speak, and by what they choose to talk about. Writers provide this information (intentionally or unintentionally) through the dialog they write for their characters. This exercise is designed to reinforce the links between character personality and both the words they choose to say and the way they choose to say them.

Time Required: 15 minutes
Goal: Demonstrate the importance of dialog as a vehicle for revealing character personality, history, attitudes, and concerns.
Directions

As a class, create a situation by defining a place and activity (e.g., "watching a fire at a mountain campground," or "coming out of a theater after a movie," etc.). Next, define six characters who could be present in this situation by defining character first impressions (see the section "The Core of the Character" in Part II for discussion of character first impressions). Finally, create one sentence of dialog for each character that the class thinks best fits this character's response, or reaction, to this situation. Work as a group to make each sentence reveal as much about the character as possible and still sound like believable, characteristic dialog.

Create a new situation and decide how each of the same six characters would react in one sentence of dialog. After creating a total of three situations for the same six characters, discuss the effectiveness of dialog in revealing a character's emotional state and personality. Analyze what makes a line of dialog sound authentic (accurately reveals the nature of the character), interesting (fun for the audience to read), and realistic (written as the character would actually speak). Can a single line of dialog do all three? Did you and the class create any that did?

Teaching Points to Emphasize

The real strengths of dialog are its abilities to reveal a character's reactions, personality, attitudes, beliefs, and inner self. However, dialog doesn't reveal this critical information automatically. The writer must plan for it. The better a writer can envision and hear a character, the easier it is to create dialog that reveals this character to a reader.

Write Right Exercise #33

Cause and Effect

Explore the cause-and-effect relationship between events in a story.

Appropriate Grades: 3+

Concept

Everyone tries to predict what will happen as they read a story. How do they do this? They assume that the law of cause and effect is operating in this story. They assume that the actions early in the story are causes that will eventually produce consequences later in the story. If John tells a lie near the beginning of a story, readers know he will regret it and get in trouble later. Cause and effect. Student writers often forget this most basic story structure while they are writing. They simply make things "happen." This exercise is designed to re-mind them of the power and flow of cause and effect.

Time Required: 15 minutes

Goal: Clearly demonstrate the inevitable cause-and-effect linkage in a sequence of story events.

Directions

Nothing is more basic in both Eastern and Western philosophies than the idea of cause and effect. One thing leads to another. Actions today cause events tomorrow. What you sew today, so shall you reap tomorrow. Karma. Cause and effect. It is a powerful and reliable story structure that can be developed in writing exercises.

This exercise should first be demonstrated to the entire class, and may then be per-formed by smaller groups of three or four students. The exercise begins with student #1, who invents and describes a fictional event. They tell about something that happened. They do not explain *why* it happened. They just tell *what* happened.

Student #1: *A cat wandered, howling, down an alley.*

Now student #2 tells *why* this event happened. That is, they invent a past event that caused student #1's event to happen in the story's present.

Student #2: *The cat was howling because it was lost and hadn't eaten in six days. On a family vacation, it had jumped out of the arms of the girl who owned it. The family couldn't find the cat and had to leave for home without it.*

If the class isn't satisfied with, or isn't sure of, this causal relationship, have student #2 explain and justify it. If necessary, amend event #2 so that the class understands the cause-and-effect relationship between events #1 and #2. This is an important part of the exercise. You must ensure that everyone understands and can accept the cause-and-effect relation-ship between these two events. Every event causes a new event, which in turn becomes the cause for the next event. Every event has a root cause somewhere in the past.

It is always surprising to observe how much more interest is created in event #1 after student #2 has provided its causal background. At this point, you might pause to discuss the direct cause-and-effect relationship in this developing story and how it defines the necessary plot line.

Now student #3 tells why event #2 happened. That is, they invent a past event that caused event #2, which in turn caused event #1.

Student #3: *The family loved their cat, Scooter. But they knew Scooter would never survive on her own while they left for a three-week driving vacation. Scooter was scared of everything and needed lots of love and attention. They decided to take Scooter with them on the car trip.*

The class must confirm that event #3 is a plausible cause for event #2. Now proceed forward. Student #4 invents the next event in the story, which follows after, and because of, the original event—event #1.

Student #4: *A man threw a shoe at Scooter and yelled at her to be quiet. Scooter collapsed, trembling with hunger and fear behind a slimy dumpster, where she met a cockroach.*

Again, the class debates and approves the cause-and-effect relationship between events. Finally, student #5 invents the final event of the story, which follows after, and because of, the event #4.

Student #5: *Scooter found that the cockroach was part of a large, friendly family. Scooter moved in with the cockroaches (even though her room was much too small) and lived happily ever after.*

A five-event cause-and-effect sequence has been established. Does it define a story? From this sequence, could students proceed backward to the core character information that defines a story? Does the class understand how this cause-and-effect sequence flows from event to event? Is event #5 more interesting because they know its causal background—events #1 through #4? Does event #5 tend to resolve the situation (or problem) naturally created in event #1?

Cause-and-effect structuring of a story is different than scene-and-sequel structuring, which focuses on the main character's external action (or interaction) and then internal re-action. Cause-and-effect structuring focuses on logical, sequential progression of the scenes, or story events. Even though the next scene appears to be inevitably foretold by the current events (causes), we still need to know how the main character feels about, or interprets, these events. This is the job of the sequel.

Teaching Points to Emphasize

Every reader expects story events to flow logically from one scene to the next. Readers often can't *anticipate* the exact direction of this flow, but they should be able to see it as being logical, if not inevitable, in *hindsight*. As a writer lays out the scenes of a story, they can use this concept to first plan, and later review and edit, the sequencing of scenes they have created.

If the story seems to drift without powerful tension and purpose, one way to repair this is to check the scenes that lead to these dull, aimless places and make sure causal events (actions) occur in these scenes that must come to fruition during that now-dull scene. Then, develop this fruition. The causal action is like hearing one shoe hit the floor. Readers can't put the story down until they've heard the other shoe hit the floor, that is, until they have read the resultant outcome.

Write Right Exercise #34

The Sentence Game

Explore some of the common ways sentences lose their power and speed.

Appropriate Grades: 3+
Concept

Stories are built on scenes. Scenes are built on sentences. There is nothing more fundamental to story writing than the mastery of a sentence. This exercise, in the form of a quiz, addresses many of the most frequent ways writers hide and dilute the power of their sentences. Fixing sentences is an editing task and requires an understanding of these common problems.

Time Required: 20 minutes
Goal: Develop a better understanding of the concepts that ensure successful sentences.
Directions

This exercise is presented in the form of a quiz. Read the pairs of sentences and have students identify which sentence is better written. They should write down their answer (sentence A or B) and a short explanation of why it's better. They earn one point for identifying the better-written sentence, and two points for identifying the correct reason. Read each pair of sentences three times, so that students will have an adequate chance to compare them. Answers and explanations are provided at the end of the quiz.

I recommend that you not read the title (designated sentence flaw) for each pair of sentences. Have students rely on instinct to hear what doesn't sound right. Still, some teachers read the titles to help their students focus on, and listen for, the problem at hand.

Questions

1. Avoid excess description.
    A. She seized the blue, tapered, nine-inch-tall pitcher, which was just over half-filled with water, and threw it across the room at him. Water splashed out, covering the rich, oriental carpet with spots, before the pitcher shattered against the wallpaper with the tiny, beige flower pattern into a spray of water and a million jagged, tiny slivers of glass.
    B. She seized the half-filled pitcher and threw it across the room at him, where it shattered against the wall in a spray of water and jagged slivers of glass.

2. Be specific, not general.
    A. Standing six inches taller than anyone else on the wooden platform, Jeremy Swindell fished his pocket watch from his vest and checked the time. The 2:10 P.M. train to Yuma was an hour late. He cursed and stomped his boot.
    B. A tall man checked his watch. The train was late. It made him feel bad.

3.   Avoid weak verbs.

   A.   Megan thought it was a nice room. There were bright posters on the wall. There was an orange rug and a desk that was full of books. There was a bright-blue flower vase on the desk. Everything seemed to be so alive.
   B.   She loved the room. Bright posters screamed from the walls. Orange rug, blue vase, desk overflowing with books—all pulsed with life.

4.   Use the sentence power position.

   A.   After all they did to keep the giant snake cornered—build a wall, post guards, aim lights on it—still it escaped.
   B.   The giant snake escaped after all they did to keep it cornered—build a wall, post guards, aim lights on it.

5.   Avoid redundant phrases.

   A.   Feeling very sad, she wept. He felt so angry he smashed his fist into the wall.
   B.   She wept. He smashed his fist into the wall.

6.   Avoid needless qualifiers.

   A.   Billy really liked pancakes that were pretty tall and mostly covered with syrup. But he was somewhat embarrassed to say very much to the waitress.
   B.   Billy liked pancakes that were tall and covered with syrup. But he was embarrassed to say it to the waitress.

7.   Avoid redundant information.

   A.   Susan saw the book. Was it the book Dan told her about? She'd peek inside to see.
   B.   Susan saw the book. She wondered to herself if it was the book Dan told her about. She thought she would peek inside to see.

8.   Avoid unnecessary adverbs.

   A.   He secretly tiptoed up the staircase, a baseball bat clutched tightly in his hand.
   B.   He tiptoed up the staircase, a baseball bat clutched in his hand.

9.   Avoid unnecessary character dialog tags.

   A.   "I'm so happy!" Carol smiled.
        So did her mother. "You did a wonderful job," she praised.
   B.   "I'm so happy!" said Carol.
        Her mother smiled. "You did a wonderful job."

10.   Use consistent parallel construction.

   A.   The two dogs were instant best friends. They loved the same things: rolling in soft grass, chasing cars, and being scratched behind their ears by Fred.
   B.   The two dogs were instant best friends. They loved the same things: rolling in soft grass, to chase after cars, and having Fred scratch behind their ears.

Answers

1.   Avoid excess description.

Answer: B

Reason: There is too much description in (A). It needlessly encumbers the action. If these details are important, establish them earlier so that the pace of this key action sequence isn't destroyed.

2.   Be specific, not general.

Answer: A

Reason: Specific references create stronger images for the reader, and create a sense of authenticity and reality. (B) is too general to create vivid images. How tall is a "tall man"? *Which* tall man? What does "feel bad" mean? Angry? Sick? Sad? Be specific.

3.   Avoid weak verbs.

Answer: B

Reason: Look at the verbs. (A) includes *were*, *seemed to be*, and four instances of *was*. These are all flat, lifeless verbs of state. They pull energy from the scene. (B) includes *loved*, *screamed*, and *pulsed*. Strong action verbs create more vivid images, propelling the reader through a story.

4.   Use the sentence power position.

Answer: A

Reason: The power position is the end of the sentence. After dropping the bombshell at the beginning (the snake escaped), readers don't care about the information in the rest of the sentence. Readers want to know what the snake does now that it's loose. Let supporting information build toward the climax of each sentence, which is the power position—the final phrase.

5.   Avoid redundant phrases.

Answer: B

Reason: Two flaws appear in these sentences. First, the phrases "Feeling very sad" and "He felt so angry" are redundant. Readers understand these emotional states from what the characters *do*, so they don't need to be told twice. If some other emotion made her cry (relief, frustration, boredom, etc.), it would be worth mentioning. Readers will assume that she's sad and he's mad based on their actions, unless told otherwise.

The second flaw is a flagrant violation of "show don't tell." Don't tell readers that she's sad and he's mad. Show the reader what they do. Worst of all, don't do both!

6.   Avoid needless qualifiers.

Answer: B

Reason: Indefinite modifiers hurt rather than help a story. *Really*, *pretty*, *mostly*, *somewhat*, and *very much* aren't needed, and they confuse the reader. Does he or doesn't he? Cut such modifiers.

7.   Avoid redundant information.

Answer: A

Reason: Writers don't need to tell readers what they obviously know. It's dead weight on the story. In this case, "She wondered to herself" and "She thought" are both redundant and needless. Who else could she wonder to? If she's asking the question of herself, of course she's wondering. That's what wondering is. Cut phrases that give readers no new information.

8.   Avoid unnecessary adverbs.

Answer: B

Reason: Strong verbs rarely require adverbs. Everyone is being secretive when they tiptoe. It's impossible to clutch something loosely. Otherwise, the word *clutch* would have no meaning. *Clutched* and *tiptoed* are strong enough verbs not to require supporting adverbs. Cut adverbs that don't provide essential information.

9.   Avoid unnecessary character dialog tags.

Answer: B

Reason: (A) has unnecessary dialog tags, or labels indicating who is speaking. "Carol smiled" and "she praised" are unnecessary. We already know this from the dialog itself. Writers should use *said* if they don't have a strong reason to use something else but feel they must use something. Most other words pull readers out of the dialog. Cut unnecessary dialog tags, or use beats (bits of character action), to substitute for a direct tag. After the beat "Her mother smiled," readers know that the mother is talking.

10.   Use consistent parallel construction.

Answer: A

Reason: Sentence (B) mixes construction forms for the list. (A) maintains a parallel construction. It flows better and is more effective and memorable.

Have students calculate their scores. Grant the best editors in the class (30 is a perfect score) a moment of fame. Then use this opportunity to discuss sentence editing concepts and have students edit their own stories.

Create additional example sentences for any concepts that your students are struggling with, or have students, themselves, create additional examples. Either way, your goal is to arm them with an understanding of the editing tools that can bring out the full and rich potential of their story.

Teaching Points to Emphasize

Stories are built on sentences. If the sentences don't work, they keep the story from working. There is no magic to writing strong, effective sentences. First, draft them with passion, emotion, and enthusiasm. Next, edit the story, then the scenes, then the sentences. There usually aren't major problems with sentences, just lots of nagging little ones—easy to fix if the student writer knows what to look for and takes the time to fix them. Remember the goals of each sentence: clarity, vividness, economy, and balance.

Write Right Exercise #35

He Entered the Room

Explore the visual power of verbs.

Appropriate Grades: 2+

Concept

Students typically imagine a scene, or a specific action, and then write it. Whatever words they write, they will always re-create an accurate and vivid image in their own mind. This is the problem. Students can afford to be sloppy with word choices because *any* words will work for them. They forget that only carefully chosen words will re-create an accurate and vivid image in the reader's mind. This problem becomes particularly apparent with verb choices. This exercise demonstrates the implications of the verb choices they make—and these choices present themselves in every sentence of every story.

Time Required: 15 minutes

Goal: Create an awareness of the necessity for using strong, precise verbs.

Directions

On the chalkboard, write "He _____-ed the room." Then fill in the blank with the word *enter*. Ask the class to describe, in detail, their image of this person entering the room. Their images will all be vague and general. Why? The verb *enter* is vague and general.

Tell the class that you want to show them how he *really* entered the room. Step out of the room and then reenter. You may enter any way you choose—saunter in, burst in, crawl in, dash in, creep in, trip in, back in, skip in, storm in, etc.

Having reentered the room, ask the class, "What's a better verb than *enter* to describe how I came in?" They can't use a phrase. They can't use similes and metaphors. They may only use a better verb.

Make a list on the chalkboard of the strong verbs offered. Again, tell the class that you want to show them how he *really* entered the room. Step out of the room and reenter. You may enter any way you choose, as long as you enter differently than you did the first time. Again, ask for better verbs.

Repeat this process several times. Perhaps allow one or more students to do the entering. Your goal is to encourage debate among the class about which is the most accurate, most descriptive verb to use to describe each entry.

Teaching Points to Emphasize

Verbs define the action, motion, and much of the emotional tone of a story. Careful choice of verbs during story writing and editing creates a much stronger sense of power and energy, and more enjoyable, more vivid imagery for the story. Strong, precise verbs provide more accurate information about the action and event being described.

Excessive use of adverbs is one sign of weak verb choices. Strong, descriptive, action verbs don't often need the assistance of adverbs. This allows the writer to cut needless words from the story.

Write Right Exercise #36

The Scene Game II

Explore the effectiveness of a student's chosen detail in conveying an image of a scene.

Appropriate Grades: 1–5
Concept

Every writer wonders if the words they choose convey an accurate image of the scenes and characters of their story. Young writers struggle even more with this concept because it is more difficult for them to assess the descriptive value of their chosen words. This exercise allows students to see the effect of their words.

Time Required: 30 minutes
Goal: Establish a clear connection between story wording and the resulting images a reader envisions.
Directions

This exercise should be used when students have completed their first draft of a story. Divide the class into groups of three students. A two-person group will work if the class isn't evenly divisible into threes.

One student in each group reads or tells one scene from their story to the other two students (the student should choose an important scene for this reading). With no further information, with no discussion, and with no chance to question the story writer, the other two students each independently draw a picture of this scene. They have five minutes to complete it.

The writer then evaluates and compares the pictures. They must evaluate the correctness of every aspect of each picture. Something is "correct" if it matches the writer's image of this particular aspect of the scene. Errors and inconsistencies are neither the fault of, nor the responsibility of, the drawers. Rather, they are a signal to the writer that the words they chose to include in their description of this scene may not be adequate or accurate. It is the writer's job to ensure that the reader's images of each scene match their own with regard to all important and critical scene elements.

A second student now reads one scene from their story for the other group members to draw. Finally, repeat the process for the third student. The students are left to decide later how to reword their scenes so that another group (if they were to repeat this exercise) would draw them more correctly.

Teaching Points to Emphasize

Every story image we envision comes from the words the writer uses. Just because the writer can imagine a scene or character doesn't mean that the reader will be able to imagine it. The writer must carefully select the right words to describe it.

Students should save the drawings of their scenes made by other students. They should evaluate which aspects of a scene were drawn correctly, which were drawn incorrectly, which were included (action, characters, setting, details), and which were omitted. If much of a drawing is incorrect, it probably means that the student didn't have a strong image of that scene in their mind when they wrote it.

Write Right Exercise #37

Where Images Come From

Explore the roles of different types of words in forming and defining our images of a story.

Appropriate Grades: 3+
Concept

Students rarely stop to consider which words really produce the images of their story, or what contributions different types of words make to a reader's understanding of the story events. However, this knowledge can be critically valuable to a writer. It's worthwhile to consider the functions and contributions of different types of words.

Time Required: 15 minutes
Goal: Understand the contributions of nouns, verbs, and modifiers to creating and controlling a reader's images of a scene.
Directions

You will read three versions of a paragraph to your class: one without any nouns, one without any verbs, and one without any modifiers. I believe that this exercise is most effective if you read each version to a different group of students, who can then compare their images of the scene. However, it is more often used with an entire class, who discuss images of this scene between readings.

Almost any paragraph of exposition will work. The one I include here works well because it relies on an even mix of nouns, verbs, and modifiers to create the overall scene.

The paragraph without **nouns**:

A scraggly old shuffled down the twisty black-top. Looked for a comfortable to sit. Found on the of a fallen, and sat, gazing at the pastoral around. In the heard a deep, resonant church. Slowly stood, rubbed his aching, and continued his to.

The common reaction to this version is that it is comical and nonsensical. Nouns create the basic images in a reader's mind.

The paragraph without **verbs**:

A scraggly old man down the twisty, black-top road. He for a comfortable place. He one on the stump of a fallen tree, and, at the pastoral scene around him. In the distance he a deep, resonant church bell. He slowly, his aching back, and his walk to town.

The common reaction to this version is that it is a disconnected string of definite images. Verbs create motion and action, and connect and complete a reader's images.

The paragraph without **modifiers**:

A man shuffled down the road. He looked for a place to sit. He found one on the stump of a tree, and sat, gazing at the scene around him. In the distance he heard a bell. He stood, rubbed his back, and continued his walk to town.

The common reaction to this version is that it is clear but flat and colorless. Modifiers paint the rich pallette of story colors in a reader's mind.

The complete paragraph:

A scraggly old man shuffled down the twisty, black-top road. He looked for a comfortable place to sit. He found one on the stump of a fallen tree, and sat, gazing at the pastoral scene around him. In the distance he heard a deep, resonant church bell. He slowly stood, rubbed his aching back, and continued his walk to town.

In all discussions, focus the class on what contribution each type of word (noun, verb, modifier) makes to our understanding of even this simple scene. As students reread and edit their own work, their understanding of the role of each type of word can lead them to identifying easily corrected weaknesses in their writing.

Teaching Points to Emphasize

Basic images come from nouns. Without nouns, the paragraph is nonsensical, meaningless. Readers don't know what to picture.

Action and movement come from verbs. Without verbs, readers don't know how to interpret the scene. They are left with disconnected images and need more information to connect and complete them.

Details come from modifiers. Without modifiers, the paragraph is lifeless and boring.

Write Right Exercise #38

The Deadwood Word Hunt

Explore the sound, identity, and common usage of words that bog down and diminish writing.

Appropriate Grades: 3+
Concept

It's much easier to *decide* to remove worthless, excess words from a story than it is to actually do it. Much of this difficulty results from a complex variety of "deadwood words." Searching for all types of needless words at once is a daunting task. Once students become more familiar with the chief culprits, and practice finding them in ordinary speech, it will be easier for them to search for and identify these words in their stories.

Time Required: Varies (typically an ongoing exercise)
Goal: Learn to identify and recognize the major categories of deadwood words.
Directions

For this exercise, each student will sift through everyday conversation for examples of the 11 categories of deadwood words. See figure 8 on page 194 for the form students should use during this exercise.

Primary grades have not yet studied some of these word forms. Eliminate from the list those that are inappropriate for your students. The goal is to improve students' writing by making them aware of the negative power of the deadwood words they encounter in every-day speech, not to overwhelm them with an avalanche of new concepts.

Discuss the 11 categories of deadwood words listed below and provide examples of each. To begin the exercise, define the physical and temporal limitations of their search. Common limitations include: for the rest of today, in this classroom; for the rest of today, anywhere outside this classroom, but still on the school campus; for the next two hours, anywhere; or for the rest of this week, anywhere.

Students now try to fill in the form by noting at least five examples of each category of deadwood words that they hear others use. Each entry should note the situation and context of its use. Many teachers make the search for deadwood words into a contest, like a scavenger hunt.

As described in the section "Do the Words Deliver?" in Part III, the 11 categories of deadwood words that students should search for are the following:

Ambiguous, abstract terms
Needless qualifiers
Needless connectors
Redundant words
Redundant phrases
Clichés
Circumlocution

Empty hyperbole
Euphemisms
Jargon
Double negatives

Options/Variations

Here are three successful variants of this exercise:

1. The first student to note the use of any category of deadwood words in class calls out verbally the word (or phrase) and the category. The teacher must approve this call before the student may add it to their list. Though potentially disruptive, this verbal system offers two significant advantages. First, the entire class is made instantly aware of what deadwood words sound like. An opportunity then exists to further discuss the particular category of deadwood words, enhancing class recognition and acknowledgment of the category. Second, each call by a student emphasizes the contest, encouraging other students to search more earnestly for deadwood words.

2. Conduct the search in assigned reading passages. The advantage of this variation is that students search through written text, not informal conversation. The context is closer to what they will face when they write. The disadvantage is that they are far less likely to find examples in well-written passages.

3. Have students complete their lists in pairs, or in teams of three. Two team members must hear the infraction to qualify it as an example usage. Working in teams allows students to immediately discuss a specific word usage, rather than forcing them to wait and learn later in class whether or not the usage really is a deadwood word.

Teaching Points to Emphasize

Often, all that robs a story of its power and punch is an excess of deadwood words. They are easy to find once you know the various forms they take and their look and sound in a sentence. Students shouldn't worry about them during a first draft. They are easier to find and remove later. This is one of the tasks of editing.

From *Write Right! Creative Writing Using Storytelling Techniques.* © 1999 Kendall Haven. Teacher Ideas Press. (800) 237-6124.

Deadwood Word Type	1	2	3	4	5
Ambiguous Terms					
Needless Qualifiers					
Needless Connectors					
Unnecessary Fillers					
Redundant Phrases					
Clichés					
Stereotypes					
Circumlocution					
Empty Hyperbole					
Euphemisms					
Jargon					
Double Negatives					

Fig. 8. Deadwood Word Hunt.

Part V

Glossary of Writing Terms

This summary contains many of the terms and concepts key to the creation, writing, shaping, and editing of a story. Listings for each term include a definition and information about the application of the concept to the creative-writing process. Listings are divided into two sections, "Story Creation" (the process of creating and drafting a story) and "Story Editing" (the process of evaluating and revising a story). Within each section, entries are listed, in a very general sense, in the order of their appropriate use in the process.

 **Story Creation**

1. **Narrative.** This general term refers to many prose forms. Narrative is that part of a prose work that provides an orderly description of events. Any event; any description. Any written description of events (excluding dialog) is narrative. Essays, theses, articles, reports, journals, and textbooks are all forms of narrative. A story is a more restrictive subset of narrative because "story" specifies characteristics of both the information presented and the form of presentation that "narrative" alone does not imply.

2. **Story.** A story is the narrative combination of four key elements: character, conflict, struggle, and goal. More completely, it is characters who struggle, at some real risk to themselves, past conflicts and obstacles to obtain something they want. Stories are about characters, not plots. What we care about is the *conflict* and *struggle*. The greater, the more dangerous these two elements are, the more readers care about character and story.

3. **Incident.** Most dictionaries define *story* as being "a narrative account of a real or imagined event or events." For the purposes of *Write Right*, this defines *incident*. In writing terms, an incident is the reporting of something that happened. Incidents are plot-based. Stories are character-based. Incidents may have strong emotion and trauma, but they lack character-based conflict and struggle, which are the hallmarks of a story. By shifting the focus of an incident from plot to character, it is possible to convert incidents into stories.

4. **Character.** Characters are the heart and soul of every story. Characters *are* the story. But what is a character? A story character is really the sum of five layers of information: **core information** (character first impression, goal, conflict—problems, flaws, risk, and danger—crucible, and struggle), **sensory** image (any information an observer's senses—sight, hearing, sound, smell, touch, and taste—could directly record), **personality** (how they relate to and interact with the world; the way they are; what they're like), the character's **history** (what has happened to them in the past), and their current **activity** (the things they do).

5. **Goal.** An objective, purpose, want, or need. Defining the goal of the main character does two important things for a story: first, it creates the basic structure for the story. It tells readers (and the writer) how and when the story will end. It tells them what the story is about. Second, it makes readers care about the main character. If readers care about the characters, they will care about the story. Goal is the first element of the core character information that draws readers into a story and makes them care about the story and about its characters.

6. **Obstacles.** Obstacles are the things and forces that block a character from achieving their goal. There are two possible kinds of obstacles: problems and flaws. Problems are any obstacles that exist outside the character. Flaws are obstacles that exist inside the character. Commonly, flaws and problems are coupled in a story. Problems arise and uncover a hidden flaw in the character. A dominant flaw creates problems. In either case, the character must overcome both.

   Obstacles are the source of conflict in a story. The bigger the story problems and flaws are, the more effectively and completely they block a character from achieving their goal, the more powerful and engrossing the story becomes.

7. **Risk and danger.** It is not really problems and flaws a reader cares about. It is the risk and danger associated with these problems and flaws that mesmerizes readers; creates excitement, suspense, and tension; and draws readers into a story.

   Danger is the consequences of failure. That is, danger is what will happen to the main character if they attempt to overcome an obstacle and fail in that attempt. Danger can be physical or emotional. Danger must be real, relevant, and believable to the reader.
   Risk is a measure of the probability of failure. The more likely it is that a character will fail in attempting to overcome some obstacle, the greater the risk is for this character. The bigger the risk and danger, the better readers like the story. We crave risk and danger.

8. **Jeopardy.** Jeopardy is the sum total of problems and flaws and their associated risk and danger. Because these elements often work in unison in a story, it is convenient to have a single term to represent all of them together.

9. **Conflict.** Conflict drives a story. Core story conflict occurs between protagonist and antagonist. This conflict results because the antagonist is the central obstacle that prevents the main character from achieving their goal. However, conflict can abound in all aspects and

scenes of a story. Small conflicts (disagreements, upsets, lack of cooperation, etc.) can be found, or created, in almost every character interaction. The wise writer searches for *dis*agreement, *dis*unity, and *dis*harmony in their story characters and events.

10. **Struggles.** To have a story, the characters must *do* something. They must *act*. If these actions are undertaken in an attempt to overcome a set of dangerous, risky obstacles, the actions become struggles. Readers want characters to struggle, whether physically or emotionally, in a story. Struggles, and the conflicts that create them, are at the core of every story.

11. **Reactions.** Reactions are the involuntary, automatic movements, utterances, and facial expressions characters present in immediate response to stressful situations. Something happens; characters react. These reactions are clear windows into the personality, values, and attitudes of the character. Readers will always believe a character's reactions over what the character claims or consciously does.

    A politician claims to support families and family values and is then caught on film sneering at a baby pushed forward for him to greet. Instantly, voters "know" that the politician lied and really hates children. Why? Because we believe that reactions reflect a character's core values and personality more truly than their planned statements and actions.

12. **"Real and relevant."** Every story must have a main character, goal, conflict, and struggles. To draw a reader into the story, each of these elements must appear to be real to the character and, more importantly, relevant to the reader. Wonderfully written stories about the fear of growing old don't make for good reading in first grade. Why? Growing old isn't relevant to first-graders. The real-and-relevant test is what writers use to rewrite stories for a particular audience. First, define the major story and character elements. Next, decide if each element is relevant to the intended audience and if that audience will believe that they seem real to the story characters. If not, adjust the story accordingly.

13. **Themes.** In one short phrase, what is the story about? Most will try to answer with a one-sentence plot summary. However, no story is about plot. Stories are about characters; more specifically, they are about character-related "themes." The movie *Braveheart* is about the power and lure of freedom for the oppressed Scots. "The Merchant of Venice" is about ethnic prejudice and the resulting urge for revenge. These are themes. "Romeo and Juliet" is about the depth of love. "Peter Rabbit" is about the consequences of disobedience.

    Themes are for the reader. A story's theme is the concept or topic the writer wants readers to ponder while and after they read the story. Love, loyalty, conflicting goals, justice, fair play, jealousy, self-sacrifice, passion, a lack of passion, revenge, history—all these and countless other concepts and topics are the fodder for themes.

14. **Story question.** A story question creates suspense in a story. A story question is planted in a reader's mind early in a story. The need to answer this question propels the reader through the story. Usually, the story question is the main character's goal expressed in the form of a question. Will they or will they not achieve their goal?

15. **Protagonist and antagonist.** The protagonist is the main character. The central force against which the protagonist struggles is the antagonist. The antagonist need not be a person. It need not even be alive. A mountain could be the antagonist. Weather could be the antagonist. The antagonist need not even be a separate being from the protagonist. Often, the best fight is the fight against oneself. Hamlet is good example of a character consumed by internal struggles; he is his own antagonist.

A story's core is the protagonist's struggle against the antagonist. A hero can only rise as high as the antagonist will let them. With nothing to struggle against, the protagonist is just an ordinary character. If a writer wants to make their protagonist seem heroic to the reader, they should not develop the stature of the protagonist, but rather should develop the antagonist into a seemingly unbeatable adversary. Then the main character automatically becomes a hero. The hero, though, can never be more powerful than the antagonist.

16. **Crucible.** The main character has a goal and faces obstacles (external problems and internal flaws) of monumental proportion. For each, the writer has created immeasurable risk and danger. At this point, the reader is likely to ask, "So, why doesn't the character just walk away and say, 'I didn't want that goal anyway.'? I would."

Something must *force* the main character to face the grand jeopardy so cleverly created for them. Something must make it impossible for them to turn away from this confrontation: the crucible. The greater the jeopardy, the stronger a crucible the story needs to keep the main character from simply leaving the story.

In a sense, the crucible creates the key to tension. At every moment, the main character is faced with two seemingly unacceptable choices: face the *un*-faceable jeopardy, or abandon the *un*-abandonable quest. Readers love this kind of tension! (Sounds a bit like Don Quixote, doesn't it? He may not have known windmills, but he knew story.)

17. **Perspective.** Omniscient, objective, first-person, second-person, third-person, and multiple perspectives are the choices for perspective. How does a writer decide which perspective to use? Why should they care?

The perspective a writer chooses define how readers will view the story. It defines how readers view each character and interpret story events. Perspective defines which events readers will be able to see, whose head they get to enter, whose thoughts they get to hear. In short, perspective is one of the biggest decisions a writer will ever make about a story.

18. **Viewpoint.** Viewpoint refers to a specific story character through whose eyes readers view the story. Viewpoint applies primarily to first- and third-person perspectives. The writer's job is to find or create the character who can most effectively tell the story, that character through whose eyes readers will most want to see the story unfold.

19. **Plot.** Plot is the sequence of events and actions presented to tell a story. Plot is determined by the obstacles that stand in the path of the main character. The plot is the sequence of actions that the character undertakes to overcome these obstacles and achieve their goal.

20. **Tension.** Readers need tension in a story. Tension makes them turn the pages, skip meals, and read straight through to the end. Most dictionaries define *tension* as "a state of emotional stress," or "the dynamic relationship between parts of a work of art set off one against the other."

Tension is created by obstacles and their associated risk and danger. The more unconquerable the obstacles, the greater the risk and danger, the longer the resolution is delayed and unresolved, the greater the tension, and the more unable the reader is to put down the story.

21. **Suspense.** A close cousin of tension and curiosity, suspense is what propels the reader through the paragraphs and pages of a story without daring to pause or take a breath. Creating suspense is the act of literally suspending the reader between a story question and its answer, between a conflict and its resolution, between the initiation of some dramatic event and its conclusion. Suspense creates a need in the reader to know what will happen.

22. **Scene.** Most dictionaries define *scene* as being a division of a play or story. We all have a sense of what a scene is. Scenes change when either the place (setting) shifts, when time shifts, or when there is a substantial shift in the mix of characters present in the story.

While correct, this definition isn't as useful in building stories as a definition of a scene taken from a different viewpoint. A scene is a segment of a story in which a specific character action, interaction, or conflict occurs. Each scene, like a mini-story, has a purpose, a scene question, a conflict, a struggle, and a resolution. Scenes are where the action of a story takes place.

23. **Sequel.** A sequel is the opportunity after a scene for the main character to reflect, to re-group, to reform their thoughts and plans, to reevaluate the events and other characters of the story. Without sequels, the story seems to rush along at breakneck speed, with no purpose or point. Readers hunger for a chance to check in with the main characters and see how they feel about what is happening.

If a scene shows *what* happens, the sequel shows what it *means*. Thus scene and sequel are like "what," and "so what."

24. **Epiphany.** Webster's defines an epiphany as a sudden realization of the essential nature or meaning of something. Epiphanies are those flashes of insight, those moments of "Ah-ha!" clarity.

There are three steps to the writing of an epiphany: the set up, the trigger, and the epiphany itself. The set up requires that a character misunderstand their situation, that their view of things be erroneous. They must then act based on that erroneous view. The best epiphanies come from characters who erroneously believe the exact opposite of the true state of affairs.

The trigger is an incident or moment which reveals the character's erroneous thinking and, thus, precipitates the epiphany. The epiphany is the moment of clarity, of understanding.

25. **Irony.** Dramatic irony is a close cousin of epiphany. The dictionary says irony is a state of affairs that is the reverse of what was to be expected. Irony, unlike an epiphany, does not require that the character becomes aware of their erroneous thinking.

There are three steps to an irony. First, a character must misperceive or misinterpret a situation, character, or event. Second, the character must act based on that misconception. Third, the character experiences unexpected, unanticipated consequences (positive or negative) from that action.

26. **Voice.** There are two separate meanings associated with the term "voice." One refers to a writer's general style; one to the tone of a specific story.

Every story has a "voice," which describes the story's general mood, its tone, and the sound of the story's narrator. The most effective voice for a story is defined by the general mood or feeling that should be created throughout this story and by the style of writing which will most effectively communicate this story.

"Voice" also refers to the writer's personal style of writing. Hemingway had an identifiable style or voice. So did Steinbeck, London, and Mark Twain. So will your students, if they write over a long enough period to develop a consistent, successful style. This personal "voice" is developed over years of writing work and should not be a concern of student writers.

28. **Passion.** Humans are all very passionate beings. Any character becomes more attractive and interesting when readers see their passions, and when readers see characters *act* on those passions.

    Usually, but not always, a character's passions somehow relate to, or are affected by, the goals and jeopardy facing that character. Passion is a key to unlocking the interest and energy of story characters, and a guaranteed ticket into the hearts and minds of readers.

29. **Climax.** Every story has a climax. That climax need not be one of heart-stopping action or cathartic, tear-inducing tragedy. Still there has to be a moment of insight, realization, irreversible action, or decision that a story builds toward.

    The climax acts as a one-way gate. Once through it, characters cannot go back to the way things were. Options are sacrificed, innocence is lost, commitments are irrevocably made.

    Viewed another way, the climax is the moment when the final obstacle is confronted, the final conflict is enjoined. Once the climax has passed and the story question is answered, readers cannot go back to the exciting time of uncertainty when that question still hung in the balance, and events could go either way.

30. **Motif.** A motif is a recurring theme, symbol, object or image appearing throughout a story. Most commonly, a reader's view of the motif changes over the course of the story as they gain insight to the story's characters and situations.

    A motif has value in that it provides a measuring rod for the reader to track the flow, progress, and change of a story.

31. **Creativity.** To effectively write stories writers have to be creative. Far too many have come to believe that they aren't creative. But what is creativity?

    The dictionary uses words like "the ability to transcend traditional thinking." Here is a working, or practical definition of creativity. Creativity is the combination of two attributes: the willingness to look like a fool, and the persistence to do it over and over again.

32. **Story seeds.** Story seeds are the root ideas that begin the process of forming and growing a story. Seeds give students a starting point for their story thinking.

    A seed does not create a story. Character core information does that job. Nor is a seed the theme of a story. "Something scary that happened on a bicycle" is neither theme nor story. It is a story seed. The irresistible power of peer pressure is a theme. A ten-year-old, freckled boy, Jason, is a decent character. That he foolishly accepted a dare from some older boys and rode his bike to a dangerous part of town, got lost, and desperately longed to get back home before pitch-black night, is a goal and decent story structure.

Story Editing

1. **Images.** A goal of writing a story is to entice readers to create vivid, engrossing images of the story places, events, and characters. But where do those images come from? Nouns create images. Modifiers add richness and detail. Verbs create motion, movement, and action. Readers need all three.

2. **"Show don't tell."** Show don't tell has become a semi-official mantra of fiction writing. In general it means that readers will become more involved in a story if the writer uses sensory information to *show* readers what a character does rather than *tell* them directly how the character feels and thinks. "Showing" forces readers to actively figure out on their own how characters feel and why they do what they do. "Telling" pushes readers into the role of passive observers of the story. Readers grow more involved with stories in which they actively participate.

   Telling is more efficient. It uses fewer words. Showing provides more detail, involves the reader in the story by allowing them to interpret the significance and meaning of a character's actions, and is more powerful.

3. **Detail and description.** Detail creates reality. Period. Detail and description create the images in a reader's mind that make the events, places, and characters of a story seem both vivid and real. However, writers and readers pay a price for that detail. Physical detail slows the pace of a story. It dissipates the story's energy.

   Details are the specific, sensory references to objects, places, events or characters in a story. Effective details perform three services for a story. First, they describe a specific thing or object. Second, they represent, and assist the reader in picturing a larger context or scene. Third, they provide insight into the characters associated with the places, thing or scenes being described.

4. **Dialog.** Dialog reveals character. Dialog moves the story forward. Dialog carries great amounts of energy. Readers are drawn to dialog that accomplishes these goals.

   What makes story dialog hard to write is that it is neither an accurate report of how real people speak, nor is it the formal narrative English used for composition. It's somewhere in-between.
   People converse in sentence fragments, endlessly repeating themselves and the person with whom they converse. Conversations digress and skip around. People typically try to avoid, or skirt around, conflict in their conversations. Real conversations are boring stuff to wade through.
   On the other extreme, formal narrative English never sounds real to the reader. It is far more structured and linear than common spoken English.
   Effective dialog walks a tight rope between these two extremes. Effective dialog emphasizes conflict and tension. It briskly propels the story forward. It reveals character and uses wording and phraseology which accurately reflects the characters. It sound like real conversation. Mastering effective dialog is like mastering a foreign language and requires extensive practice.

5. **Deadwood words.** Deadwood words are words that do not positively contribute to a story, and, like rotten planks of wood, take up space and weaken the structure around them. There are a dozen common types of deadwood words with which student writers should become familiar in order to ferret them out of their writing.

6. **Simile.** "The door looked like a tombstone." That's a simile. A resemblance has been created between two functionally dissimilar items (or concepts) which have been connected by either "like," "as," or other equivalent phrase. Similes create fresh, vivid images through which readers better understand story characters, settings, and events. Similes are a powerful element in a writer's bag of forms of effective detail.

7. **Metaphor.** "His arms became steel pistons, ramrodding blows into the mass of dough at a hundred RPM." That's a metaphor. The central item or concept isn't *compared* to a second, more visually distinct item, it is ascribed that item's traits, characteristics, abilities, and properties.

    Metaphors create more powerful imagery than do similes. But that power also means that they risk pulling a reader out of the story, making them aware of the writing. Similes are weaker in their visual power, but flow more naturally.

8. **Repetition.** In the name of brevity, repetition has gotten a bad reputation among new writers. Many of America's best writers (adult as well as children's writers) rely on repetition to guide a reader through a story. Situations are repeated. Key character lines are repeated. Sentence structure and phraseology are repeated (as in this paragraph). Selected language is repeated. Repeated lines are used to create humor. Far from being a word-wasting evil, intentional repetition can be a powerful writing tool.

9. **Humor.** Humor is good. Everyone loves to and needs to laugh. While dozens of books have been written on humor writing, they all boil down to one golden rule: If it's funny, it's funny.

    Categories of humor, styles of humor, techniques of humor are all worth studying by a student writer. Humor draws readers in and holds them in a story. It breaks long stretches of tension. Like a good palate pause, it refreshes the senses of the reader for story situations to come.

10. **Foreshadowing.** It's a delicious moment for the reader to squeal with satisfaction, "I *knew* that was going to happen!" How did they know? The writer foreshadowed the event. Foreshadowing is a hint of things to come, a promise to the audience that specific dramatic events lie just around the corner and across the page, a hook, a tension builder.

11. **Beats.** What writers call "beats," actors call "stage business." Beats are little bits of physical action or internal reflection interspersed through the dialog of a scene.

    Beats are physical detail. Beats enable the reader to picture a scene's action. They reveal a character's habits, mannerisms, and personality. They break up long passages of dialog, vary the pace, and make the passage more visual.
    BUT, beats also intrude on the power and energy of dialog. Beats diffuse, or at least mask, the power and tension of dialog. They break the flow and pace of dialog.

12. **Stereotypes.** A stereotype is a set of traits or characteristics ascribed to a group defined by some other common trait or characteristic. An absent-minded professor rushing clumsily across campus wearing a bow tie is a stereotype. A fat, jolly baker is a stereotype.

    We use stereotypes all the time to quickly and efficiently describe characters by defining the group to which they belong and then allowing the reader to infer that the common, stereotypical traits of that group apply to this individual character. The danger comes when the sets of stereotypical traits are derogatory and demeaning. Writers can and do use stereotypes but must be very careful to ensure that the stereotypes they use will not be offensive and inflammatory.

13. **Author intrusion.** Once a writer has created a perspective, viewpoint character, and voice for a story, the entire story must read as though it comes from that one narrator's voice. Occasionally (and it usually happens when the author has some impassioned, heart-felt point to make) the writing stops sounding like the narrator and begins to sound like a lecture from the author.

    This intrusion distracts readers. The author is not supposed to be in this story. The narrator is. That's why writers create and use narrators to tell the story.

14. **Balance.** The art of writing is all about balance. Pace versus detail, description versus action, narrative versus dialog, foreshadowing versus telegraphing your plot, character development versus plot motion, tension versus humor, rich and elaborate imagery versus concise and efficient writing, balance between scenes and emotional states, etc., etc.

    Enhancing one aspect of a story often comes at the expense of some other aspect. The concept of balance can be a helpful guide to deciding when "some" becomes too much and when a little isn't nearly enough. The finished story needs balance even more than it needs any individual aspect of the story or of writing, which the writer is trying to juggle.

15. **First paragraph.** The opening paragraph(s) of any story are the most critical. If they don't grab the reader, none of the other paragraphs will ever be seen. These paragraphs also serve a greater variety of story functions of any paragraph(s) in a story. Because of its vast importance, it is far easier to construct an effective first paragraph *after* the entire story has been written.

16. **Title.** Do it last. After the final version of a story has been written search the text for themes, motifs, or wording that will make a short, memorable, interesting title while still conveying the essence of the story. A title is more a marketing tool *for* the story than a part *of* the story.

17. **Active versus passive voice.** In passive voice, things happen to the subject. ("The paper was laid on the table.") In active voice, the subject does the acting. ("He laid the paper on the table.")

    Active voice carries more energy than passive. Active voice creates more specific and complete images for the reader to visualize. Active voice commands a reader's attention more. Active voice avoids those deadly verbs of state. (Deadly because they suck the life out of a sentence.)

Writing References

Libraries and bookstores house shelves of books about how to write. These are the references I have found most useful and dependable.

Magazines

Berkin, Bernard, ed. *Writing!* Middletown, CT: Weekly Reader, 1995– . Quarterly.

Clark, Thomas, ed. *Writers Digest.* Cincinnati, OH: F & W Publications, 1963– . Monthly.

Books

Allen, Roberta. *Fast Fiction: Creating Fiction in Five Minutes.* Cincinnati, OH: Story Press, 1997.

Boles, Paul. *Story-Crafting.* Cincinnati, OH: Writer's Digest Books, 1984.

Brohaugh, William. *Write Tight.* Cincinnati, OH: Writer's Digest Books, 1993.

Browne, M. Neil, and Stuart Keeley. *Asking the Right Questions.* Englewood Cliffs, NJ: Prentice-Hall, 1981.

Browne, Renni, and Dave King. *Self-Editing for Fiction Writers.* New York: Harper Perennial, 1993.

Card, Orson. *Characters and Viewpoint.* Cincinnati, OH: Writer's Digest Books, 1988.

Cheney, Theodore. *Getting the Words Right.* Cincinnati, OH: Writer's Digest Books, 1983.

Chiarella, Tom. *Writing Dialog.* Cincinnati, OH: Story Press, 1998.

Delton, Judy. *The 29 Most Common Writing Mistakes.* Cincinnati, OH: Writer's Digest Books, 1985.

Fredette, Jean, ed. *The Writer's Digest Handbook of Short Story Writing.* 2 vols. Cincinnati, OH: Writer's Digest Books, 1988.

Helitzer, Melvin. *Comedy Writing Secrets.* Cincinnati, OH: Writer's Digest Books, 1986.

Highsmith, Patricia. *Plotting and Writing Suspense Fiction.* New York: St. Martin's Press, 1983.

Hood, Ann. *Creating Character Emotions.* Cincinnati, OH: Story Press, 1998.

Kercheval, Jesse Lee. *Building Fiction.* Cincinnati, OH: Story Press, 1997.

Klauser, Henriette. *Writing on Both Sides of the Brain.* San Francisco: HarperSanFrancisco, 1987.

McCutcheon, Marc. *Building Believable Characters.* Cincinnati, OH: Writer's Digest Books, 1996.

Noble, William. *Show, Don't Tell.* Middlebury, VT: Paul Eirksson, 1991.

———. *Conflict, Action & Suspense.* Cincinnati, OH: Writer's Digest Books, 1994.

Nyberg, Ben. *One Great Way to Write Short Stories.* Cincinnati, OH: Writer's Digest Books, 1988.

Olmstead, Robert. *Elements of the Writing Craft.* Cincinnati, OH: Story Press, 1997.

Peck, Robert. *Fiction Is Folks.* Cincinnati, OH: Writer's Digest Books, 1983.

Saks, Sol. *The Craft of Comedy Writing.* Cincinnati, OH: Writer's Digest Books, 1985.

Swain, Dwight. *Creating Characters.* Cincinnati, OH: Writer's Digest Books, 1990.

Tobias, Ronald. *Theme and Strategy.* Cincinnati, OH: Writer's Digest Books, 1989.

———. *Twenty Master Plots.* Cincinnati, OH: Writer's Digest Books, 1993.

About the Author

A former research scientist, Kendall Haven is the only West Point graduate to ever become a professional storyteller. He holds a Master's Degree in Oceanography and spent six years with the Department of Energy before finding his true passion for storytelling and a very different kind of "truth." He has now performed for close to 3 million people in 40 states, and has won awards for his story-writing and storytelling. He has conducted workshops in over 20 states on storytelling's practical, in-class teaching power, and has become one of the nation's leading advocates for the educational value of storytelling.

Kendall has recorded five audio tapes and published six books of original stories. He has also used his writing talent to create stories for many non-profit organizations, including the American Cancer Society and the Institute for Mental Health Initiatives. He recently created a national award-winning adventure drama for National Public Radio on the effects of watching television. His first Teacher Ideas Press book of 50 science stories, *Marvels of Science*, makes the history and process of science fascinating and compelling. *Amazing American Women* illuminates 40 fascinating and little-known women's stories in American history. His third book, *Great Moments in Science*, was released in early 1996. Haven continues to develop other books.

Haven's most recent awards include the 1995 and 1996 Storytelling World Silver Award for best Story Anthology, the 1993 International Festival Association Silver Award for best Education Program, the 1992 Corporation for Public Broadcasting Silver Award for best Children's Public Radio Production, and the 1991 Award for Excellence in California Education. He has twice been an American Library Association "Notable Recording Artist," and is the only storyteller in the United States with three entries in the ALA's *Best of the Best for Children*.

Haven is founder and Chair of the International Whole Language Umbrella Storytelling Interest Group, and is on the Board of Directors as well as the Educational Advisory Committee of the National Storytelling Association. He is a co-director of the Sonoma Storytelling Festival, past four-year Chair of the Bay Area Storytelling Festival, and founder of storytelling festivals in Las Vegas, NV; Boise, ID; and Mariposa, CA.

He lives with his wife in the rolling Sonoma County grape vineyards in rural Northern California.